SHANGHAI
SACRED

SHANGHAI SACRED

The Religious Landscape of a Global City

BENOÎT VERMANDER

LIZ HINGLEY

LIANG ZHANG

PHOTOGRAPHS BY LIZ HINGLEY

UNIVERSITY OF WASHINGTON PRESS
Seattle

Shanghai Sacred was made possible in part by a grant from the
Chiang Ching-kuo Foundation for International Scholarly Exchange.

University of Washington Press
www.washington.edu/uwpress

Library of Congress Cataloging-in-Publication Data on file

ISBN 978-0-295-74167-3 (hardcover), ISBN 978-0-295-74168-0 (pbk),
ISBN 978-0-295-74169-7 (ebook)

Cover photograph: Animal Release gathering, Shanghai ferry port, 2015, © Liz Hingley

CONTENTS

Plates 1–16 follow page 60, plates 17–32 follow page 124, and plates 33–48 follow page 156.

MAPS

PREFACE

Our exploration of Shanghai's religious spaces and practices started with a simple premise: The religious fabric of a city cannot be studied independently from the factors that determine and modify its social dynamic and texture. Consequently, the agency of worshippers' communities had to be stressed, how they were managing interactions among their members and with external actors, crafting spatial arrangements, and organizing rituals.

Observation would lead us to formulate or reformulate questions about the nature of "sacredness" in a global metropolis, the state-led manufacturing of civic shrines and rituals, and the interplay between "Chinese" and "global" characteristics of Shanghai religiosity. This would in turn prompt us to conceptualize the religious spaces that four chapters of this book endeavor to explore (landmarks, compounds, homes, and waterways) and also to realize that the intensity of sacred spaces fluctuates according to specific calendars. Therefore, the framing and coexistence of different religious space-times would soon appear to constitute the very fabric we aimed to describe.[1]

FROM START TO FINISH

Each of us brought a distinct contribution to the task, and yet we researched and wrote this volume together in such a way as to transcend individual distinctions and make it ours. A word about the encounters that shaped our project may be in order: Benoît Vermander joined the Department of Religious Studies at Fudan University in 2009. Liang Zhang (Zhang Liang 张靓), a native of the city and a research assistant in the Institute of Religious Studies of the Shanghai Academy of Social Sciences (SASS), had worked on the history of both Protestant missions and local Muslim communities and was planning to research one of the oldest Catholic parishes in the metropolis. Liang and Benoît had exchanged ideas on a possible religious mapping of Shanghai. Meanwhile, photographer and anthropologist Liz Hingley was concluding an in-depth visual exploration of religious diversity in one street of Birmingham, United Kingdom. Liz and Benoît met at the colloquium

"Seeing and Believing in Contemporary Christianity" organized by the University of Birmingham in February 2012. Their exchanges led to the development of a research program. Liz settled in Shanghai in June 2013 and would make the city her home until October 2016.

Around March 2013, we had agreed on the following objectives: together, we would attempt to map Shanghai's religious diversity, to trace the networks and social styles that different groupings nurture, and to evaluate the degree of separateness or interaction among the various denominations across the metropolis. In addition, we would privilege a visual approach, paying close attention to the way spaces are crafted, decorated, and inhabited. Liz worked full-time on the project and used photography as a way of meeting and engaging with communities. She started exploring diverse areas around the terminal stations of Shanghai's metro system, one of the largest networks in the world. This gave her an appreciation of Shanghai's exceptional dimensions (the municipality encompasses an area of 6,341 square kilometers, compared to 1,572 square kilometers for Greater London) and of its ever-evolving peripheries. Students from the university's Department of Religious Studies accompanied her on this preliminary exploration. This initial endeavor fostered a small group of friends and collaborators who would actively participate in our research during the following years. Their names are listed in the acknowledgments that conclude this preface.

Subsequent expeditions often involved Liang and Liz, who developed a network of contacts together. Sometimes with friends and students, and later often by herself, Liz researched the majority of case studies in this book. Liang underwent an in-depth immersion in the Zhangjialou Catholic parish, which led to an exploration of Shanghai-based Catholic networks; she also gathered material on the Shanghai Muslim community and local history in general. Providing initial contacts and hypotheses, Benoît supported Liz and Liang on a number of case studies, conducted independent research on popular religiosity and civic sacredness, and attempted to connect our various cases into a global narrative. Relying largely on Liz's and Liang's research reports, he took over the writing of the final draft.

Our introduction, "Sacredness and the City," lays out the questions that guide our research and narrative. It explains our approach to sacredness, starting with French sociologist Émile Durkheim's (1858–1917) landmark theory on the way the distinction and interplay between the sacred and the profane are constitutive of the social fabric. As detailed in the introduction, Durkheim's focus on the spatial and temporal landmarks that structure the psyche and self-representation of a community remains a safe and inspiring starting point for exploring contemporary religion, while discrepancies between this conceptual apparatus and practical observations allow the researcher to point out what might be specific to Chinese religious traditions and to present-day metropolises. The nature of our exploration explains why the chapters are organized according to spatial metaphors. Chapter 1, "Mapping Shanghai," outlines narratives about the religious and political past of the metropolis as well as the trajectories through which decision makers, ordinary citizens, and worshippers crisscross the city space. Chapters 2–5 explore four constitutive dimensions of the space-times through which beliefs and rituals are experienced, shared, and performed.

In Shanghai, one meets with Buddhists, Catholics, Protestants, Orthodox Christians, Daoists, Muslims, Hindus, Baha'is, Sikhs, New Agers, Reiki healers, Yoga masters, Hare Krishnas, worshippers of the deities proper to the Jiangnan region, and many more; the faithful and their interlocutors happen to be at the same time fishermen, entrepreneurs, taxi drivers, students, expats, computer geeks, elderly women, migrant laborers, ethnic minorities, and government officials, among others. The reader is thus invited to enter the labyrinth, as we did. The conclusion complements and corrects the classical notions of the sociology of religion, with which we started, by presenting Chinese metaphors and concepts, concluding with that of resonance (*ganying*), so as to give a global account of Shanghai's sacred spaces and communities as so many "echo chambers" in which worshippers and visitors internalize a nexus of experiences.

HOW TO DO THINGS WITH SITES

According to the statistics provided by the city government, Shanghai counts around 430 official places of worship operated by the five state-recognized religions. Among them, we studied 19 sites that are Buddhist, 9 Daoist, 17 Catholic, 10 Protestant, and 8 Muslim. The choice was determined partly by the religious urbanism of the city, which differs somewhat from the relative number of worshippers; most temples, for example, are Buddhist, while Daoist buildings are few.[2] The relatively high number of Catholic places of worship we visited is partly the result of the fact that the Church operates more than 100 buildings (it was more than 400 before 1949) and that several are historic landmarks, although Protestants are now more numerous than Catholics. In contrast, the 8 mosques we visited represent the grand total of places officially designated for Muslim worship.

Some of these 63 places are citywide landmarks: they are physically and symbolically inscribed into the urban space in a way that made their listing and study a requisite. Others can be classified as compounds that first and foremost serve the needs of a faith community in a setting that is officially recognized for this purpose. Around the middle of our fieldwork, we endeavored to balance our sample across religions and neighborhoods, looking actively for venues serving categories that were until that point underrepresented in our study. This is, for instance, how we embarked on the study of three local Buddhist temples in the northeastern Baoshan District.

Some sacred landmarks belong to congregations that are not officially recognized, such as the Ohel Moishe Synagogue and the Orthodox St. Nicholas Church. Besides including these in our survey, we added a few sites that illustrate the state's effort toward cementing civic worship. More important, a number of places of worship that are not officially recognized by the state are full-fledged compounds or spiritual homes (discussed in chapters 3 and 5). For obvious reasons, we cannot mark these places on the maps, but they were significant to our research. We visited several unregistered Protestant places of worship and one underground Catholic church (a scarcity supplemented by a number of interviews), and Buddhist worship outside temples was a focal point of our research (see chapters 4 and 5). Chapter 5 also includes a map of sites for the study of alternative spiritualities that, without being overtly religious, contribute to diversification of the city's spiritual offerings. Additionally, home visits and meetings in public spaces (planned or unplanned) were too informal and too numerous to be counted. We visited most places several times, and experienced in-depth, repeated encounters with members of the congregation. We feel that the number and diversity of the places we visited produced a representative sample, with only a few missing elements. Makeshift mosques catering to migrant workers, for example, proved to be too sensitive a fieldwork venue.[3]

Besides images or feeling engraved on the memories of the observers, visits and encounters naturally produce discourses that vary in nature, and can be read at several levels. Speaking of ghosts and ancestors carries a different weight, and takes on different tones when done in venues such as a coffee shop, at home during New Year's Eve, or at cemeteries during visitations for the Tomb Sweeping Festival or the winter solstice. The guiding principle remains to consider both what is said and what is done, as one's worldview is lived and expressed through words and practices. We thus took care to both converse and participate in worship with the people and communities we met.

The vast majority of exchanges took place in standard Chinese (Mandarin). Thanks to Liang and some of our students, the Shanghai dialect was very much part of the conversation. A number of mainly young respondents — students, professionals — engaged with Liz in English. We checked these results for creation of bias, and in a number of cases it appeared that the use of English encouraged freedom of expression and that shifting between languages deepened some connections. The global character of Shanghai largely accounts for this. We decided, however, that additional information had to be secured directly in the Shanghai dialect. Our concerns had to do with calendrical observances, on the one hand, and with a vocabulary on sacredness that would be specific to the Shanghai language, on the other.

From November 2015 until February 2016, Chen Jiaren, our research assistant at the Xu-Ricci Dialogue Institute, conducted interviews that focused on both topics. These interviews helped us check facts and notions in a way that sometimes are not allowed in casual interactions.

ICONIC KNOWLEDGE

The tapestry we finally wove out of these distinct elements of our research remains as much (or probably more) a work of art than an objective portrayal. We did select cases, lines of interpretation, and what we considered to be salient features. The truth it communicates aims at echoing experiences that are not easily quantified or objectified. But could it have been otherwise? Reflecting on the visual element that is part and parcel of our research will help us further clarify what we sought to achieve in this book.

Any research project led by ethnography requires admission into new places and trusting exchanges between investigators, individuals, and groups. Picture taking can be part of such a process, fostering interactions between observers and practitioners that can be transformative for all parties involved, while making practitioners and photographers associate in producing knowledge.[4] Besides, the photographic endeavor builds on the recognition that ethnographic understanding emerges as much from sensory as from intellectual reflection.[5] It reveals how bodies and senses take part in ritual performances "within a specially constructed space, simultaneously defining (imposing) and experiencing (receiving) the values ordering the environment."[6] This sensory involvement in religious performances makes us approach the rituals performed throughout various locations — both private and public — as art forms, and therefore as productions and constructions, rather than as mere reflections of preexisting sets of representations and relationships. The photographs in this book constitute genuine research results to the extent that they are authentically artworks. As a result, photographs taken on such occasions should be considered derived art forms, which not only express but also re-create the effects of such performances and even create or construct new affects and effects. Going one step further, rituals and photographs are to be seen as synergetic art forms, originating from a shared experience and together creating a sequence of effects. The layers of intentions and reality expressed through religious choreography enter the photographic imagination. It produces in turn artworks that extend (and bend) the spiritual journeying from the participants to the researcher and photographer, before continuing to readers and viewers.

The photographs displayed throughout the book reflect the interactions that triggered them, hence their diversity. Some pictures are staged in the sense that subjects wished to convey a message about their beliefs or the ritual actions in which they were engaged. This is not to say that pictures were created by the subjects or that the photographer did not make choices. For instance, plate 1 shows a picture taken during a Catholic-organized workshop on foot massage techniques. Another picture showing pairs of practitioners exercising beneath a large crucifix hanging on the wall was taken during the same event but composed on the initiative of one of the organizers. Such a picture, he said, would testify to the "religious nature" of the event. The one chosen for this book seemed to all three of us to communicate the atmosphere of this day more potently than the photograph that the organizer had requested.

In the text, we refer the reader to photographs relevant to the cases being discussed. Mentions do not follow a strictly linear order, as the sequence of photographs follows its own visual logic. The circulation from text to images and from images to text gives the viewer-reader a variety of perspectives on Shanghai's religious space-times. Images are by nature polysemous. The viewer brings his or her own associations and perspectives into the frame. Instead of imposing a single meaning, contained in context or caption, the work of interpretation confronts "the image itself as a textual analysis."[7] Interactions throughout the photographic process at times create icons that encapsulate forms of social and personal relations to sacredness, somehow still alive in the effects produced by the image.[8] Thus the viewer enters a form of iconic knowledge that complements and possibly corrects the discursive knowledge produced by narratives and data analysis.

GLOBAL CITY, GLOBAL RELIGION?

Shanghai is a global city whatever the criteria.[9] Its population, more than 24 million in 2016, makes it the most populous municipality in the world. Its metropolitan area comprises around 35 million inhabitants, and Shanghai is the epicenter of the Yangzi River Delta Megalopolis, 88 million strong. It now ranks among the ten wealthiest cities in the world by GDP and sixteenth in the 2016 edition of the *Global Financial Centres Index*.[10] Its cultural hardware and attractiveness are consistently on the rise, though Shanghai is not yet considered on a par with other comparable global cities. Estimating diversity is a more delicate matter: statistics show that more than 250,000 non-nationals reside in Shanghai, 170,000 on average being non-Chinese (the others coming from Hong Kong, Singapore, and Taiwan), constituting around 25 percent of the total number of foreigners in China. As the figure may be underestimated and does not include short-term residents and visitors, one may estimate the number of foreigners in Shanghai at 1 to 2 percent of its total population. Diversity is notably increased by people from all over China who are drawn to the city (40 percent of the population does not hold a resident permit.) Last but not least, Shanghai's global outlook is nothing new for a city that had been, at the end of the nineteenth century, the symbol of cosmopolitanism and Asian modernity, a status that it lost only from the time of the Sino-Japanese war till the beginning of the 1990s.

The study of global cities as religious hubs has recently attracted much interest.[11] Such studies tend to focus on the religious diversity that characterizes many such metropolises and on its consequences for identity politics and social reconfigurations. But could global cities also foster a form of global religion? This ambiguous term may refer to one of the existing global religions that nowadays crisscross the entire globe, one form or several forms of them benefiting from globalization fostered by urban dynamics and cultures. It may also evoke a religion or religiosity in the making, promoted by the reshaping of the human condition that life in giant metropolises entails. Somehow, this epochal change would eventually reshape creeds and religiosities as much as the progressive passage to agriculture or the advent of modernity have done in the past. Seen from our fieldwork, the metropolitan religious tapestry seems rather to be a collage, or alternatively a montage,[12] of faith communities living more or less in isolation from one another. There is no perceived trend toward the sharing and mixing of creeds or ritual practices.

However, the question triggers observations that suggest how Shanghai as a religious space might be unified by a specific dynamic. First, city dwellers navigate a series of religious markers in space (buildings and other sites) and time (festivals) that they apprehend as part of their overall urban experience. Some will give special weight to a set of markers, doing so according to their religious proximity or affiliation, but they remain conscious of the inherent plurality of such markers, integrated into the metropolis's shared space-time. Second, interactions between locals, migrants, and foreigners continuously reshape the ethos and practices of most faith communities. This process is facilitated by the inhabitants' consciousness of being part of a modern, global city, which makes the scope of the continuous evolutions affecting the city and the religious communities active in its midst characteristic of Shanghai's identity and mission. Third, the experience of living in Shanghai and the consciousness of what it entails become part of religious expressions proper: it colors religious architecture; it determines ways of behaving within and outside of one faith's community; it weaves in different patterns of social and spiritual networking; it permeates impressions received from an array of spiritual traditions and communities, making such contacts and feelings slowly resonate in one's own psyche. What is entailed in sharing a space that is both local and global and how the urban experience is part of one's spiritual journey are evoked in various ways throughout our narrative.

ACKNOWLEDGMENTS

The Xu-Ricci Dialogue Institute, a research center under the School of Philosophy at Fudan University, funded this project and ensured its management from June 2013 onward. We thank the institute's manager, Liang Zhun, for facilitating the smooth running of the project. During the last year of fieldwork, AsiaCentre and its director Jean-François Dimeglio provided additional technical support. Chen Jiaren, who joined the institute in March 2015 as a research assistant, made a decisive contribution with a series of interviews; she also located research material, checked the bibliography, and acted as the contact person for Yu Jin, who expertly designed the maps for this volume.

Special thanks are due to Shanghai Academy of Social Sciences for hosting Liz as an invited researcher for the duration of her stay. The head of its Institute of Religious Studies, Yan Kejia, was instrumental in securing the necessary approvals and showed much interest in our project from the start. We also address our sincerest thanks to Benoît's colleagues at Fudan's Department of Religious Studies. Among them, Li Tiangang was a most precious interlocutor, sharing his thorough knowledge of Shanghai's religious and social history with us. He and Yu Zhejun introduced us to Jinze Township, and Yu Zhejun also helped us navigate the history of the city god temple and popular processions. Zhu Xiaohong was very generous in sharing her knowledge and contacts, providing an introduction to the Catholic fishermen's community of Qingpu District. During his sabbatical time at Fudan in 2015–16, Mark Larrimore, New York School of Social Studies, was a most helpful interlocutor, sharing valued contacts and insights. Our heartfelt gratitude goes to Violet Mount, who reread the entire manuscript and contributed numerous editorial remarks. Katherine Swancutt, King's College London, provided precious final advice when we tried to recapture our approach and the adventure we experienced through our project in this preface.

Ji Yiwen, Zheng Mali, and Jiang Kongkong were the students at Fudan who associated more directly with our research. During the three years of fieldwork, Ji Yiwen accompanied Liz and sometimes Benoît to Daoist and Buddhist sites; Zheng Mali helped in building trust with local Protestant communities; and Jiang Kongkong introduced both Benoît and Liz to her native township of Chuansha. Special thanks are due to Sun Weiqiao, who volunteered at the Longhua Buddhist temple during the academic year 2015–16 and allowed us to integrate data from his reports. He also accompanied Liz to several Buddhist and new-spiritualities sites. Pastor Jing Jianmei, a doctoral student in Fudan's program of religious studies, offered much help in approaching and understanding the parish communities of Shanghai's official Protestant Church. In 2011, Xie Hua worked with Benoît on a survey of young Catholics' liturgical and missionary outlook. Additionally, our gratitude goes to Mose Yiluo, a student at Shanghai University, who introduced us to the city's ethnic Yi community, in which she is an active participant, and helped in our fieldwork around the Buddhist temples of Baoshan District. Anlun, as he prefers to call himself, provided us with useful introductions to some Daoist and Buddhist sites. Bertrand Cristau, a longtime French resident of Shanghai and a friend of Benoît's, drove us to Chongming Island several times, shared our discoveries there, and provided useful introductions to a number of practicing Catholics, both Chinese and foreign.

This is where we should give thanks and recognition to the true coauthors of this book, our informants. However, most of them must remain anonymous; we use the same pseudonym for each person throughout the course of the narrative. For those who did not require anonymity, mention of their names in the text must be read as a token of gratitude in itself.

Some venues helped us test and discuss our hypothesis as well as exhibit pictures and draw lessons from the reactions they triggered. Besides workshops at Fudan University and Shanghai Academy of Social Sciences, a colloquium held at Renmin University in April 2015, organized by Yang Huilin and David Jaspers, of Glasgow University, provided the first opportunity to publicly discuss our approach with Chinese and foreign scholars. Ray Arts Center (a leading place for research on photography in Shanghai) organized the first exhibition in August–September 2015, as well as a series of talks by Li Tiangang, Yu Zhejun, and the three of us. Special thanks go to Shi Hantao, then director of Ray Arts Center, for his generous advice and support on the creative elements of this project. During the meeting of the Society for the Scientific Study of Religion held at Newport Beach, California, in October 2015, we joined Jin Lu (Purdue University) and Henry Kuo (Graduate Theological Union, University of California, Berkeley) on a panel that gave us further opportunities to spell out our approach. A colloquium and photo exhibit organized by the Institut d'Études Catholiques de Paris in June 2016 greatly helped in finalizing our conclusions. Liz also found much profit in sharing our findings at seminars organized by Clare Dwyer at University College London and David Jasper at Glasgow University and at various seminars within the artistic field.

At the University of Washington Press, Lorri Hagman encouraged us greatly with her interest in the project and guided us toward its completion. The comments of two anonymous readers gave us precious help with our final revisions. Also at the University of Washington Press, several other people were instrumental in planning, editing, designing, and producing this book. There is not enough space here to detail all the support they gave us, but we would like to thank Niccole Coggins, Julie Van Pelt, Laura Iwasaki, and Katrina Noble. Lynn Greisz was most helpful with the proofreading and Scott Smiley with the indexing of the book.

SHANGHAI
SACRED

Sacredness and the City

ON SEPTEMBER 28, 2013, MORE THAN TWO HUNDRED PARTICIPANTS from ethnic minorities and the five recognized religions attended a multi-faith gathering at the Songjiang Experimental High School basketball court, an event organized by the United Front Work Department of Songjiang District (plate 3).[1] Laywomen from the nearby Buddhist Xilin Temple opened the floor with a dance performance. An ethnic minority choir followed, and Protestant women from the Yong'en Church (Yong'en Tang) wearing pink outfits continued with an "eternal praise" dance. Afterward, young men studying at the Daoist College of Dongyue Temple (Dongyue Xinggong) performed a tai chi demonstration, followed by a show of Muslim sportsmen, and a Catholic choir from the Holy Heart Church concluded the performance. The last activity of the day was a game of tug-of-war, which was won by the representatives of the local mosque.

All groups had rehearsed very seriously, anxious to emphasize their congregation's contribution to the community; at the same time, the competition among religious groups was made apparent by the tug-of-war game. Congregations were authorized to showcase and compare their achievements while operating and somehow competing within a state-controlled environment. Interreligious and cooperative ventures are organized by the Chinese state, which also decides on their content and format. This explains why most believers show little appetite for such activities and would rather concentrate on their own organizational growth. Turning interreligious encounters into recreational activities is indeed a good strategy for making them palatable, and even enjoyable, for communities that rarely leave their own sacred spaces. Thus, a basketball court was transformed for a few hours into a place of celebration shared by a variety of religious and ethnic groups, as well as by the authorities that regulate the public expression of sacredness.

The Chinese state recognizes Buddhism, Daoism, Islam, Protestantism, and Catholicism as religions (*zongjiao*). At the same time, other faiths, popular practices, and unofficial expressions of the five recognized religions are proliferating well beyond the official domain. Major Chinese cities are among the prominent loci where the religious sphere is being reshaped, and the trend is particularly visible in Shanghai. With more than 24 million inhabitants, Shanghai is one of the world's leading metropolises.[2] Its complex history, economic development, and urban and architectural inventiveness have been objects of in-depth exploration. In contrast, its religious and spiritual vitality, which shapes cultural trends in China and globally, is not yet fully appreciated. In 2014, the city's official website listed 430 official places of worship operated by the five state-recognized religions, places that attracted around 20 million participants in 2013. The same website lists a number of operations run by religious organizations, among them four institutes of religious higher learning.[3] Buddhist temples and communities seem to be flourishing. According to official statistics, there are 119 temples in Shanghai and 1,183 members of the Buddhist clergy, and in 2014, more than 5.5 million people participated in Buddhist ceremonies.[4] Furthermore, due to the city's heritage and present urban policies, Shanghai boasts the largest number of official Christian places of worship of all Chinese cities (169 for Protestants and 108 for Catholics), and 18 churches are listed among 632 heritage protection sites.[5]

Shanghai's religious dynamism manifests itself in multiple ways with interaction between local and international faith communities. Jewish, Sikh, Hindu, Mormon, and Baha'i communities, to name a few, reclaim or claim spiritual space, and new religious groups continue to appear and recruit in this effervescent urban context.[6] People moving to Shanghai from other parts of China or from abroad contribute to the city's religious vitality as they rediscover their faith or enter new congregational networks.[7] Observation of Shanghai's cityscape thus opens up new ways of thinking about how religious lines of demarcation are drawn, policed, and challenged in today's metropolises.

SACREDNESS: USES AND MISUSES

Like the multicultural, multifaith city itself, the language used by the religious practitioners of Shanghai when speaking of their spiritual practices is composed of many layers — local, national, and global. At the same time, researchers on religion and spirituality refer to a lexicon that supposedly covers all related phenomena throughout the world. The relevancy of this lexicon is often called into question when it comes to Chinese or, more largely, non-Western contexts. We thus need to ponder two intertwined linguistic sets: the vocabulary used by believers for giving an account of their experience and the lexicon that scholars mobilize for describing the religious realities of a city like Shanghai, which is both Chinese and global. The following discussion is merely an entry into this lexical field. Throughout the book, we pay special attention to the language and notions put into play by our interlocutors.

The original Latin term for the word "sacredness" refers first and foremost to a judicial quality attributed to an object, a person, a space, or a moment in time by a given institution: "Considered sacred is what is dedicated and consecrated to the gods."[8] While the sociology of religion has taken up this etymology for discriminating between the sacred and the profane, debates have arisen as to whether or not such a distinction is to be deemed universal. This question has direct implications for our research.

Sacred times, spaces, and objects are meant to connect different levels of reality through the enactment of rituals and offerings. Conversely, in Western classical thought, "things profane are those that are not subject to the religious laws of a sanctuary"[9] or those "that — once taken out from the religious or the sacred — revert to being owned and used by humans."[10] This approach, focused on the definition of sacredness as a construct constitutive of social cohesiveness, has been theorized and universalized by the French sociologist Émile Durkheim. However, some scholars of religion mobilize the same notion of sacredness when accounting for the way a specific order of reality (often described as more "real" than the mundane world) happens to be personally experienced by the people who relate to it. Among Chinese scholars of religion, the perspective developed by Romanian historian of religion Mircea Eliade (1907–1986), central to this second approach, remains popular today.[11]

In *The Elementary Forms of Religious Life*, a seminal work on the sociology of religion, Durkheim identifies the contrast between the sacred and the profane as a measure of a community's cohesiveness.[12] Such a distinction, he writes, is of a classificatory nature; all known religious beliefs inscribe the entirety of ideal and real things into one or the other of these two classes.[13] The scope of sacred objects "can vary infinitely from one religion to another,"[14] and there is nothing substantial to refer to when it comes to the distinction between these two classes. The common feature that distinguishes these sacred objects or entities is that "they are withdrawn from general circulation; they are separate and set apart."[15] Society never stops creating such new sacred things,[16] conferring moral power on mortals or even on ideas (such as equality or freedom), through the attachment of dogmas, symbols, sacred places, and days.

Durkheim further distinguishes between different calendar phases (low-intensity, ordinary time versus effervescent collective moments), some set apart as "sacred." He recognizes that in modern societies the continuity between these two phases blurs the experience of sacred time.[17] He reflects on the rigorous prohibitions that usually regulate contacts between profane and sacred moments, spaces, or things, which, he explains, are necessitated by the "contagious" nature of that sacredness,[18] for even indirect contact with religious forces enables them to invade all that passes within their reach. Durkheim further states that sacredness is marked by a basic ambiguity, comprising not only things that are pure, holy, and beneficial to the persons who relate to them but also elements that are evil and impure: "The same object can pass from one to the other without changing its nature," for "what makes a thing sacred is the collective feeling of which it is the object."[19]

Durkheim has been criticized for according too much importance to religious phenomena and to sacredness in particular. Later scholars (notably anthropologist Claude Lévi-Strauss, although he never engages in direct discussion with Durkheim) have challenged the preeminence Durkheim gives to religious rites and beliefs in explaining the crystallization of social structures. These scholars focus instead on linguistic, matrimonial, and symbolic exchanges, making religion (and notably rituals) a nearly irrelevant dimension of the superstructure. An opposite line has criticized Durkheim for conceding far too little to religion and sacredness, as he links them inextricably to social structures and collective states of consciousness.

Throughout this book, we consider sacredness as a social construct, while noting that personal experiences color the use of the term. Thus, for the purpose of our inquiry, the following enclosures or areas are sacred spaces: spaces and buildings that have been dedicated to religious worship by the legal authorities; other spaces and buildings used by specific groups for the same purpose, on a permanent or sporadic basis, independent of legal recognition; areas of the city designed for public commemorations that foster public sacredness; and, in some instances, parts of or even an entire urban space that some groups perceive as in need of special care and respect because of the desecration it may have suffered due to urban and social transformation. In today's Shanghai, Buddhist practices of Animal Release, which will be discussed at length in this book, constitute a good example of the latter.

We thus assume the following: In contemporary societies, and within the same environment, different groups and instances define different types of sacredness. The more such collectives create sacred objects, spaces, and time periods that submit to a number of rules (e.g., restrictions on use and transactions), the more they may be called religious in nature. Conversely, if there is ultimately no restriction or taboo imposed on its use, it becomes quasi-impossible to qualify an object or space as sacred. Although we would hesitate to consider a commercial space as sacred in any way, such a space may incorporate some kind of sacred enclosure on its premises, such as the Thai Buddhist shrine that was erected on the esplanade of a mall in Shanghai (plate 2).[20] Finally, different types of sacredness can associate, compete with, or stand alone in the city's complex, multilayered environment.

SACREDNESS AND THE CHINESE WORLD

Is the dichotomy between the sacred and the profane universal? Or is this distinction too ethnocentric for use outside certain cultural contexts?[21] Some scholars have claimed that what Durkheim describes are not religions in general but rather communal religions, including Greek and Roman polis religions. The sacred-profane dichotomy applies so well to ancient Greek and Roman cities that some specialists have criticized the comparative character of his analyses. In their view, Durkheim should have limited himself to the set of communal religions that are best explained by his theory without attempting to appraise the religious phenomenon in its totality, as he did by relying mainly on material on aborigines and Polynesian societies.[22]

This conceptual approach has nevertheless inspired sociologists of religion outside the European context, including that of China. Sinologist Marcel Granet (1884–1940), a loyal pupil of Durkheim's, draws a sharp distinction between two seasons when describing rural ancient China. One season is dedicated to work (with different tempi for men and for women) within the household or village. The other, the season of "sacred effervescence" (as Durkheim put it), was divided into two periods—the beginning of spring and the end of autumn—and was the occasion for the gathering of larger communities. Granet insists on the contrast between these two periods, the profane and the sacred, and recognizes in the second a catalyst of all developments in "Chinese religion." Opposition between domesticated spaces and untamed "holy sites" complements this calendar distinction. During sacred periods, holy sites attracted crowds anxious to benefit from the hallowed forces at work there. Granet analyzes latter-day religious practices as developments of these "elementary forms." He notes that, although the distinction between sacred and profane is not as pronounced as it is in the West,[23] the division between auspicious and non-auspicious days and the territorial prohibitions and rectifications proper to the art of geomancy were still observed in both the cities and the countryside around 1920.[24] Granet ends with a meditation on the possible demise of the old religious order after the May Fourth Movement of 1919. A century later, many features noted by Granet remain relevant today. Even if religions in China *do* change (and how would it not be the case?), their development may be partly understood through concepts and insights provided by Durkheim's *Elementary Forms of Religious Life* and the works that build on it.

The relevancy of the sacred/profane distinction in China has been supported by comprehensive studies on Chinese religion (from ancient times to the end of the empire). The crucial importance given to rituals (and, notably, sacrifices) for maintaining both cosmic and social order, the attention placed on orthopraxis rather than on orthodoxy, and the inscription of religious functions within the social and political fabric all clearly situate Chinese religion within the model of communal religions. The community of practices that defines Chinese social and religious milieus requires participants to respect ritual proceedings and the prohibitions attached to them, to symbolically configure spaces and times, and to deal cautiously with the impure and devastating forces that the sacred can liberate. From the time of the Western Han dynasty (206 BCE–9 CE) onward, the system has combined different sacrificial spheres in a whole. And the inclusion of the local religious sphere in state orthodoxy was systematized during the Ming dynasty when the creation of a city god temple (*chenghuang miao*) in each county and prefecture was made compulsory:

> Certain aspects of the state cult [in early China] were off limits to ordinary Chinese — beginning with the most sacred sacrifice to Heaven personally performed by the emperor at the winter solstice. There were also times of coexistence and even cooperation between official rituals and popular celebrations. . . . Thrice a year in every single county, the City God had to travel from his temple to an altar situated outside the city walls, where he would preside over a sacrifice to appease the suffering souls of victims of bad death, notably fallen soldiers. This was both an official ritual, presided over by local officials, and a wildly popular celebration, with the whole city taking part in the boisterous procession.[25]

Even if the above shows that religions are inscribed into social realities in ways that are comparable from one civilization to another, use of the English word "sacredness" with regard to societies in which concepts have not been shaped by the Indo-European lexicon can distort the study of phenomena that are better encapsulated by endogenous concepts.[26] Terms describing the organization of the Chinese cosmological worldview are helpful in supplementing and contrasting with the (Latin-based) sacred/profane dichotomy.

For instance, a character commonly found in oracle-bone inscriptions dating to around 1000 BCE, *zhu* 祝 combines the graph that signifies spirit(s) or the spiritual (on the left) and the graph for the ancestor(s) (on the right), signifying primarily "prayers addressed to an ancestor." *Zhu* can also refer to a public servant in charge of ritual offerings. In certain contexts, it is also used for expressing the idea of "linking, attaching to" and even the action of cutting one's hair, which can be considered ritual. Even more interestingly, the earliest Chinese dictionary, *Shuowen jiezi*, written during the Han period (206 BCE–220 CE), hypothesizes that the second part of the character may refer not to ancestors but to the mouth (*kou* 口), with special reference to the act of cursing. Indeed, rarely, the character may be pronounced *zhou*, thus identifying with the homonym *zhou* 咒, "to curse." In contemporary Chinese, *zhu* means "to congratulate, to wish well, and to call for blessings upon."[27]

In *The Book of Rites* (Liji), rituals (*li* 礼 / 禮)[28] are conceived of as figurative knots (*ji* 纪 / 紀) that hold society, time-space, and the universe together. In the *The Book of Rites* itself, and in the ancient Chinese philosophical corpus as a whole, the character *li* can be understood in two ways: restrictively, as ceremonies through which spirits and gods are honored, and extensively, as all rules defining proper and decorous behavior. The common denominator is the reverence (*jing*) to be shown to spirits when performing rites and toward other human beings when fulfilling duties.[29] Rites enact boundaries; they define gender and social distinctions as well as cosmological ones. *The Analects of Confucius* (Lunyu) and other writings can be legitimately read as a demythologization of the sacrificial ceremonies that were at the origins of the concept of ritual.[30] Confucius, however, vigorously maintained the necessity of blood sacrifices and the efficacy of rituals in sustaining a world order based on clearly established divisions.[31] *The Analects* has been described as redefining the secular as sacred.[32] This would mean, however, that the frontiers of the sacred were redrawn, not erased.

In Chinese religions, sacrifice (*ji*) was always preceded by purification (*zhai*). Traditionally, the killing of animals was prohibited during times of purification. The agents presiding over sacrifices were subjected to periods of reclusion and prohibition, including any polluting contact. Ritual purity remains the rule in both Buddhist and Daoist Chinese temples. Similarly, a number of regulations surround places (mainly mountains and temples), images, and other material culture that are deemed sacred. The delineation of the ritual space, the use of liturgical language, and the role given to liturgical texts (which may themselves become objects of sacrifice, notably by burning) function as markers separating the sacred and profane realms.[33] Chinese rituals are thus comparable to the Roman *sacra* (rites).

There is, however, a difference: The Latin-based lexicon Durkheim used draws a sharp distinction between sacred and profane. In China, ritual permeates all aspects of existence. This is due in part to the difference that defining a term entails for both cultures. In ancient Chinese thought, the meaning of any concept deemed central in the understanding of human and cosmic realities will be progressively enlarged.[34] Going one step further, the relationship between the cardinal Confucian virtues of ritual (sense of properties, ritual expertise) and benevolence (*ren*) suggests a corrective to the sacred/profane dichotomy: While the sacred/profane distinction is about discontinuities, Chinese texts and terminology stress necessary continuation in life processes. Different orders in collective existence are associated with different models of conduct. There are different space-times (including the ones induced by the distinction between sacrifices and festivals, on the one hand, and everyday work and life, on the other), but their alternation and combination are indispensable for ensuring the community's sustainability as a whole. Ritual observance allows one to lead life based on benevolence, while the deployment of benevolence enables one to express to the fullest the inner meaning of ritual. Then the distinction between the sacred and the profane is better perceived as a continuum.

The alternate stress on separation and continuity may be inherent to mental representations. Generally speaking, symbolic systems and ritual practices develop a number of hermeneutical circles between taking into account the discontinuities inherent in life (birth and death, differentiation of species) and, conversely, the need to ensure life continuity through links and transitions that balance or deny death and finitude.[35] This latter dimension is probably an aspect of the representational processes that Durkheim overlooked and that structural anthropology stressed and investigated in reaction. Chinese society managed continuities and discontinuities in communal and personal life processes through a symbolic organization that the sacred/profane dichotomy helps one approach but does not fully describe.[36]

At the same time, the sacred/profane dichotomy is now inscribed into the lexicon of contemporary Chinese, introduced through the appropriation of Western concepts and adoption of neologisms from the mid-nineteenth century onward. The compounds *shensheng* (sacred), *shenshengxing* (sacredness), *shenshenggan* (sense of the sacred), and *shisu* (profane) are common in writing. Their use in speech varies from quite often to not at all; in the Shanghai dialect, for instance, the compound *shensheng* normally is not used.

The compound for "sacred" is composed of two characters: *shen*, referring to the divine, and *sheng*, referring to sainthood or sagehood. *Shensheng* can be translated as "sacred" or "holy" (however, "holy" and "holiness" are preferentially expressed by the use of the second character, *sheng*, alone).[37] Additionally, *shengjie* is used for speaking of purity or holiness and refers to inner versus external holiness. *Shisu* can translate as "secular," "mundane," or yet "profane." The second character, *su*, traditionally applies to anything that is common or vulgar. These neologisms do not express the original meanings of the Latin terms *sacer* and *profanus* but are translations of religious realities shaped in nineteenth-century Europe when experiencing a personal relationship with the Divine was a defining feature of religion for liberal Protestantism. Accordingly, *shensheng* seems ready-made for rendering the title of comparative religionist Rudolf Otto's classic book *Das Heilige* (The Holy), and *shenshenggan* echoes with the undertones of the German word *Religiosität* (religiosity). In other words, the introduction of these neologisms into Chinese reflects the way Western scholars approached notions related to religion and sacredness from the mid-nineteenth century until the 1930s.

The regular use of these terms by young Catholics from Shanghai and adjacent cities, when asked in 2012 to assess the situation in the Church, was striking.

> The way of evangelization is too utilitarian, and catechism classes look very secular (*shisu*). Sometimes many people are baptized, but a lot of baptized people do not go to church. Or they come to church just to eat, drink, and make friends. (*Male, 26 years old, company staff*)
>
> Catholicism now has lost the characteristics of Catholicism, and it looks like Protestantism. Liturgy has no sacredness (*shenshengxing*); it has introduced many modern elements — singing, dancing. . . . There is no sense of the sacred (*shenshenggan*). In the catechism classes one talks about "Love", one does not speak about Truth, and one blindly tries to attract people, like if it were a commercial activity. Non-believers feel that people within the Church lead a life that is no different from the one led by the Profanes (*shisu shang de ren*), and evangelization, of course, is not effective. (*Male, 25 years old, company staff*)[38]

Is the stress on sacredness then linked primarily to the specifics of the Catholic ethos, or does it illustrate viewpoints and concerns that are shared among Chinese faith communities at large? The answer is complex and will be detailed throughout the book. Younger residents spontaneously make use of the "sacredness" lexicon. Older Shanghai residents, especially those who assert Buddhist beliefs, tend to associate the above-mentioned lexical compounds with Christianity.[39] The identification is reinforced by the fact that terms such as *shensheng* and *shenshengxing* are not part of the Shanghai dialect and must be borrowed from standard Chinese. The same respondents will instead use the term *shenmi* (mysterious, occult) to describe something that Buddhist temples embody and offer while spontaneously likening "sacred" and "mysterious." Throughout the book, interviews further detail the subtleties of these lexical uses, which differ according to social, generational, and religious backgrounds. We need to navigate between the sacredness-related lexicon as used by social scientists and the inclusion of the words "sacred" and "sacredness" (or their near equivalents) in the vocabulary of ordinary believers, who give these terms meanings that vary from one community to another. Such ambiguity is common, and words such as "power," "consciousness," or even "household" take on different resonances according to the cultural context in which they are used.

THE RITUALS OF EVERYDAY LIFE

The centrality we have given to religious *language* needs to be balanced with a focus on social *practices*.[40] Religious communities initiate and maintain social networks, care for older people, and interact with their neighborhood. Volunteers organize workshops and charity events in Buddhist temple compounds, religious fellowships orchestrate funerals in ways more sensitive to the grieving than are state-sanctioned rituals, mosques provide professional training, and Protestant and Catholic networks offer members a breadth of social, cultural, and spiritual life. These initiatives contribute both to their inner growth and to the vitality of civil society at large. Such practices can be seen as *tactics*, rather than full-fledged *strategies*. Strategies are composed of sequences of rational decisions made by agents of power who can abstract themselves from the constraints of a given environment. In contrast, people and communities devise tactics that help them cope with the decisions taken by those who hold power over their lives. "[A] tactic depends on time. . . . It must constantly manipulate events in order to turn them into 'opportunities.' The weak must continually turn to their own ends forces alien to them."[41]

And indeed, as the account of our fieldwork shows, the shaping of Shanghai's religious landscape depends first on an ever-changing combination of tactics: in contrast to the urban and religious strategies devised by decision makers, religious practitioners proceed by way of "wandering lines," errant trajectories, becoming in the process "poets of their own acts" as they continue to transform, for their use, the mental and sometimes material landscape of Shanghai.[42] In this respect, and in alignment with the way activities such as cooking or conversing have been studied by anthropologists, rituals can be seen as *bricolage*, engaging worshippers in trajectories of *braconnage* (poaching) within the urban territory designed by the state's strategy of modernization. Still, believers engage in ritual observance with more consciousness and deliberation than they apply to the activities of everyday life. Cooking, for instance, can legitimately be described as "ritual" regardless of setting, but its inclusion in a religious context (such as cooking for friends gathered at one's home for scripture reading) increases its meaning and ritual density.

The urban religious landscape is shaped not only by tactics devised by communities of believers who try to carve out a space for themselves but also by the interplay between these tactics and the strategies developed by decision makers. Chapter 1 shows how strategies of urban transformation affect religious buildings and symbols. It also details how the strategies engineered by state or local governments include the shaping of events and urban spaces that foster a feeling of civic sacredness to be experienced by all citizens. Still, these buildings and events are used, lived, or interpreted by urban dwellers in ways that may modify the original intent of the state.

The chapters that follow provide a sense of how the interplay between all actors translates into practices that tend to be *ritualized*: religious or civic rituals not only are crucial to the sense of identity nurtured by a community, small or large, but also tend to organize and permeate all of the community's other activities. At this stage, we need to enlarge what is usually meant by the word "ritual," so as to understand how coordinated social practices can be fruitfully interpreted as "ritual figurations" that contribute to mapping the urban territory.

RITUAL FIGURATIONS

The ever-evolving networks of relationships from which individuals grow and concurrently help forge have been described by sociologist Norbert Elias as interdependent practices of "figuration" or "configuration."[43] He illustrates these relationships with three analogies: a group of dancers whose gestures are meshed and synchronized with those of other dancers;[44] a game of chess in which each move produces a countermove (the metaphor applying to both individual and collective interactions);[45] and four people playing cards, their dealings forming "a flexible lattice-work of tensions."[46] Minutely choreographed dancing was an essential element of Chinese court rituals;[47] anthropologists have described the world of chess players as deeply ritualized;[48] and the small-group-building rituals surrounding card playing are the sort of activities that, like cooking and shopping, could be considered practices of everyday life through which social actors craft and inhabit their environment. Notably, two of the three analogies involve games, while dancing and playing are intricately linked activities. Roberte Hamayon has proposed considering all game playing as a ritual representation, making the study of "playing" a window into the global symbolic organization of a society (as much as is the case for "giving").[49] "Playing" and "giving" are both characterized by a mixture of *cooperation* and *competition* among players. Religious rituals can usefully be approached as a form of playing. Cooperation among participants is needed, but competition, in different garb, is never very far away: relationships between the faithful and spiritual entities easily take the form of bargaining (or even jostling when these entities are deemed to be nefarious), the performance of rituals often reveals underlying conflicts in the community, and different faith communities compete in assessing their privileged or unique relationship with the Divine. Study of religious playing in the playground constituted by the city involves paying particular attention to the following:

- The way performances shape space and time while engaging actors and spectators in a dynamic of participation
- The cooperative and competitive dimensions of religious activities, which contribute to their integration into a global ethos
- The shaping of polarities and spatial constellations induced by religious playing

Focusing on religious figurations will enable us to enter the complex game of interactions between congregations and political powers, among various congregations living in the same urban space, and among members of the same congregation. It will also show how rituals discipline and police (but possibly also liberate and empower) the participants and how the entire social space is fathomed through the ritual configurations enacted in its midst. These all make up the religious fabric of Shanghai, a textured landscape, which is to be understood and described as a whole.

ENTERING SHANGHAI

Shanghai can be described as a web of sacred spaces that resonate differently from one community to another. These spaces are constantly activated through ritual enactments, and their combination charts a sacred geography. The frontiers and functions of religious spaces—from recognized landmarks to ad hoc meeting places—can be porous and evolving, as the city's religious geography is always being created and re-created through the resourcefulness of believers.

Recent studies of Chinese sacred geography depart from the earlier practice of separating the sacred and the profane into exclusive categories and instead see the sacred as constructed and contested by various influxes, not only religious or spiritual but also sociopolitical and historical.[50] However, this process is more intense, involves more actors, and is more conspicuous in the metropolises of today than in rural landscapes or in China's ancient sacred mountains in the past. In Shanghai, as in other global cities, sacredness is stored, engineered, and circulated in various ways.

Sacredness is *stored* in the sense that religious and quasi-religious spaces are integrated into the general fabric of the city, becoming part of its identity, carrying both shared legacies and conflicting significances. Sacredness is also *engineered*: spaces such as offices, factories, hotels, and waterfronts are regularly used for ritual purposes and sanctified by the presence of a worshipping community. Sacredness is also a commodity that is *circulated* through networks and along circuits, and in Shanghai, waterways offer an apt metaphor: they made Shanghai a unified territory, as the metro systems and the highways now do. Within a shared territory in which they can easily circulate, people carve out mental spaces that are not restricted to spatial enclosures.

This is akin to saying that our experience of space is mentally shaped by a sense of *presence*; in such a sense of presence, the faithful locate the experience of sacredness. Presence can be static, as with Chinese sacred mountains,[51] but it can also be carried dynamically along highways and waterways, in which case it disrupts official frontiers: the tactics by which Shanghai's city dwellers redefine the religious landscape — electing new worship sites, elaborating new ritual expressions, and associating in networks — transgress and disrupt the ordering engineered by city planners and policy makers. Similar to Shanghai's global cityscape, the religious landscape we are now going to explore is both anchored in the history of the city and in a state of constant transformation. More importantly, it is woven through the interplay that takes place between actors whose inventiveness and sense of adaptation manifest themselves in rituals, space arrangements, and communal ways of living.

The same scenery is perceived very differently from one viewpoint to another. Likewise, we need to appreciate Shanghai's religious landscape from the perspectives taken by its makers, each seeing it in relation to his or her contribution. Only in the concluding chapter of this book have we combined all dimensions into a whole, circulating between the individual, the communal, and the global. Our vision will necessarily remain what the contemplation of any landscape is by nature — always changing. And it will probably lead the reader to decide on a given perspective, centering on a particular community or, conversely, widening to encompass the whole of China or toward other global cities. Such a broadening of perspective is called for by our subject matter: Shanghai's social and religious landscape is inserted into a mental and a spatial continuum that the reader, once the book is closed, can focus on or expand at will.

CHAPTER 1

Mapping Shanghai

SHANGHAI, LIKE ALL CITIES, IS MAPPED BY ITS HISTORICAL LEGACY, its city planners, and its urban dwellers. Mental maps are created through routine trajectories and occasional wanderings, by the use of the transportation system as well as cultural and leisure venues, by perception of landmarks, and by memories of events. Religious mappings are located within this array.

A WALLED CITY AND ITS SURROUNDINGS

Studies of the Shanghai of the first decades of the twentieth century have emphasized its prominent role in bringing China into the era of "modernity."[1] Chinese researchers are still debating whether this focus on modernization may have twisted or shadowed the study of Shanghai as a locus of revolutionary history.[2] Both modernity and revolution are inscribed into the city's architectural landmarks. The affluent district of Xintiandi (New Heavens and Earth) includes the site of the first congress of the Chinese Communist Party (CCP), held in July 1921, memorialized by a museum; the Longhua Revolutionary Martyrs' Cemetery (Longhua Lieshi Lingyuan), next to the Buddhist Longhua Temple (Longhua Si), commemorates Party members and other activists who died during the revolutionary struggles of 1928–37; and the Monument to the People's Heroes stands at the northern end of the Bund, next to the former headquarters of several Protestant missionary societies. Religious landmarks and symbols of public sacredness inform the city's global narrative.

Modernization has long been linked to Shanghai's religious development.[3] The county gazetteer of 1504 mentions around one hundred Buddhist and Daoist temples.[4] The conversion to Catholicism of Xu Guangqi (1562–1633), a Shanghai-born scholar and statesman, resulted in long-term religious and social changes from 1608 onward. After 1842, the majority of Protestant mission societies in China were headquartered in Shanghai, bringing profound transformations in education and health care. The city was also central to the aggiornamento of Buddhism in the Republican era (1912–49) and the shaping of an urban Daoist culture.[5] More recently, the internationalization of contemporary Shanghai has been accompanied by an expanding and increasingly diverse religious landscape.

Shanghai is part of the Jiangnan (South of the River) human and geographic region, historically composed of two prefectures in Zhejiang and three prefectures that were, for some time, under imperial "direct rule" (*zhili*) and known as the Southern Zhili (Nanzhili) region until the Qing dynasty. Besides Shanghai Municipality, this territory today encompasses the southern parts of Jiangsu and Anhui, as well as the northern parts of Zhejiang and Jiangxi. The geographic, economic, and cultural identity of Jiangnan can still be seen in the religious settings and rituals of the westernmost part of today's Shanghai. Jiangnan local religion often housed local gods in Buddhist temples, while integrating them into the Daoist celestial bureaucracy.[6] Inhabitants of the region nurtured a sense of community through shared beliefs and rituals that evolved together with economic and social transformations.[7]

An early and continuous process of urbanization also contributed to shape today's metropolis. The name Shanghai ("On the Sea") first appears in 1291, in reference to a new county in Songjiang Prefecture, located fifty kilometers east of Huating, the capital. Geographic conditions were both promising and risky, with streams and rivers frequently changing course.[8] The shift of influence from Qingpu (on the west) to Shanghai is linked to the shrinking of the Wusong River and the widening of the Huangpu River.[9] As waterways flowing through the Yangzi River delta toward the ocean linked the rich prefecture of Songjiang and the commercial center of Suzhou to the nation and world, Shanghai's location fostered its commercial development. Excellent conditions for rice cultivation and active trade in salt and cotton provided a basis for further expansion. A certain Woman Huang (Huang Daopo) was said to have taught other women advanced techniques of cotton weaving at the end of the thirteenth century, techniques she had supposedly learned from the aborigines of Hainan Island. This tale was spread by the reconstruction of her temple in 1836: when local leaders tried to counter the cult of the sea goddess Mazu, which Fujian merchants promoted, they elevated Woman Huang to the status of a seafaring deity.[10] The weaving of cotton made cultivating the crop much more profitable, and Shanghai cotton and embroidery were sold all over China at the beginning of the sixteenth century. As early as 1391, Shanghai had more than five hundred thousand inhabitants, and by the beginning of the seventeenth century, it may have approached the one million mark, making it the most populous county in China.[11]

Though it was seen more as a place of business than of culture, Shanghai had its fair share of degree holders from the very end of the fourteenth century onward. Artistic and intellectual pursuits flourished, among them calligraphy, painting, and the art of gardening. At the same time, the social gap was growing; famines and brigandage drove literati from Pudong and other rural settlements for the safety of the county seat. The ravages caused by brigandage eventually led to the construction of a city wall in 1533, a development of both practical and symbolic significance. This came with religious change as well; a shrine to the God of War (Guandi) was set up on top of the wall. Less than a century after the wall was built, three more shrines and a new statue of the God of War were erected in Shanghai.[12] Gardens and elaborate buildings adorned the city, while rural villas were closely connected to the urban center, and some of the land around the wall was gradually developed. After 1842, foreign concessions developed outside the walled city, and the wall itself fell in 1912 as a result of political upheaval.

Dong Qichang (1555–1636), the greatest painter and calligrapher of the late Ming dynasty (1368–1644) and a native of Shanghai, must be mentioned among those who contributed to the development of Buddhist institutions in the city. In addition to donating calligraphy to the Guanyin monastery, he launched an appeal for construction of a library in Longhua Temple (Longhua Si). Jing'an Temple (Jing'an Si), just northwest of the walled city, also received support from members of the gentry. Already, by 1504, the local gazetteer wrote, there were around one hundred Buddhist and Daoist temples in the county. The 1588 gazetteer testifies to further institutional growth.

In the Shanghai region, as was true elsewhere in China, the boundaries between Daoist, Buddhist, and popular religions were not easy to delineate. Apocalyptic frameworks and messianic hopes transcended religious affiliations. Daoist and Buddhist specialists came to share a common ritual idiom, the range of ritual practices at the local level encompassed all schools and denominations, and local practices and strategies were pivotal in the construction of the main pilgrimage centers.

After the imperial ban on maritime trade was lifted in 1684, Shanghai started to trade with Japan and the countries of Southeast Asia. The city's growth triggered its elevation from a district (*xian*) to a circuit (*dao*). At the beginning of the nineteenth century, when transport by sea replaced transport on the Great Canal, the construction of seagoing junks and the development of credit services went hand in hand. This may have triggered the development of the Green Gang (Qingbang), which eventually organized and policed almost all criminal activities in Shanghai. The Green Gang probably originated from "altar communities" (*shetuan*) formed by boatmen operating in the Ming-Qing grain tribute system on the Grand Canal. The development of steam-powered transportation on the sea may have turned their members toward other activities.[13]

As Shanghai was developing into a commercial center and surpassing comparable locations, artisans and other skilled migrants, attracted by the city's growth, gathered into "native-place associations" (*huiguan*) and networked with "common-trade associations" (*gongsuo*) based on the skills they had to offer.[14] Temples were erected outside the city walls, and philanthropic activities developed. The common-trade associations, started by Shanghai merchants, were all located inside the walled city, with many favoring the area around the City God Temple (Chenghuang Miao) and Yu Garden, where eight associations had their headquarters. In contrast, with one exception, the native-place associations were located outside the walls, almost all on a south-north axis facing the Huangpu River.[15] Different native-place groups identified with different temples and calendars.[16] They took care of burial arrangements for sojourners of limited financial means.[17] Public processions were also a way for the associations and their leaders to display their wealth and prestige. While the leaders of the native-place associations gradually distanced themselves from such activities, workers and craftsmen continued to use their premises for religious purposes.[18]

ACCOMMODATING NEW FAITHS

Daoism, Buddhism, and Confucianism did not compose the entirety of Shanghai's early religious field. Islam developed there in a relatively early period, before Christianity made the city a center of its operations in China.

The Muslim Presence in Shanghai

The Songjiang Mosque (still operating today) was probably built around 1295, and a local Muslim community had developed even before its construction.[19] Mongol rulers had relocated army officers and soldiers from Central Asia, as well as their families, to this area. The Muslim presence continued throughout the Ming and Qing dynasties. Around 1573, a mosque was built in Qingpu County, which would be destroyed during the anti-Japanese war (1937–45). Several legal disputes also testify to the Muslim presence within Shanghai's social and cultural milieus.[20]

The Western powers intended the First Opium War, which broke out in 1839, "to force China to recognize and accept the new capitalist order of the world."[21] The main stipulations of the subsequent Treaty of Nanjing (1842) had to do with freedom of trade, including implicit toleration of opium smuggling. Five ports, Shanghai among them, were opened for foreign trade and residence. Shanghai was carved up into two autonomous concessions and an area administered by China, an arrangement that would last until the Japanese invaded in 1937. It became an important industrial center and trading port that attracted both foreigners and Chinese migrants. Starting with the English presence, Indian Muslims also played a role in the history of Islam in Shanghai, despite their limited numbers. In 1855, an Indian Muslim financed the construction of a mosque and a cemetery on Zhejiang Road, and the place grew into an important local Muslim outlet.

Chinese Muslim newcomers were mostly ethnic Hui. During the Taiping Rebellion (1851–64), many Hui Muslims from Nanjing settled in Shanghai. Others came from Jiangsu, Anhui, Shandong, Henan, and Hubei. Local identities endured and continue to influence the ethos of Shanghai's Muslim community today. Hui people from Nanjing lived around Little Southern Gate (Xiao Nanmen) and Sandals Bay (Caoxiewan), while those from Shandong gathered along Malisi Road (present-day Dagu Road).

This influx led to the construction of around twenty mosques. The North Mosque on Fuyou Road (built in 1870), the Xiao Taoyuan Mosque (or West Mosque), and the Huxi Mosque (built in 1921 by Hui people from Shandong and Henan) are still in activity. Among other centers of worship, the Mosque on Jiangning Road, a base for people from Shandong, closed in 1959. Before 1949, there were five Muslim women's schools in Shanghai that also served as centers of worship known as "women's mosques." Hui migrants developed expertise in jewelry, jade, and antiques.[22] They also opened numerous halal restaurants, which became favorites among local non-Muslim people. Muslim-owned businesses such as Shanghai Xiexing Company (an import-export firm founded in 1914 with a head office in Shanghai, a transfer station in Hong Kong, and a subsidiary in Colombo, Ceylon [now Sri Lanka]) subsidized the creation of a modern school system and supported the Shanghai Muslims' Board (Shanghai Qingzhen Dongshehui). This board, founded in 1909 and composed of eighty-three members, mainly wealthy businessmen, managed ten departments. It initiated ambitious projects, such as setting up the Islamic Normal School in 1928. Translations and publications, funerals, and charities were also prominent concerns.[23]

During the Cultural Revolution (1966–76), when activists forcibly stopped all religious activities, mosques were closed or converted to schools or plants. By the mid-1980s, there were about 50,000 Muslims residing in Shanghai, with seven mosques to serve them. Since then, the number of official mosques has increased only by one. According to the 2010 census, there were at that time around 85,000 Muslim residents, 78,163 Hui people and 5,254 Uighur.[24] Non-resident Muslim migrants, especially from northwest

China, make up a larger number, probably bringing the total to around 250,000, with a subsequent rise in the number of makeshift mosques.

From Xu Guangqi to "Catholic Shanghai"

Shanghai became the cradle of Chinese Catholicism thanks to the efforts of the first Chinese Christians and missionary work proper. Adquainted with the Jesuit missionary Matteo Ricci (1552–1610), and having been baptized in 1603, the great statesman and scientist Xu Guangqi (1562–1633) returned home to Shanghai in 1607 for the prescribed period of mourning following his father's death and asked another Jesuit, Lazzaro Cattaneo (1560–1640), to instruct his household in the faith. In 1609, Xu presented sixty candidates for baptism. His properties, in the part of the city now known as Xujia-hui, became the headquarters of the Catholic mission. His granddaughter Candida Xu (1607–1680) commissioned the building of more than thirty churches in China. By 1665, missionaries had built sixty-six places of worship, mainly chapels, in Songjiang Prefecture, and converts numbered as many as fifty thousand. A local community developed in prosperous Jiading County (now part of Shanghai Municipality) as early as in Songjiang, thanks to another convert, Sun Yunhua (1581–1632), a close friend of Xu Guangqi's. In 1627, Jiading was the site of a decisive meeting of missionaries and some converted literati about the proper translation of basic Christian terms. Evangelization in Chongming County also began during this early period.[25]

In the last decades of the eighteenth century, edicts from Rome and imperial persecution chased away the missionaries and forced the Chinese church underground. The church had already been weakened by the "Rites Controversy" (around 1645–1742), during which missionaries, Roman prelates, the imperial administration, and Chinese literati engaged in bitter arguments as to the civil or religious nature of the ceremonies held in honor of Confucius and the ancestors. One can legitimately see in the Rites Controversy the first debate as to whether or not the Western terms "sacred" and "secular" apply to the Chinese context. When the Jesuits returned to Shanghai after 1842, some of Xu's descendants were still practicing the faith. They had built a small house alongside the river to use as their chapel. The Jesuits decided to establish their mission there.[26] Until the Chinese Revolution in 1949, the continuous growth of the Shanghai church made it the center of Chinese Catholicism. The Franco-Chinese treaty of 1844 allowed for the return of the missionaries and the retrocession of churches confiscated in the preceding century. The first French consul, Charles de Montigny, cemented a strong alliance with the French Jesuit missionaries who had arrived in 1842, after repeated requests for their return from the Christian communities of the region.[27]

The missionaries accumulated land and properties in a way that gave considerable autonomy to themselves and the communities under their care; in 1845, the Chinese administration devised a system granting land to the different foreigners' communities outside the walled city. Perpetual property rights were recognized, but an annual rent was still to be paid. No Chinese could claim ownership of these settlements. At the same time, missionaries, like all foreign settlers, were developing an intricate web of relationships and negotiations with the locals, who were far from being merely passive recipients of foreign actions. The commercial civilization that had developed around the Yangzi deltas had fostered material and virtual channels of communication controlled by well-organized guilds by which foreigners entered into a negotiated cooperation. As a consequence, Shanghai became the crossroads where a Chinese modernity took shape and was diffused. Cultural production and visual aesthetics became the mirror through which the city came to understand itself.[28] Shanghai was nurturing a subversive, creative spirit that was escaping both imperial and foreign attempts to control it.[29]

In 1856–59, the Vatican divided the Chinese territory into apostolic vicariates assigned to different religious congregations. The Jesuit Province of Paris was placed in charge of the Jiangnan region, which included both urban areas (Nanjing and Shanghai) and countryside. Operating in isolation from the imperial edicts of persecution until 1842, the Christian communities of Shanghai and its surroundings were governed through local Catholic clans in charge of the management of churches, with the help of consecrated virgins who led liturgical assemblies. In 1842, the apostolic vicar, Monsignor Louis de Besi, was indignant, "They are not only singers, but deaconesses, and more powerful than those of Christian antiquity."[30] Returning foreign missionaries were soon asserting their control over both temporal goods and women's initiatives, which would be contained by the arrival of French feminine congregations. However, even if the missionaries' stiff governance at times met with resistance, Shanghai Catholics were nevertheless proud of the abundant material and intellectual resources converging on their city. The Jesuit headquarters in Xujiahui ("Zikawei" in the local dialect) established a very large church, a seminary, a library, a high school, a museum of natural history, an observatory, an orphanage, a vocational school with a printing press and several artistic workshops, and similar institutions managed by religious sisters. After 1903, Aurora University would crown this "state within a state."[31] Today, the renovation of these buildings supports the official narrative woven by the authorities of Xuhui District. The museum constructed on the site of the former orphanage and vocational school (opened in 2010), the reopened Jesuit library, and the Higher Seminary (renovated in 2016) complement the Xu Guangqi Memorial Hall. The hall is located in the small park that also bears the name of the Shanghainese statesman and convert (officially honored as an outstanding scientist and patriot), which includes a "sacred alley" (*shendao*) leading to his gravesite, desecrated during the Cultural Revolution.

A variety of Catholic parish cultures arose from a mix of local traditions and the devotional style common to world Catholicism. Catholic devotions as lived in Europe and elsewhere found solid ground in Shanghai. Thus, the good deeds of the eighty-nine male members of the Apostolate of Prayer sodality of St. Francis parish for 1869 were recorded as follows: "2,547 masses; 467 via dolorosa; 2,167 rosaries recited; 2,859 morning and evening prayers; 3,386 other prayers; 1,005 offerings of meritorious actions made; 222 acts of patience; 495 victories over oneself; 261 alms; 89 Holy Communions; 192 baptisms of pagan children; 34 exhortations to the pagans." And, the anonymous narrator adds, "Were I to take the women's records, I would find much higher figures on some items, especially for Holy Communions. But I preferred to [mention] men's records."[32]

This rather inward-looking devotional culture continues to shape the local Catholic ethos. Nevertheless, in the wake of the rapid development of Shanghai's civil society, the first half of the twentieth century witnessed the rapid development of active Church charities, exemplified by the colorful figure of Joseph Lo Pahong (Lu Baihong) (1875–1937), a devout, enterprising, and very wealthy philanthropist.[33] During the Japanese invasion, the Jesuit Robert Jacquinot de Besange (1878–1946) undertook the immense task of designing, securing acceptance by all parties, and managing a security zone where civilians would be protected from the hostilities. The Jacquinot Zone hosted around three hundred thousand refugees from 1937 to 1940.[34]

From Protestant Headquarters to Indigenous Church

The first British consul, George Balfour, arrived in Shanghai fifteen months after the Treaty of Nanjing was signed. The missionary-interpreter Walter Henry Medhurst (1796–1857) was already in the process of founding the London Missionary Society Press and led the team in charge of securing a Chinese translation of the Bible (known as the "Delegates' Version"). His fellow missionary William Lockhart (1811–1896) founded the first Western hospital in Shanghai around the same time. Their followers would continue to stress translation, publication, health care, and charities, while continuing to rely on the protection of the Western powers. In 1846, Balfour's successor, John Rutherford Alcock, used the threat of cannons to obtain reparation after three British missionaries were molested in Qingpu. During the years that followed, the Western presence in Shanghai was similarly bolstered by gunboat diplomacy.[35]

Shanghai has been the base of operations for Chinese Protestant churches from the start and remains so today. Of the five recognized religions,

Protestantism is the only one that does not have its headquarters in Bei-jing. Protestant Shanghai is anchored in architectural memories, with a con-centration of buildings on or near the Bund, the waterfront area defining the former Shanghai International Settlement. The Anglican Holy Trinity Church, one of the tallest buildings on the Bund in the nineteenth century, was built in 1847, upgraded to cathedral in 1875, and had to be rebuilt several times. Union Church was erected in 1864 and relocated in 1886 and 1924. In 1932, the celebrated architect László Hudec designed the majestic building that stands at the corner of Huqiu and Yuanmingyuan Roads, where the Christian Literature Society, founded in 1887, and the China Baptist Pub-lication Society used to have their headquarters. One of the society's early directors, Edward Selby Little, who had come to China with the Southern California Episcopal Conference, epitomizes the mix of missionary, politi-cal, and commercial motivations typical of several Western figures living in Shanghai during this period. The Baptist Publication Society published the journal *True Light* (Zhenguang), which eventually gave its name to the building. The Young Women's Christian Association Building, also on Yuanmingyuan Road, was known as the "women's building." Even after the YWCA soon shifted its focus to social work, the building hosted the offices of the missionary journal *The Chinese Recorder*. Two doors down on the north side was the Missions Building, home to the National Christian Council, the American Bible Society, the National Bible Society of Scotland, the Lon-don Missionary Society, and the China Council of the Presbyterian Church. YMCA headquarters were located on Huqiu Road, in a building described as "a monument to the brotherhood of commerce and Christianity."[36] By 1922, the YMCA's 450 paid staff members across China were being supervised from Shanghai by the national staff led by David Yui.[37] Under its middle-class leadership, the YMCA was fostering community self-help. It attracted "the best young men in Shanghai," a staff member in that city reported in 1901.[38]

The US Anglican All Saints Church, built in 1925, and the Methodist-Episcopal Moore Memorial Church (MMC) were located not far from the Bund. Shanghai was also home to the Seventh-Day Adventists' headquarters in China. *The Signs of the Times* (Shizhao yuebao), also based in the city, was the most widely circulated Christian periodical in the mid-twentieth century, with around 130,000 copies sold per issue in 1937. The periodical was both a missionary tool and a vigorous advocate of hygiene education.[39] The influence of Protestantism on Shanghai's overall course of development could hardly be overestimated. St. John's College, founded in 1879 by US Episcopalians (a leading figure among them being Russian-born Joseph Schereschewsky, who had entered the Episcopal Church in New York), became a full-fledged university accredited in the United States in 1905. Its associated middle school attracted the children of Shanghai's Chinese elite, including T. V. Soong, premier of the Republic of China; K. H. Ting, the Anglican leader who was to mediate the relationship between the Protestant Church and the new regime; and the architect Leoh Ming Pei. In terms of social awareness, the YMCA, present in China since 1890, initiated a child labor campaign and programs of popular education in various factories that became large-scale in the 1930s under the leadership of Cora Deng. These programs trained a large number of activists, many of whom would later organize popular resistance against Japan.[40] The number and diversity of Protestant congregations in Shanghai explain the multifaceted outlook of the city's local churches today. They contrast with the dominance of the China Inland Mission tradition in Wenzhou and the preponderance of Anglicanism and Methodism in Fujian.[41]

Shanghai thus became the hotbed of a truly indigenous Protestant Church infused with Christian nationalism. The aftermath of the Boxer Rebellion (1899–1901) played a crucial role in the process of indigenization. In 1902, a few Shanghai YMCA activists started an independent Christian Union in order to distance themselves from legal actions seeking reparations initiated by the Western powers each time missionary personnel or properties were harmed or damaged. Thereafter, an independent Presbyterian parish was established in Zhabei District and soon became a nexus of like-minded individuals and local congregations. In 1907, one hundred years after the arrival of Robert Morrisson, the Centenary Missionary Conference was held in Shanghai. It called for the eventual formation of a Chinese Church that would at some point pass beyond missionary control and guidance. Yu Cidu (1873–1931), a woman preacher who played a major role in evangelical revivalism, organized her influential preaching sessions in the Jiangwan suburb northeast of the city center.[42] The legacy of some Shanghai-based figures of the Republican era still exercises a decisive influence on present-day Christianity. Among them, Ni Tuosheng (Watchman Nee) (1903–1972), leader of the Christian Assembly (Jidutu Juhuichu), commonly known as the Little Flock, deserves special mention. Ni remained in the International Settlement in Shanghai during the troubled times of the anti-Japanese war. Denounced as a counterrevolutionary in the 1950s, he died in 1972.[43] The vitality of Protestantism in today's Shanghai is thus anchored to a rich and diverse tradition, yet the factors that support its current growth differ from those of the first half of the twentieth century.

CHINESE RELIGIONS AND RELIGIOUS MODERNIZATION

Catholicism and Protestantism were driving forces in Shanghai's modernization. Muslims were also part of the surge toward a civil society promoting schooling, internationalization, self-organization, and managerial techniques. At first glance, it seems that "Chinese religions" were going against the current. This might even have been the assessment of some among the Chinese elite beyond the Christianized gentry. Between 1905 and 1914, the ephemeral Chinese City Council "forbade gambling, worshipping traditional Taoist and Buddhist deities, sailing 'dragon-boats', acting as spirit-medium, or playing children's games in which there was an element of gambling."[44] The city council was not without its own religious undertones, since its members showed pietistic Confucian inclinations.[45]

In fact, Buddhist and, to a lesser extent, Daoist elites led the drive toward the aggiornamento of their own faiths, furthering Shanghai's overall modernization. At the beginning of the twentieth century, the growth of Christianity and related social organizations such as the YMCA was for Shanghai-based Buddhist leaders "both a pressure and a model to follow."[46] It was in Shanghai that the celebrated reformist monk Taixu (1890–1947) gave defining speeches on the tasks of "humanistic Buddhism" (*renjian Fojiao*). His vision of a reformed Buddhism was close to the liberal, socially oriented Protestant thinking that was flourishing in some of Shanghai's parishes. The city had also been the place where prominent Buddhist monks created the General Buddhist Association of China (Zhonghua Fojiao Zonghui). Other societies created during this period include the Shanghai Buddhism Preservation Society (1926); the Chinese Buddhist Association (1929), founded by Masters Yuanying, Taixu, and Renshan; the Shanghai Buddhist Society (1929), directed by Master Dabei; and the Association of Buddhist Disciples for Salvation and Peace (1936). In the 1910s and 1920s, Buddhist scholars returning from Japan found new ways of introducing the doctrine. Shanghai's prosperity allowed for growth in the number of temples, publications, and meetings, making Shanghai the center of Buddhist revival in the Republican era.[47]

A laity-led Daoist renewal centered first on individual practices rather than on communal devotions.[48] At the same time, temples belonging to the monastic Quanzhen School started to complement those affiliated with the ritualistic Zhengyi School. The Quanzhen temples were established with funding from native-place associations and guilds from northern Jiangsu and other areas.[49] The shift in the outlook of Shanghai Daoism took place along with its opening toward modernity. In 1917, the establishment of the Shanghai Psychical Research Society (Shanghai Lingxuehui) linked the divinatory practice of spirit-writing with the new popular interest in parapsychology.[50] The success of such pursuits helped initiate new Daoist networks, based no longer on communal affiliations but rather on shared interests and even on political concerns regarding the nation's physical and moral regeneration. Daoism thus adopted the codes of Shanghai-led modernity, and its urban elite propagated the faith through popular magazines, as occurred with other religions.[51] The religious fabric of Republican-era

Shanghai was interwoven with a level of activities and networking in civic circles that was unheard of elsewhere in China.[52] The Japanese invasion and subsequent political developments were to change the course of this dynamic.

1949–PRESENT: REMAPPING SACREDNESS

After 1949, while as the new Communist regime of the People's Republic of China (PRC) banned and repressed all "sects and secret societies" (*huidaomen*), it created a legal framework for the five authorized religions (Buddhism, Daoism, Catholicism, Protestantism, and Islam) and endeavored to ensure the loyalty of the religious leadership through the creation of ad hoc associations and personnel renewal. Secularization of society at large (notably by discouraging rituals for ancestors and other expressions of popular religiosity) was another central objective. Mourning was permitted only in public funeral parlors; cremation, instead of burial, became the norm; expressions of grief and mourning dress were strictly regulated and constrained; and the work unit rather than the family was in charge of funeral matters.[53]

Monastic wandering and Daoist household clergy were early targets for rectification. Buddhist leaders were soon enrolled in national causes such as mobilization in support of the Korean War effort.[54] Slow to organize, and subject to increased criticism for their "feudal" outlook, Daoists created the Chinese Daoist Association only in 1957, with Chen Yingning (the leader of the Daoist renewal movement in Shanghai during the Republican era) as secretary-general and later on as chairman. In these capacities, he played an important role in the rise of *qigong* in the People's Republic of China.[55] The Great Leap Forward (1958–61), the campaign aimed at moving China toward a collectivist economy, led to the purge of many prominent religious leaders and the closure of most churches. In Shanghai, the number of Protestant churches fell from two hundred to eight.[56] On June 15, 1953, a police raid at the Faculty of Theology in Xujiahui closed the last Jesuit institution in China. On the night of September 8, 1955, Bishop Gong Pinmei, seven Chinese diocesan priests, fourteen Chinese Jesuit, two Carmelite sisters and three hundred influential laypeople were arrested, an event still commemorated by the local community. Other arrests followed. Before the end of the month, around 1,200 Catholics were imprisoned. Their confessions were part of the evidence used in 1960 in the final trial of the bishop of Shanghai and fourteen other defendants.[57] Shortly afterward, the Cultural Revolution engulfed all the actors in this drama in a common torrent. Decisions made after 1979 by the local Catholic leadership as to whether or not to cooperate with the government divided the community. After his return to the

Shanghai diocese around 1982, the Jesuit Aloysius Jin Luxian (1916–2013), who would be the official bishop of Shanghai from 1985 until his death, met with harsh criticism from underground priests and laypeople. His memoirs allude to these conflicts, their psychological impact, and their effect on Rome's policy toward China.[58]

The Shanghai Protestant Church held its first accusation meeting in 1951, with Western missionaries and reputedly pro-Nationalist Chinese pastors as the main targets. Ni Tuosheng was imprisoned in 1952, to the applause of the Three-Self Patriotic Movement's local leadership.[59] He was sentenced to fifteen years' imprisonment in 1956. The Party used different tactics with different Protestant Churches.[60] When it came to the Seventh-Day Adventists, the Party organized frustrated church workers into a new core leadership that opposed the current leaders, who were mainly missionaries (unlike other Protestant churches, Seventh-Day Adventism was still directed mainly by missionaries), and those who defended them. This created deep antagonisms within the congregation, which resulted in more arrests. Finally, the Adventist Church was integrated into the Three-Self Patriotic Movement.[61] At the beginning of the 1960s, through strategies tailored to the situation of each group, Shanghai authorities had religious leaders firmly under their control.

In Shanghai, as in other Chinese cities, Red Guards from Beijing instructed their Shanghai counterparts to raid temples and churches, burn books, and persecute and parade their victims.[62] Nien Cheng's celebrated memoir *Life and Death in Shanghai*, published in 1987, describes what was in store for people who were targeted as "counterrevolutionaries." Memories of the destruction are still alive. Visitors to Xu Guangqi Memorial Park, near the Xujiahui St. Ignatius Cathedral, are still likely to meet elderly Catholic residents of the neighborhood who are quick to stress that the grave of Xu Guangqi, vandalized during the Cultural Revolution, once occupied the place where a memorial now stands. Stones bearing the original Latin inscription of 1903 (erected in commemoration of the four hundredth anniversary of Xu's baptism), also vandalized during that period, remain on display in the park.

Other aspects of the Cultural Revolution in Shanghai, however, are specific to the city itself. First, the campaign began in Shanghai, when Jiang Qing, Mao Zedong's wife, recruited the writer Yao Wenyuan to pen a far-reaching criticism of the historical drama *Hai Rui Dismissed from Office* in an essay published in November 1965. Over the next ten years, Shanghai's writers groups would continue to play a leading ideological role nationwide. Second, the early victory of the workers movement's rebels against the Conservatives (i.e., supporters of the CCP apparatus) paradoxically spared Shanghai some of the murderous infighting that would desolate other

Chinese cities. The strength of the workers' movement is another feature of Shanghai's experience throughout the Cultural Revolution. Finally, the paradoxical nature of the movement's leadership deserves special attention, as it highlights the uneasy relationship between Shanghai and the northern part of the country. Although the Gang of Four is sometimes known as the "Shanghai clique," two of its members were from Shandong.[63] Other radical leaders active in Shanghai were also from northern China.[64] This explains, in part, the overpowering reaction of Shanghai's population against the last radical bastions when their militants tried to resist the fall of the Gang of Four in October 1976.

During the Cultural Revolution, all public religious activities were forbidden. This unprecedented level of repression was foreshadowed during the Great Leap Forward, with its stepped-up campaigns against "feudal superstitions." At that time, the state apparatus linked rumors caused by famines and other disasters to the upsurge in superstitious activity, which it sought to counter by implementing such campaigns. These rumors were not limited to the countryside, and spread through big cities like Shanghai.

> In June 1962, the party cell at the No. 9 State Textile Mill in Shanghai asked nine women workers to give their views about the causes of the famine. Six were convinced that the disasters had been sent by the gods (*pusa*). Thirty-nine-year-old Wang Jinxiu said: "During the past years, there have been an awful lot of natural disasters — first we hear of floods, then of droughts, then of hailstorms, then of whirlwinds. This is all because people no longer believe enough in the gods. Buddha has sent us the famine." . . . In April 1963, the General Labor Union of Shanghai Municipality reported that workers at the No. 9, No. 12, and No. 17 State Textile Mills, at the No. 4 Printing and Dyeing Mill, and in the working-class district of Yangpu were gripped by a rumor that a "toad spirit" (*hama jing*) was roaming the suburb of Pudong — just across the Huangpu River from Yangpu. The toad weighed 2.5 *jin* (1.5 kg) and was able to speak. Like its prototypes in Jilin, it forecast: "This year more than half of the old people will die," but added that they might survive if they ate a toad before the first day of the fifth lunar month.[65]

The fact that such hearsay was already spreading in the early 1960s explains the increasing repression of all religious activities (considered part of the "four olds" — old thinking, old culture, old customs, and old habits) and the messianic and apocalyptic aspects of the Cultural Revolution. The emergence of a Mao cult was noticeable from the beginning of the new regime onward, as when a local newspaper reported in 1950: "From now on you should not buy incense paper anymore. Believing in gods is nonsense. Only Chairman Mao and the Communist Party are the real living divinities who relieve the poor and the sufferers."[66] Although such words targeted popular religion practices, they are loaded with strong Buddhist undertones: Mao Zedong was somehow presented as the Enlightened One, saving the poor from the sea of suffering. At the same time, the movement was not simply engineered by the state or by Mao himself. The emotional and ritualistic expressions of the Mao cult displayed by the Red Guards during the first years of the Cultural Revolution were the product of their own agency, resulting in the enactment of political-religious rituals.[67] The religious element that permeated the new regime at key moments of its tumultuous history cannot be described as mere ideological fabrication but was rooted in a popular sense of sacredness that sometimes overflowed its bounds and could not be controlled.

The shaping of this alternative sacredness implied the desecration of concurring manifestations. All temples and churches were closed and, in many cases, converted into factories. In 1966, at the beginning of the Cultural Revolution, Red Guards from Beijing vandalized the St. Ignatius Cathedral, smashing all its stained glass windows. For the next ten years, the cathedral would serve as a grain warehouse. The adjacent house, which formerly hosted the Jesuit community, "had become a parasol-handle factory where all those who had been priests and nuns worked during the Cultural Revolution."[68] Desecration was not enough. Symbolic separations had to be enacted through and through: "The Dongjiadu cathedral was hidden from view, concrete sheds were slapped around the building, and workshops were set up inside.[69] A light bulb factory had its boiler room behind the altar."[70] Similar stories are still being told about all major religious edifices in Shanghai.

RELIGIONS AND THE MAKING OF A GLOBAL METROPOLIS

After the Cultural Revolution ended, Shanghai was one of the first cities to plan and encourage the reopening of religious edifices. Between the end of 1978 and the end of 1979, Jade Buddha Temple, Xiao Taoyuan Mosque, and Moore Memorial Church reopened. After 1980, cadres invited Bishop Jin Luxian to participate in Catholic reconstruction under the auspices of the Open Door policy.[71] Buddhist temples soon benefited from special attention, as they were rebuilt, aggrandized, and embellished though public-private partnerships. With the Three-Self Patriotic Movement and the China Christian Council both headquartered in Shanghai, Protestantism was also a recipient of state investment; the 18,470-square-meter East China Theological Seminary was founded in 1985. Daoism and Islam seem to have received less official attention. The lavish rebuilding of the City God Temple owes less to its importance as a religious center than to its status as a symbol of civic sacredness.

The progressive rebuilding of Shanghai's religious cityscape — in terms of places of worship, institutions and believers — does not mean that such reconstruction is complete. In 2010, sociologist Yang Fenggang observed,

> In Shanghai, the 280 Protestant churches present in 1949 were reduced to twenty-three by 1990, the 1950 Buddhist temples dropped to nineteen, the 392 Catholic churches to forty-three, the 236 Daoist temples to six, and the nineteen Islamic mosques to six. According to an oral briefing by a government official at a meeting in 2006, there were 375 religious sites in Shanghai in 2005, including eighty-five Buddhist temples, fifteen Daoist temples, seven mosques, 104 Catholic churches, and 164 Protestant churches. It is true that there has been a rapid increase in the reform era. However, the overall number has remained far less than that of the pre-PRC era. Moreover, the Chinese population has approximately tripled since 1949, from about 450 million to 1.3 billion today, and the increase has been even greater in the Beijing and Shanghai metropolises.[72]

The presence of at least 430 official places of worship in 2014 shows that religious reconstruction is still in progress.[73] Unofficial places of worship are flourishing with little government interference, certainly less than in other cities or provinces, although incidents have occurred. For instance, in 2009, a home church in Minhang District with a membership of around 1,200 was forced to disband.[74]

More important, the Shanghai government's policies for creating and managing places of worship have been closely linked to overall urban planning.[75] The post-1992 urban dynamic that affects the religious landscaping of the metropolis includes the development of nine new satellite cities, sixty new towns, and six hundred central villages within its administrative area. The outlying settlements were intended to provide public revenue through the conversion of formerly non-priced land into a land-lease market.[76] Present-day Shanghai corresponds roughly to what its planners had envisioned, with clearly differentiated neighborhoods (map 1). The suburbs now include high-priced residential communities that have become urban centers of their own.[77]

The distinction among neighborhoods is mitigated by the extension of the metro system, which grew exponentially in the years leading up to Expo Shanghai 2010 and continues to expand today. Now the world's largest transit system by route length, Shanghai Metro links territories that otherwise

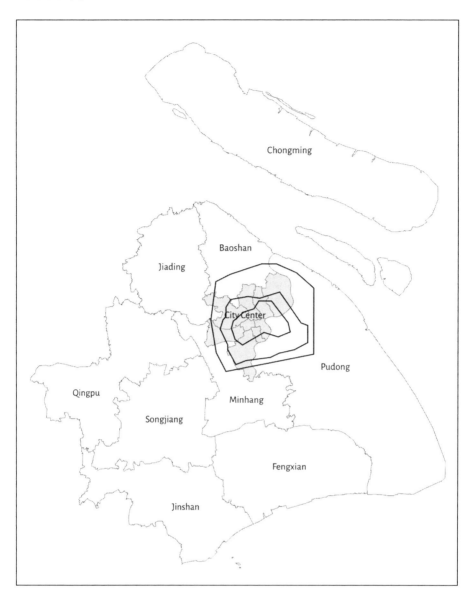

MAP 1. Shanghai Municipality (Administrative Districts and Ring Roads)

could be seen as having been artificially gathered into a municipality and lacking organic cohesiveness. In 2016, the network's daily traffic rose to 8.4 million trips.[78] If the metro system makes the entire city a lived reality for city dwellers, the basic urban experience remains that of the micro-district (*xiaoqu*) or residential community. Micro-districts are experienced as "expanded homes," the more so because almost all of them are walled.[79] These communities, around 5,700 in the whole of Shanghai Municipality,[80] vary in size, some with only one high-rise and no communal area, but most comprise between four to sixty apartment buildings and a range of common spaces. Communities belong to one of the 208 administrative wards that make up the sixteen districts that compose Shanghai Municipality.

At the same time, the Shanghai urban imaginary retains memories of the *lilong*, or *longtang* (a form of residential development centered on lanes or groups of lanes), though this form has been disappearing from the urban landscape over the past two to three decades. Neither fully enclosed nor truly open, "jointly produced by foreign landowners and Chinese builders, the *li* combined the vernacular and the translocal (or the colonial), incorporated residential and commercial functions, and accommodated elite and lower-class residents."[81] Today, the *lilong* imaginary speaks nostalgically of solidarity between the street and the compound, while echoing the dream of freedom and adventure that had set the sojourners of colonial Shanghai in motion.

The spaces, buildings, and communication networks of the metropolis are home to official and private memories, urban myths, and public or furtive practices that foster a sense of what it means to dwell, work, and move in a given environment. Thus, the city — a place of encounters and estrangement, of constraints and wanderings, of conflicting discourses and unifying visions — naturally becomes a nexus of meanings that are constantly constructed, questioned, and combined in its midst.[82] The lived sacredness of the city is the privileged expression of a quest that both unites and scatters the inhabitants of a shared urban territory.

CIVIL RELIGION, CIVIC SACREDNESS

Sacredness is engineered both by religious congregations and by the state. The more the state involves itself in the engineering of sacredness, the more it asserts a religious function and nature. From its outset, the state unites society within a single system of beliefs and practices, known as "civil religion." At yet another stage, the pluralization of religious organizations may induce the state to adopt one of the creeds active in its territorial sphere of influence as a state religion, or, while protecting (or repressing) all of them, the state may develop forms of communal worship that mobilize, mimic, or frame religious rituals.

Civil religion is generally defined as "a system of symbols, beliefs, and rites of a reverent and celebratory kind, concerning the myths, history and destiny of a people that is used to establish and express the sacred character of their social identity and the civic and political order associated with it."[83] It gathers a collection of beliefs, values, rites, and symbols that give sacred meaning to the life of the community.[84] The rituals celebrated for those killed in war "strikingly express such characteristics," though "these processes are far from being straightforward, unambiguous or uncontested."[85]

There is a further distinction to be made between *civil* religion and *civic* religion, the latter often called "polis religion" when referring to the model offered by Greek and Latin antiquity. Civic religion is to be understood as the public display and management of sacredness within a given city. In the ancient Greek polis (or Latin *civitas*), the divine powers being celebrated within the territorial limits of the city were somehow co-citizens (*municipes*) of the people who worshipped them. Civic religion embodied the contractual relationships between the cities and their gods, the latter ensuring prosperity and safety in exchange for the ceremonial and sacrificial recognition they received.[86] This idea is not absent from the Chinese model of local religiosity. As noted, disasters that happened during the Cultural Revolution have sometimes been attributed to the interruption of such sacrificial recognition. Even more to the point, the celebration of revolutionary martyrs or other prominent civic figures may be associated with a city's destiny as a whole. However, rather than using the term "civic religion" when dealing with present-day metropolises, it might be more appropriate to speak merely of a sphere of "civic sacredness" that anchors a nation's civil religion to a specific environment while complementing or correcting this national model as it may ignore or contradict some tenets of local memory and identity. Thus, Shanghai will celebrate its past in ways that the national discourse engineered from Beijing would not allow if specific local events and metaphors were not put into motion. In other words, civic sacredness contextualizes the national civil religion (whatever its prevalence and its degree of formalization) according to the resources provided by the local ethos.

Local authorities do not act alone in the process of investing the city's space with meaning. Rather, a complex interaction takes place among the municipal power, religious groupings, and city dwellers. People gather in spaces inscribed into the urban geography, the "second nature" shaped by the polis. Such spaces may or may not be officially sanctioned; they may be citywide or part of a small neighborhood; they may offer large, public facilities or be limited to a quasi-private street corner. In any case, spaces are made functionally sacred, even temporarily, by the way they are marked for specific practices. Within these spaces, further spatial arrangements facilitate the performance of rituals. Memorial squares, designated buildings, or a site where a disaster has occurred and where people come to pay tribute, all define different levels and moments of celebration or mourning.

The frontiers of civic sacredness are porous. Three maps in this volume illustrate three levels of analysis. First, at the level of symbolic Shanghai, some privileged landmarks offer an image of the city as variously experienced by different stakeholders (map 2). Second, sites of civic sacredness are those designed as such by the authorities; they draw up a dominant narrative of the city's history and mission (map 3). Finally, religious landmarks are significant in various ways at different moments of the year (see map 4 in chap. 2).

For officials, city dwellers, and visitors alike, symbolic Shanghai certainly includes such sites as the People's Municipal Government Building and the Shanghai Museum on People's Square. Together with its surroundings, the new Shanghai Museum, in the shape of an ancient bronze sacrificial vessel, exemplifies the way city landmarks may symbolize the local ethos by combining layers of the past in a synthesis that speaks of the city's present and the way it envisions its future.

> The Shanghai Museum . . . has emerged as something of a visual symbol of the new Shanghai. Completed in 1996, the museum is a centrepiece in the newly-fashioned People's Square, which like Tiananmen Square for Beijing is the political, cultural and symbolic heart of Shanghai. People's Square, radically transformed from its socialist legacy (which was itself a radical transformation of the site during its colonial days), is also framed by the Grand Theatre, the headquarters of the Shanghai city government and the Shanghai Municipal Urban Planning Exhibition Centre. Taken together these represent the official face of Shanghai: the government headquarters is the political and economic present; the Urban Planning Exhibition Centre embodies, both in its exterior and in its exhibitions, a progressive commercial future; and the Shanghai Museum conveys a glorious past. The museum and the Grand Theatre present to the world a cultured image of the city that is crucial to its larger image as a global economic powerhouse.[87]

The reconstituted Yu Garden neighborhood connects contemporary Shanghai to its origins as a walled city. Far to the west, Xu Guangqi Memorial Park and Memorial Hall celebrate the opening of the city to the world and to modernity a long time before Western powers effected such opening by force. The Bund and Xintiandi District speak not only of the time of the foreign concessions, when Shanghai was already a world metropolis, but also of the national and revolutionary struggles through which the city decided its own fate. The Shanghai Jewish Refugees Museum (formerly Ohel Moishe Synagogue) has become a symbol of Shanghai's openness and generosity during the period when no visitor needed a passport to enter. Grand buildings constructed on the eastern side of the Huangpu River for the development of Pudong after 1993 testify to Shanghai's global destiny. The year when its status was confirmed by the celebration of Expo Shanghai 2010 is commemorated by the China Art Museum.[88] And from 2016 onward, the sacrosanct towers of Sleeping Beauty's Castle at Shanghai Disneyland echo the heights of the Peace Hotel (completed

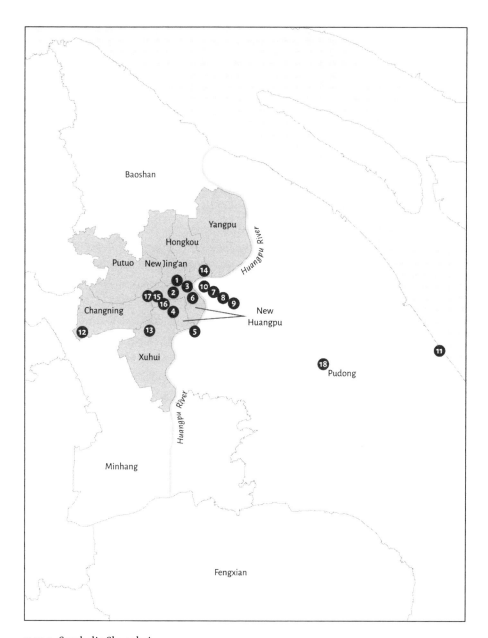

MAP 2. Symbolic Shanghai

1 Shanghai Government
2 Shanghai Museum
3 The Bund
4 Xintiandi
5 China Art Museum (Chinese Pavilion of Expo
   Shanghai 2010)
6 Yu Garden (Yuyuan)
7 Shanghai Tower
8 Jin Mao Tower
9 Shanghai World Financial Center

10 Oriental Pearl Radio and TV Tower
11 Pudong International Airport
12 Hongqiao International Airport
13 Xu Guangqi Memorial Park and Hall
14 Shanghai Jewish Refugees Museum
    (former Ohel Moishe Synagogue)
15 Shanghai Exhibition Centre
16 Former residence of Sun Yat-sen
17 CWI Children's Palace
18 Shanghai Disney Resort

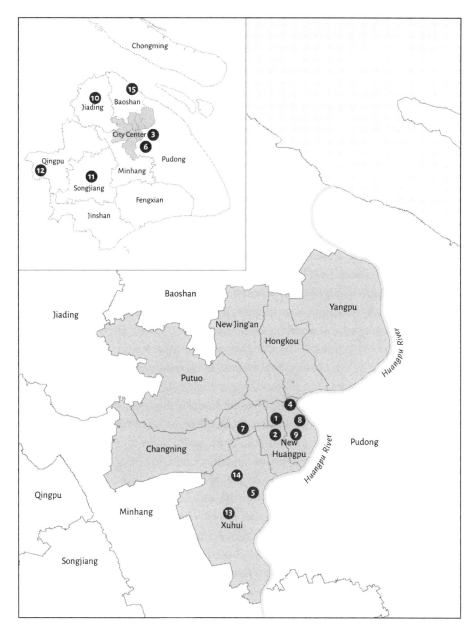

MAP 3. Landmarks of Civic Sacredness

1 People's Square
2 Memorial Hall of the First National Congress of the CCP
3 Shanghai Municipal History Museum
4 Shanghai Monument to the People's Heroes
5 The Longhua Revolutionary Martyrs' Cemetery
6 China Art Museum (Chinese Pavilion of Expo Shanghai 2010)
7 Shanghai Exhibition Centre
8 City God Temple of Shanghai
9 Shanghai Confucian Temple
10 Jiading Confucius Temple and Examination Museum
11 Songjiang Guangfulin Relics Park
12 Fushouyuan Cemetery Park
13 Longhua Crematorium and Funerary Museum
14 Xu Guangqi Memorial Park and Hall
15 Shanghai Songhu Anti-Japanese Campaign Memorial Hall

in 1929), the Shanghai Exhibition Hall (1955), and the 632-meter-high Shanghai Tower.

Several of the places mentioned above, complemented by other spaces and buildings, are clearly sites of civic sacredness: they celebrate the city as a collective being marked by a destiny, a life, and mission that transcend individuals and time spans. Such places are subject to restrictions and reverence, which identify them as sacred, that is, dedicated to the worship of the symbolic being formed by the city in association with the country to which it belongs. At the same time, Shanghai city planners had to take into account different layers of civic sacredness, fostered by political and historical factors. Detailing these layers will allow us to better comprehend the delicate balance that Shanghai must maintain when dealing with its own past, on the one hand, and its inclusion into a national narrative, on the other.

The first layer of civic sacredness is centered on New China, encapsulating the decisive break of 1949, contrasting New China with earlier periods, and upholding the hopes of socialism's advance. To this day, "red tourism" has been a way of maintaining or reviving pilgrimages along Shanghai's revolutionary holy sites.[89] The Longhua Revolutionary Martyrs' Cemetery (discussed in chap. 2) exemplifies this type of civic sacredness. The Shanghai Exhibition Centre, on Yan'an Road, is also highly significant. Built in 1955 as a symbol of Sino-Soviet friendship, with the central tower designed on the model of Saint Petersburg's Admiralty Building, it was the tallest building in Shanghai until 1988 and, until 2011, the site of all major political meetings in the city.

The second type of civic sacredness, Eternal China, marks a shift (but not a break) from the New China model. The shift began in the mid-1990s, and the redesign of People's Square at that time represents the beginning of a trend that the China Art Museum would carry through several decades later. The China Art Museum hosted the China Pavilion at Expo Shanghai 2010, often termed the "Oriental Crown" (Dongfang Zhiguan). Like the Shanghai Museum, its shape was inspired by ancient sacrificial vessels, enlarging progressively from bottom to top, with a rooftop designed on the nine-square-grid layout typical of classical Chinese urban planning, an image of the universe. The color of the structure, "Chinese red" (Zhongguo hong), may be its most striking feature. A combination of seven shades created especially for the project, it differs from both the "oriental red" (dongfang hong) typical of the revolutionary years and the purple (zi) shades typical of the Imperial Palace.[90] The idea of stability associated with a four-legged sacrificial vessel opens up to that of China's "eternity."

The third and fourth types of civic sacredness duplicate to some extent the division between the epochal and the eternal represented by the first and second layers but at the level of the city proper.

The third layer focuses on the time of foreign dominance, the foreign concessions, and the anti-Japanese war. Ambiguous by nature, it recalls a history of suffering, humiliation, resilience, and pride. Monuments and symbols merge revolutionary representations with a Shanghai-based aesthetics influenced by Christianity and the West. For instance, in the Longhua Revolutionary Martyrs' Cemetery, the gigantic sculpture of a figure lying on his side and partially embedded in the ground has an arm raised as if announcing resurrection (plate 4), and the wax figure of Mao in the Memorial Hall of the First National Congress of the Chinese Communist Party is the only one standing, in a scene reminiscent of the Last Supper (plate 5).

The fourth and final layer of civic sacredness takes the history of the city as a whole, from its origins to its resplendent future. It is notable for integrating three places emblematic of what the "Chinese city religion" was meant to be: the city god temple (discussed in chap. 2) and two temples inscribed into state-sponsored Confucianism. Renovated in 1997, the Shanghai Confucian Temple (Shanghai Wenmiao), an institution that changed its location four times in the course of its tormented seven-hundred-year history, is home to a weekly book fair recalling its historical status as a school-temple centered on a cult of literacy.[91] Its promotional brochure presents it as a "sacred place (*shengdi*) of Confucian culture." Several high schools are located in the neighborhood. The trees in the gardens are adorned with yellow cards bearing blessings written by students pleading for success on exams, and tourists use the cards to pray to "Dear Confucius" on behalf of family members or for world peace. The Jiading Confucius Temple (Jiading Kongmiao), which houses the Shanghai Museum of the Chinese Imperial Examination System, testifies to the intellectual reputation of Jiading, once a prosperous county-level city. It hosts a number of Confucian gatherings in its impressive settings. The Shanghai History Museum, located in the 468-meter-high Oriental Pearl Tower, itself a vibrant hymn to Shanghai's modernist spirit, is another landmark that celebrates the destiny of the metropolis. Guangfulin Relics Park, a huge cultural complex in the Songjiang District, might be the most inclusive attempt at redesigning civic sacredness. It combines an archaeological site with the remains or evocations of past dynasties, newly founded Buddhist and Daoist temples, and futuristic-looking buildings. Its twin status makes it both a site of civic sacredness and a religious landmark.

LANDSCAPING RELIGIONS

Manufacturing civic sacredness differs from what we call the "landscaping of religion," referring to the way city planners integrate religious buildings into the cityscape, treating them as defining elements for creating lines and atmospheres. From the 1990s, Shanghai urban planners have not been shy about doing so. The renovation of New Union Church (Xintian'an Tang), built on a riverside site in 1924 and presently not open to the public, serves as an example. The building with its Gothic steeple now stands as a landmark of the Rockbund Project, a feature of contemporary Shanghai.[92] Similarly, the traveler who exits the Longde Road metro station and descends from the nearby bridge walks a sinuous path that crosses an elongated lawn; at the end stands St. Michael's Church, which presents a clear contrast to the skyline. The lawn and the church, which was built in 2010 after the old church, located near the canal, was destroyed, are the products of a joint design that has made them a neighborhood landmark. Church buildings have similarly been conceived as integral parts of the landscaping in Shanghai New Towns. For instance, Anting German Town in Jiading District has a striking, contemporary church building on the main plaza. Built with bricks, in a more traditional style, the tall Protestant church erected in Nanqiao New Town, in Fengxian District, similarly stands out. Pagodas and temples are also privileged assets for urban design. At the same time, the architectural codes governing such buildings are strict, and when it comes to temples, their massive walls offer little conceptual space for integration with the outside environment. Nevertheless, some Buddhist landmarks, such as Jing'an Temple, play a prominent role in Shanghai's cityscape. Jiading Town's urban renewal has been organized around the forty-one-meter-high Fahua Pagoda and Confucius Temple.

Local worshippers do not always approve of such attempts at landscaping. In Nanqiao Old Town, there is a Catholic church built in 1862 in honor of the French admiral Auguste Protet, who died during the Taiping Rebellion. The old church, not visible from the street, is shaped and decorated on the model of an ancestral hall. The uncertain fate of this historical building led to the construction of another Catholic church in Nanqiao New Town, near the Protestant church just mentioned. Reflecting the opinions of the local congregation, the seminarian assisting the local priest complains about the main door "through which a cross cannot even pass [during the Holy Week ceremonies]. This church has been conceived by people who know nothing about the faith!"

At the frontier of private religiosity and civic sacredness, landscaping cemeteries has become a growing business. Fushouyuan is an expensive 402,034-square-meter cemetery park located in Qingpu District, adjacent to Sheshan (plate 6). Combining public and private interests, the group that owns and maintains the park is listed on the Hong Kong stock market.[93] Well-tended alleys, gardens, ponds, pagodas, and bronze statues of celebrities compose a harmonious landscape. The graves and statues of Communist heroes are grouped in dedicated sections of the lawn. The complex smoothly integrates successive strata of civic sacredness: in September 2015, the Jewish Memorial Park opened in Fushouyuan, with memorial stones dedicated to a Chinese diplomat and twenty-four Jewish people.[94] A Buddhist-managed space allows for the celebration of final rites before the urn is placed in a grave or cabinet. A pagoda offers a series of rooms, more luxurious the higher one ascends, with private cabinets for ash boxes and memorabilia. Here, next to pictures of relatives, family members deposit plastic flowers, miniature furniture, toys, or packs of cigarettes. A cabinet may hold nothing more than a crucifix; others may contain exuberant exhibits of everyday paraphernalia and Buddhist imagery. The sculpture studio on the top floor of the pagoda occupies an immense room.

In the cemetery, a burial plot formerly owned by the Catholic Church is known as the "church graveyard" (*jiaohui mudi*). One Sunday morning in November 2014, a week after the Catholic Church celebrated All Saints Day, the Guo family regrouped in the church graveyard. There were about fifteen people present, most wealthy Shanghainese with connections in the United States. A few months before, the ashes of the grandparents had been moved from a cemetery in Suzhou and laid to rest in the Fushouyuan columbarium while a new grave was prepared. A priest said a blessing, and the two boxes containing the ashes were placed in the two compartments at the foot of the grave. The ash boxes came with a set of fabrics and ribbons to be placed on top before the flagstone was sealed. Hesitantly, family representatives chose the fabrics likely to suit baptized Catholics, discarding those that hinted at Buddhist or popular-religion symbols. The short ceremony ended with a series of kowtows, the first performed by the adults and the second by the children. As they exited the Catholic enclave and walked through the alleys, one family member expressed satisfaction at seeing the grandparents' grave relocated. "In the Suzhou cemetery, peasants were always asking for alms, and this beautiful place allows us pay respects to the dead while having a restful, meditative Sunday walk. A good place to join the folks once the time comes."

Some traces of religious landscaping can be found even in as secular an environment as a university cafeteria. Fudan University has three halal canteens, designed primarily for its Muslim students. Emma (the English name chosen by a Kazakh from Xinjiang) dislikes the food, which is prepared by Hui Muslims whose tastes are different from hers. The newest halal canteen, opposite the university's East Gate, is inside the main students' refectory. Its entrance is decorated with a minaret-style pointed dome, the inner walls display mosque-dotted skylines, and the back wall depicts a desert with camels. At the serving station, a veiled worker sorts bright green plastic bowls, plates, spoons, and chopsticks. All workers are Hui people from Gansu.

Private entrepreneurs also contribute quasi-religious symbols to the urban landscape. The Shanghai Museum of Glass is an ambitious project occupying a former glass-manufacturing site in Baoshan District. Inside the complex, the Rainbow Chapel (Caihong Litang) can be rented for weddings and other rituals. Encased in a square white frame, the round structure associates water, earth, and sky symbolism. Inside the chapel, 3,060 glass panels painted in sixty-five translucent colors create circles of colored light.[95] Performing Chinese music in the chapel is reported to give the music new meaning, with listeners feeling as if they were "burning incense and meditating (*fen xiang er zuo*)."[96]

Urban legends also load the cityscape with meaning. A highway pillar sculpted to represent nine rising golden dragons stands at the Chengdu North Road and Yan'an Road intersection. Thus, a popular story has developed around the structure. The construction of the city's Yan'an elevated highway (1995–99) had been going smoothly until the crew ran into trouble. A Buddhist master (identified by several interlocutors as the former abbot of Jing'an Temple) finally determined that a sleeping dragon had been awoken. The story concludes that the pillar was created in atonement. In fact, this intersection is the merging point for all the city's major highways; the pillar's massive scale proved to be an aesthetic problem, which designers solved by creating the so-called Nine Dragons Pillar.[97] According to another version of the same story, the monk who located the sleeping dragon and suggested the creation of the pillar was the abbot of Longhua Temple (*long* meaning "dragon," and *longhua* referring to the dragon flower tree). In Ancient China, a dragon pillar was the center of a ritual area that integrated previously chaotic, barbarian territories into an imperial symbolic order. Therefore, this second version of the story hints at the "civilizing process" that the construction of the highway embodies and speaks of the hallowed destiny of the new Shanghai. The location of the intersection near People's Square and the crucial importance of the highway system in Shanghai's urban planning both explain the interest generated by the Nine Dragons Pillar design. Such a story also speaks indirectly of rituals that did not take place, of urban and ecological transformations that did not respect ritual prescriptions and natural equilibriums. And, finally, the Nine Dragons Pillar story speaks of the sacrificial exorcisms necessitated by urban transformations. Several versions of the story conclude with the death of the ritual master who propitiated the dragon sometime after the pillar was erected.[98]

◆　◆　◆

From the Republican era onward, the state has remapped "sacred" spaces, buildings and practices. These actions have affected the expressions of sacredness defined by the political ethos as well as those fostered by various religious groups. The present state strategy is still based roughly on the principles of the Reform and Opening policy enacted around 1978-82, even if subsequent developments provoked several adjustments. Since the 1990s, the massive scale of urban planning and the aggrandizement of Shanghai, accompanied by renovation, destruction, and construction of public and religious edifices, have complicated the matter. Religious practitioners have responded by devising different tactics: optimizing state guarantees on the use of approved religious spaces, creating new religious spaces without state approval, inscribing religious spaces into the sphere of privacy, and asserting one's presence in the history and geography of the city based on memories and trajectories proper to specific congregations. Religious inventiveness is still part and parcel of the process through which Shanghai's modernity continues to be displayed and engineered.

CHAPTER 2

Calendars and Landmarks

CALENDRICAL RITUALS AND RELIGIOUS BUILDINGS THAT MARK OUT urban spaces belong both to specific religious communities and to the city as a whole. They encompass symbols and narratives that are shared by all or that may be interpreted differently by specific groups. Time and space markers are flexible, even more so within a culturally diverse urban environment. Many calendrical rituals specific to a group are, if not adopted, at least partly appropriated and reinterpreted by the overall social environment in which they are enacted. New landmarks may emerge in any urban landscape and reshape the way its inhabitants experience it. Feasts and landmarks are not only the places where sacredness is stored and displayed. They also work as entrances through which traditions make contact and participate in the building of a city's symbolic space. The nature and role of religious/sacred feast days and spatial landmarks is sometimes ambiguous. The two are interwoven, as landmarks often accrue particular significance at certain times of the year. Religious spaces combine with sacred moments in the map of Shanghai's symbolic space-time. How these spatial and temporal markers combine is what we endeavor to explore.

MARKS ON THE CALENDAR

Officially, China follows the Gregorian calendar, but it is Chinese New Year, or the Spring Festival (Chunjie), that marks the start of a new annual cycle, even in the global metropolis of Shanghai. The first day of the festival is celebrated sometime between January 21 and February 20, based on the lunisolar calendar. The preceding period is the busiest season of the year as everyone attends to resolving all pending affairs (debts, ongoing business, hiring, and lay-offs) and reestablishing links with his or her networks, including colleagues, employees, suppliers, and clients, through celebratory dinners or gift exchanges. Thoroughly cleaning the home and getting a haircut before the Spring Festival are among the customs still observed, as is decorating one's home and front door with couplets written on red paper. Inscriptions or images may also adorn rooms or the family altar.

Some of the customs observed during the twelfth month of the lunar calendar prepare people for entry into a new year, such as a special porridge, *labazhou*, made on the eighth day of the twelfth month, which some Buddhist temples even offer on the street. Many still associate the dish's preparation with the ancient "winter sacrifice" (*laji*) and offerings to ancestors.[1] Informants stress that the day coincides with Bodhi Day (the celebration for the Awakening of the Buddha). They also repeatedly mention the "sending" of the Kitchen God (Zaoshen, known familiarly as Zaojing Gongong among older Shanghai residents) on the twenty-third evening or twenty-fourth early morning of the month. In the past, a paper horse was burned at the doorway of a home, which was meant to serve as the passage through which Zaoshen journeyed to the court of the Jade Emperor, where he reported on the family's deeds during the year.[2] The god was welcomed back at the end of the festival.[3] While the sending of the Kitchen God coincides in northern China with what is usually known as the Little New Year (Xiao Nian), the cessation of normal activities, in Shanghai this name is usually given to the twenty-ninth day of the twelfth month. On this date, an evening dinner was, and sometimes still is, served to the family's ancestors (plate 7). Nowadays, however, a visit to a temple where ancestors are offered a symbolic meal, supplemented by the reading of scriptures, has taken the place of the dinner, as many people consider the new ritual more efficacious in improving their ancestors' destinies. In Shanghai, the year-end meal (*nianyefan*) can take place on either the twenty-ninth or thirtieth day of the last lunar month.

The customs and feast days mentioned here are only a few of those inscribed into the exuberant Chinese popular tradition. They are the ones spoken of in today's Shanghai, although the diversity of origins and family traditions makes it impossible to offer a comprehensive appraisal of the calendar marks woven into the life of the metropolis. For instance, we have found rare mentions of specifically Daoist rituals, such as the anniversary of the Jade Emperor on the ninth day of the first lunar month.[4] However, the closer one gets to the periphery of the city, especially in the areas bordering Jiangsu and Zhejiang, the more one finds that Daoist festivals may give rise to local festivities.[5] Women usually act as the guardians of the calendar. Male interviewees generally were vague about calendrical observances. Degree of resilience and ways of interpreting such traditions vary. Mrs. Wang Zhen (pseud.), an elderly Zhabei resident, commented:

In the past, one was closing the well [in the courtyard of one's household] on the thirtieth of the twelfth month, and one could not open it before the third day of the new year. Many young people have never even witnessed customs like this one. People like me are still practicing a few of them because we saw what our elders were doing. I have two daughters. The younger one still knows that when you reach the age of sixty-six, you have to cook sixty-six pieces of meat. The elder has gone out for studies, so she doesn't know any of these things. Look: now we all use gas stoves, so the youth don't know how to send away the Kitchen God. In the past, we used a big, wood-burning stove, and we glued an image of Zaojing Gongong on the top of it. On the twenty-third day, we'd burn the image, and that was enough for sending the god away. The lanterns and all that stuff, on the day of the Lantern Festival, that was for welcoming him back and when we attached a new image. Now, with gas stoves, most people don't use an image, but still, some will offer some fruits and put them on the stove.[6]

As Chinese New Year approaches, the majority of those whose families are located outside Shanghai (migrant workers and other non–permanent residents) leave the city. And nowadays, a number of native Shanghai residents spend their holidays abroad. On New Year's Eve and the first day of Spring Festival, Shanghai is at its quietest. A family dinner is the main event on New Year's Eve. It may begin and pass without obvious religious connotations; however, a thanksgiving prayer inspired by Chinese religious traditions or Christianity may be heard around some tables. Compared to the practice in more traditional cities, in Shanghai, people tend to spend New Year's Eve with their nuclear families, and members of extended families invite one another to restaurants and hotels in the days leading up to New Year's Eve. Family gatherings are further enlivened by music from the CCTV (China Central Television) New Year's Eve Gala (Chunwan) — now a tradition within the tradition, dating back to the early 1980s — and the sounds and colors of fireworks. The fireworks begin with a first round, just after dinner, and conclude with a second round, between midnight and one in the morning. Whether or not the midnight fireworks are a way of "welcoming Heaven and Earth deities," as is often said, they symbolize a rite of welcoming. In the past, the Shanghai city government tried repeatedly to restrict or prohibit the use of firecrackers, yet complaints of noise and air pollution continued. In 2016, however, the prohibition was strictly implemented and respected.[7]

Larger Buddhist temples offer devotees the opportunity to contribute the "first incense" (*touxiang*) on New Year's Eve, often for a significant fee. Visits to local neighboring temples generally take place early in the morning of the first day, which traditionally is dedicated to deity worship (*jishen*). Ancestor worship (*jizu*) and deity worship are distinguished by a difference in ways of kowtowing, which grandparents promptly remind their grandchildren to observe. Kowtowing to the deities is done with the palms turned toward the sky, while kowtowing to ancestors (ghosts, spirits) is done with the palms turned toward the ground. In Shanghai today, kowtowing to the ancestors takes place mainly during the Tomb Sweeping Festival and winter solstice; it occurs much less frequently during Spring Festival.

On February 19, 2015, the first day of Chinese New Year, a long queue forms before 8:00 a.m. in front of Sanguan Temple (Sanguan Tang), a little Buddhist temple in the Jiangwan neighborhood, in northeastern Puxi, home to a small community of nuns. On this day, fences have been installed, and there are a good number of security personnel present. Just in front of the entrance stands a white tent with security gates equipped with a scanning system. The queue stretches far beyond the fences, twisting in an orderly fashion from one street to another, until it encircles the whole neighborhood. In the queue and inside the temple, the Shanghai dialect is the only language in use. At this time of year, it seems like the locals are retaking possession of the city. By 3:30, the queue to enter Sanguan Temple has dissipated, but there is still a continuous influx of visitors. The ¥20 fee pays for an entry ticket and three sticks of incense. The temple is filled to capacity. Coins pile up on the metallic lotus leaves at the feet of the statue of Guanyin, and visitors sprinkle themselves with the water that flows from her jar. Individuals conduct their devotions as they please: incense burning, offering of spirit money, fruits, and drinks, bowing and prostrations, specific requests, and devotional formulas are layered and combined like syntactic elements, creating a ritual essay that each practitioner composes throughout his or her visit. A cohort of volunteers maintains the temple grounds, burning the paper offerings left by the faithful in the furnace. At 3:50, security staff begin closing the doors of the main hall. It is business as usual.

In Shanghai, residents still welcome and celebrate the God of Fortune (Caishen) on the fifth day of the new year. Elder people like to say that the seventh day is dedicated to the common man, now that Heaven and Earth have been duly worshiped. Knowledge, observance, and interpretation of the customs linked to almost every day of the fifteen-day Spring Festival may vary among families, but everyone celebrates the Lantern Festival (Yuanxiaojie), which marks the end of the festivities. Located in the historical heart of Shanghai, Yu Garden (Yuyuan) boasts the largest number of lanterns. Although the festival lasts fifteen days, most people return to work five days to one week after New Year's Eve.

The Chinese traditional calendar indicates a number of regular observances and celebrations throughout the year. On the first (first moon) and fifteenth (full moon) days of the month, the number of temple visits rises sharply, especially in the early morning. For the Buddhist faithful, visits to temples on these days may be accompanied by other observances, such as keeping a vegetarian diet. The second day of the second month used to be an important communal event, associated with the anniversary of the God of the Soil (Tudi Gong or, familiarly, Tudi Gonggong, Grandfather of the Soil), but today most people remember this festival as a day for getting a haircut, which they normally avoid during the first lunar month. Indeed, most Shanghainese women do not have their hair cut during the month that follows the New Year, though other hairdressing services, such as perms or coloring, continue to be offered.

The nineteenth day of the second month, Guanyin's birthday, is recognized by much of Shanghai's population. Two other days are dedicated to Guanyin, whose cult has been flourishing in Shanghai since the Ming dynasty. Guanyin was and remains the most popular figure both in temples and on family altars, a testament to the devotion she inspires.[8]

The next communal event is the Tomb Sweeping Festival, which is dedicated to deceased family members and observed with visits to graves or columbaria. The festival falls on the fifteenth day after the spring equinox, now harmonized to April 5 in the Gregorian calendar. Memorial visits generally start a week or two beforehand and may also be postponed until after the festival. The custom of eating *qing* dumplings (*qingtuan*), glutinous rice mixed with wormwood (*aicao*) and filled with red bean paste, remains popular in Shanghai.

A visit to Jing'an Temple two days before the festival, on April 3, 2015, made its liturgical and emotional importance clear. In a room below the Great Hall (Daxiong Baodian),[9] around fifteen monks were chanting the Lotus Sutra. The room had been specially arranged for the festival, with the names of the souls for whom the ritual was performed inscribed on a wall. Nearby, faithful onlookers folded spirit money, dividing the tasks to make an assembly line. For some of the faithful, making paper money while listening to the monks chanting gave added meaning to the process. One family, who had two members of their older generation pass away within a year, explained that they had been preparing for the Tomb Sweeping Festival for two weeks. The names of their dead relatives were inscribed on the wall along with the others. In the period leading up to the festival, the largest Buddhist temples in Shanghai often hold the elaborate Water and

Land Dharma Service (Shuilu Pudu Dazhai Shenghui) for the liberation of deceased souls, which they organize two or three times a year.[10]

In 2014, a few days before the festival, Hu Jianwei (pseud.) and his parents were back in their hometown of Zhujiajiao, a water town inside the administrative limits of Shanghai, visiting the cemetery where his maternal relatives going back to his great-grandfather's generation are buried. Rows of vendors had set themselves up outside the gates, selling incense and flowers to the visiting families. This week, Jianwei and his family were visiting the graves of his mother's relatives; the week before, they had visited the graves of his father's relatives. His father had spent the morning cooking his grandfather's favorite foods, and Jianwei commented, "We don't cook food for great-grandfather as we don't know what he liked." At each grave they placed flowers and fruits, lit incense, cigarettes, and candles on the tombs, and burned homemade spirit money in buckets provided by the cemetery. When paying a visit to the cemetery, Jianwei's mother "speaks with her ancestors," he observed.

He continued, "During tomb sweeping, I feel very happy, close to my ancestors, and I know they enjoy the food — especially because they can eat only once a year! You need to be careful about the way you worship ancestors. My great-grandmother on my father's side believed in Jesus, so we don't burn incense for her; burning incense is a Chinese tradition, not a Western [Christian] one." The same caution, he added, applies to the process of returning to the profane world after such sacred moments. "After tomb sweeping, we go to the supermarket or to some other noisy place, a place where there are many people, so as to feel the real world and put the ghosts and spirits behind us. Then we go back home and wash our whole body to get rid of the ashes. Tomb sweeping is quite a dirty activity!" Other informants mentioned that they often kindle a fire with a newspaper or whatever is at hand just before entering their apartment complex, confirming their return to the world of the living, or yang world.

Sacred dates inevitably overlap. In 2015, Ash Wednesday fell on February 18, the same day as Chinese New Year's Eve. Chinese Catholic bishops traditionally instruct the faithful that they need not observe the fast during the Spring Festival, but a notice at St. Joseph's Church encouraged parishioners to fast regardless. That same year, an even more significant overlap occurred, when Tomb Sweeping Festival coincided with Easter. In an underground evangelical church in Pudong, the preacher did not shy away from the contrast between the festival and the holiday, noting that one is about death and the other a celebration of new life. He congratulated those who had come to the service instead of visiting graves, although most among the congregation of migrant workers would have been unable to make the trip anyway. On the same day, the homily given at St. Francis Xavier Church on Dongjiadu Street was more conciliatory in tone; the juxtaposition would help the faithful remember that the dead will revive in God.

The feast of Easter does not have the public appeal of Christmas; nevertheless, the Easter liturgy is carefully prepared and performed. The newly baptized receive certificates, a party is thrown for them, and the parish announces post-catechumenal classes that help them progress further in the faith. Special musical events also take place, and foreign musical groups occasionally enliven the Chinese-language service. For instance, the 2015 Easter service at St. Francis Xavier Church featured Swiss accordion and horn players, who were much appreciated (and photographed) by the local audience. Most parishes follow the custom of distributing eggs to congregants after mass.

While Buddha's Birthday is normally calculated according to the lunar calendar, formerly on the eighth day of the fourth month and now commonly on the fifth day of the fifth month, celebrations are often held on April 8, a short time after the Tomb Sweeping Festival, in accordance with the Japanese custom. Tim, a young Buddhist convert, calls it the "Buddhist Christmas" and stresses its devotional importance. What could be seen as a competition between Buddhist and Christian evangelists has revived the importance of the celebration, especially since the day has become a holiday in several East Asian countries and cities, including Hong Kong. The lack of consensus on a date remains an obstacle to the holiday's popularity.

As the calendar turns toward summer, events written in popular tradition continue to take place. In the lunar calendar, the "beginning of summer" (*lixia*) coincides with the seventh solar term. During the fifth month of the traditional calendar, the Dragon-Boat Festival (Duanwujie) is marked by a variety of customs aimed at avoiding disease and pestilence, especially those caused by insects, heat, and humidity. This festival is a public holiday in China. The feast of Guandi or Guangong (both honorific titles for the historical Guan Yu) is celebrated in Shanghai on the thirteenth day of the fifth month, although none of our informants considered this a truly significant day.[11] On the nineteenth day of the sixth month, some Shanghai residents celebrate Guanyin again, the feast commemorates her "ascent to the rank of bodhisattva" (*cheng dao*).

The Ghost Festival (Zhongyuanjie or Yulanpen) is celebrated when the summer heat declines,[12] which is said to happen in the middle of the seventh month on the traditional calendar. During the entire seventh month, the ghost month (*guiyue*), it is known that the spirits of the dead wander among the living. Therefore, travel and other enterprises are considered with caution. Offering food to the spirits is advisable, as is the burning of spirit money and other items. The customs that surround the seventh month are not limited to the worship of ancestors but extend to all souls and ghosts. On the fifteenth day, the channels of communication between the realms of the living and the dead are most permeable, and everyone is required to contribute offerings, participate in rituals, and take precautionary measures so as not to be contaminated by wandering souls. Toward the close of the month, specific rituals accompany the souls who return to the lower realm on the thirtieth day. In the Buddhist calendar, that day is set apart for worshipping the bodhisattva Dizang, helper of souls suffering in the underworld, although many Shanghai residents identify the date with the celebration of Tudi Gong. Traditionally, families light incense sticks in front of their houses or apartment complexes. The custom is far from universally respected but is considered important, and elders do not hesitate to remind their sons and daughters to comply. The great popularity of Ghost Festival celebrations in late Qing and Republican-era Shanghai probably reflected the concerns of poor sojourners who identified themselves with solitary, wandering ghosts.[13]

On the fifteenth day of the eighth month, the Mid-Autumn Festival (Zhongqiujie) signals an end to the dangerous bargaining with "impure sacredness" (as Durkheim would put it) that characterizes the ghost month and a return to the reassuring ordinariness of the profane world. In ancient times, the summer harvest was by then safely stored in preparation for winter. Feelings of togetherness, moon cakes, and rabbit-shaped lanterns all contribute to the sense of change conveyed by the celebration. Festivals are not merely privileged dates; they also function as doors from one period into another, with each festive period achieving its own balance of ordinariness and sacredness.

FROM AUTUMN TO WINTER

Since 1950, China has celebrated National Day on October 1, a grand fete on a par with Chinese New Year. If the Spring Festival is about cosmic and social renewal, National Day speaks of the harvest at long last reaped and shared by a nation rebuilt after a long history of hardship. The Spring Festival and National Day represent the two poles of the year, although National Day has lost some of its appeal now that it is no longer followed by an eight-day holiday.

The Double Yang Festival (Chongyangjie) falls on the ninth day of the ninth month, as nine is considered a yang number. "Climbing a height" (*denggao*) and drinking chrysanthemum liquor are recommended antidotes for excess yang energy. It is a day for showing filial respect to both the living and the dead. Generally, Buddhist temples in Shanghai organize a Water and Land Dharma Service around that time or shortly afterward. In its recent efforts to revive popular feelings of filial piety, the state has deemed this day

Elders' Day, to stress the importance of regularly visiting one's parents. On the nineteenth day of the same month, the popularity surrounding the figure of Guanyin is again demonstrated by her third feast day of the year, this time celebrating her vow to save all sentient beings.

As the end of the Gregorian year approaches, celebrations intensify. It may seem strange to count Thanksgiving Day (Gan'en Jie) among them, but the word "thanksgiving" (*gan'en*) has prompted people to send messages expressing special gratitude to, for example, helpful teachers or supportive friends. As in the United States, Christmas symbols pop up throughout the city from Black Friday onward, and interest in the holiday peaks as Christmas Eve approaches. When we planned to attend the Christmas Eve service in 2014 at Moore Memorial Church (Mu'en Tang), a landmark Protestant congregation in People's Square, we were warned to arrive two hours early in order to get seats, because "everybody is Christian on Christmas Day!"

On the third Sunday of Advent in 2015, just before the 10:00 a.m. service, volunteers at Moore Memorial Church were hanging Christmas decorations as the building filled beyond capacity. In addition to the main hall (560 seats), the balconies (380 seats), and the choir (60 seats), another hall and a large upper room were packed in latecomers who watched the service on screens. The chief pastor, Jiang Xili, delivered the homily in a confident, almost conversational way, "Do not stick to a literal interpretation of the Bible. Rather, try to harmonize the meaning of different passages of the Scriptures and to interpret them according to their spirit. And don't go to extremes, such as refusing to give your parents the financial help that they may need under the pretext that your money goes to support the Church. You must give to the Church only after having fulfilled your human duties." However, her most important lesson that day was yet to come. During every Christmas period of Pastor Jiang's twelve years serving with Moore Memorial Church, there have been incidents among worshippers and volunteers. She believes that it may be due to overcrowding in the church building but stressed that the "Evil One" is obviously at work during Christmastime. "Each year, people quarrel over seats and even beat each other, then call 110. When the policemen arrive, they ask the first antagonist: 'Do you believe in Jesus?' and, on hearing the answer, ask the second one the same question. And then they conclude, 'Then ask Jesus to arbitrate between the two of you!' What a loss of face for Christians!" She admonishes her listeners to behave better this year, adding, "We're the salt of the earth, not its chili."

The celebration of the winter solstice on December 22 is another day consecrated to the dead and tomb sweeping. In 2015, it was estimated that traffic increased by 20 percent on this particular day, meaning an additional 1.1 million people were driving to cemeteries,[14] and about 2.5 million people visited cemeteries in the ten days preceding the solstice.[15] The figure may seem high, but it is considerably lower than cemetery visits recorded for the Tomb Sweeping Festival.[16] Interestingly, some informants told us that the day of the Tomb Sweeping Festival was for visiting graves, while the winter solstice was an occasion for kowtowing to ancestors in the privacy of one's home. The winter solstice is another example of overlapping sacred temporalities. A plaque in the funerary chapel of St. Francis Xavier Church states that masses for the deceased are celebrated at least four times a year: on Tomb Sweeping day, sometime in November, the winter solstice, and the eve of the Spring Festival. The inclusion of the winter solstice, just before Christmas Eve, is particularly significant.

The atmosphere surrounding Christmas may vary according to the public mood and political climate. In 2014, many churches were filled beyond capacity. The popularity of the event generated lively discussions on social networks, with some criticisms and laments coming from Buddhist and pro-government netizens. Christmas greetings were routinely exchanged on campuses, although universities organized compulsory events for that day. The popular appeal of Christmas has given rise to creative initiatives, often with commercial undertones. For example, apples are being marketed as the Chinese "Christmas fruit." The apple (*pingguo*) was christened "the fruit of peace" (*ping'an guo*), and even in the global metropolis of Shanghai, convenience stores started packaging the red fruit in Christmas-themed boxes suitable for gifts. The display of Christmas symbols and the flurry of Christmas-related activities throughout the city are a contrast to the popular perception of Christmas as a holiday for foreigners — a sort of "foreign winter solstice" — in Shanghai during the Republican era.[17] Today, although Christmas remains a festival linked to the religion of a minority, it has become part of a shared temporality, with different groups and people experiencing and interpreting its sacredness in their own ways.

Despite the Christmas festivities, work in the last week of December carries on uninterrupted. Many young people go out on the evening of December 31. Before the New Year's Eve stampede of 2014, which took the lives of thirty-six people, the Bund was a popular spot for gathering and counting down to the new year. In the month following the tragedy, strict controls were in place around the temples, enforcing orderly behavior on the first day of Spring Festival. Chinese New Year was observed in the shadow of an event that had scarred the passage to a new year according to the Gregorian calendar.

January 1 is not usually classified as a religious festival. In the Catholic calendar, however, it is known as the Octave Day of Christmas and the Solemnity of Mary, Mother of God. This feast is celebrated in some enclaves of Catholic Shanghai. Since January 1 is a holiday in China, members of the Catholic faith have an opportunity to come together. Such is the case for

Catholic fishermen in Qingpu District, adjacent to Jiangsu and Zhejiang. In the beginning of the 1970s, the local government decided to group fishermen who had been operating on rivers and lakes in "fisheries villages" (*shuichancun*). Huaxin Township is the center of one of these villages.[18] On January 1, 2016, around 150 people gathered at a communal meeting place that serves as a chapel for monthly mass services and special occasions. Inside the room, the choir and churchgoers began chanting Christmas canticles and after some time began to walk along the narrow streets of the village. A group of women at the head of the procession beat drums, followed by the parish priest and two of his confreres. Upon returning to the chapel, fireworks were set off at the beginning of the mass and again at the close of the service. The village also performs this ritual on Christmas Eve and Easter night, adamantly refraining from doing so on Chinese New Year, although they offer fruit and wine at church on that day and hold a prayer service for their ancestors. In Chinese popular religion, processions have been linked to exorcism rites, and the beating of drums and use of firecrackers recall such traditions. Inland fishermen, a marginalized population for many centuries, were not participating in Chinese peasants' worship traditions, which facilitated their conversion to Catholicism. This small community has endowed January 1 with a celebratory meaning within the confines of its own specific space-time.

ALTERNATIVE TEMPORALITIES

The Chinese and Gregorian calendars have combined to offer a framework for most religious expressions. However, other temporalities contribute to shaping life for sectors of the urban population. The most obvious example is the Islamic calendar. In Shanghai, as in other regions of the world, it works as an alternative to the dominant seasonal approach of liturgical time. The Islamic calendar transcends the solar and lunar years, as Allah transcends the human and natural worlds. Most Muslim rituals have no fixed relationship to the seasons, moving eleven days from their position the preceding year.[19]

The three main celebrations for Muslims are Eid al-Fitr (Breaking-the-Fast Feast) ("Kaizhaijie" in Chinese) at the end of Ramadan, on the first day of the tenth month; Eid al-Adha (Festival of Sacrifice) ("Gu'erbangjie" in Chinese), which starts on the tenth day of the twelfth month; and Mawlid ("Shengjijie" in Chinese), the birthday of the Prophet Muhammad, on the twelfth day of the third month. The limited number of official mosques creates greater exclusivity and importance for these gatherings. At least at the Huxi Mosque, white cloth is often rolled out on the street in order to accommodate the overflow of devotees (plate 8).[20]

In 2015, Eid al-Adha was celebrated on September 24. On that day, the generally quiet neighborhood where the Xiao Taoyuan men's and women's mosques are located, a police car and a few street peddlers offering roast mutton, snacks, yogurt, or dried fruit, transformed the small road into a bustling main street. Neighbors saw the congregation gather before 8:00 a.m., wondering why there were so many people, as it was not a Friday, the day of the week when Muslim believers congregate at the mosque. One old man complained, "Outsiders, they're all outsiders . . . What a nuisance." Speaking to the congregation (women watched the service on television in their mosque), the imam stressed that although the three religions of the Book all record Abraham's sacrifice, only Islam celebrates it as a holy day. Despite his joy over the large turnout, he lamented the fact that, according to the register, less than twenty of them had reserved a sheep at the cost of ¥1,000. Why were they unwilling to participate in what is "more than a sacrifice"? One sheep was enough for a family, and Muslims in need could be invited to a family's feast as an act of charity. In any case, he added, worshippers could still change their minds after the prayer and reserve a sheep. The sacrifice had been arranged to take place at Fuyou Road Mosque, not far from the Xiao Taoyuan Mosque. By the time the congregation had made its way to the other mosque, halal restaurants nearby were offering bowls of soup with fresh meat.

Other minorities testify to alternative ways of dividing and experiencing the flow of time. The Yi minority of southwestern China traditionally divides the year into ten solar months of thirty-six days each, with the remaining five to six days dedicated to the celebration of the new year (the number varies according to local custom). On November 21 and 22, 2015, around forty Yi students and workers gathered in Shanghai's Songjiang District at a villa owned by a Yi entrepreneur from Guizhou. The two days were filled with games, theater, and music, with a strong emphasis on ethnic culture and language.

Are new feast days still in the making? The Alibaba Company launched China's Singles' Day, essentially an online shopping festival that encourages singles to pamper themselves, in 2009. It chose November 11 because the four ones in the date represent four singles. Reaching far beyond its original intended audience, Alibaba reported $14.3 billion in sales on November 11, 2015. Alibaba's main rival, e-commerce company JD.com, recorded around thirty-two million orders on the same day, compared with fourteen million the day before.[21] The future of new Internet-era rituals founded on the principles of consumption is unclear. Strategically situated between the "profane" period of harvest, celebrated from the end of September through the middle of November, and the "sacred effervescence" that arrives with the beginning of winter, Singles' Day may become an established tradition that speaks to the move into a virtual world and evolving consumption habits and illustrates how an imagined ritual can become calendrical and shape the practices of participants.

RELIGIOUS LANDMARKS

In traditional Chinese cities, with the exception of Beijing, the most official religious landmark was the local city god temple. City god temples, rooted in earthly god cults, were widespread in rural China and became a state institution when the founder of the Ming dynasty, Hongwu (r. 1368–98), made creation of a city god temple compulsory in every county and prefecture.[22] In Shanghai County, an existing temple was converted into the municipal city god temple.[23] City god temples had been present in the surrounding counties since the Song dynasty,[24] and some can still be found in the present administrative limits of Shanghai, the largest one being located in the Jiading District. In addition to the City God Temple, religious buildings listed as official city landmarks include the Jade Buddha, Jing'an, and Longhua Buddhist Temples; the Shanghai Confucian Temple; the Sheshan Catholic Basilica; the Xujiahui Catholic Cathedral; the Protestant Moore Memorial, Huai'en, and Hengshan Community Churches; the Songjiang and Xiao Taoyuan Mosques; and the Baiyun and Qinciyang Daoist Temples. St. Nicholas Orthodox Church and the Jewish Refugee Memorial Hall are mentioned on official publications and websites, though neither Orthodox Christianity nor Judaism is an officially recognized religion in China.[25] Such places serve as markers from which the symbolic geography of the entire city develops (map 4).

The Landmark That Is Not

Religious landmarks are sometimes multipurpose. Religious buildings were converted during, or even before in some cases, the Cultural Revolution for use by the state. After 1980, the buildings were gradually returned to their congregations, provided they were affiliated with and approved by the government.

Orthodox Christianity is not one of the five recognized religions, so the status of St. Nicholas Church in Shanghai remains ambiguous. Located on Gaolan Road in Luwan District,[26] St. Nicholas Church was built in 1934 by the same architect who designed another Orthodox church (now gone) between the International Concession and Zhabei District. Built on a Greek-cross plan, the St. Nicholas building is of modest, elegant proportions and tastefully decorated. The church was shut down around 1950 and was converted into a warehouse, then a laundry, and later a washing-machine factory. Like other religious buildings around Shanghai, it was preserved from

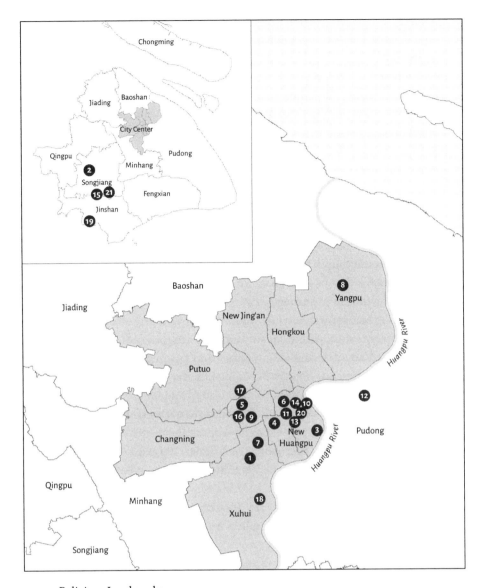

MAP 4. Religious Landmarks

1   St. Ignatius Cathedral (Xujiahui Church)
2   Sheshan Basilica of Our Lady Help
    of Christians
3   St. Francis Xavier Church
    (Dongjiadu Church)
4   St. Nicholas Church
5   Former Ohel Rachel Synagogue
6   Moore Memorial Church
7   Hengshan Community Church
8   East Shanghai Church
9   Grace Church
10 City God Temple of Shanghai

11 White Clouds Monastery
12 Qinciyang Hall Daoist Temple
13 Xiao Taoyuan Mosque
14 Shanghai Fuyou Road Mosque
15 Shanghai Songjiang Mosque
16 Jing'an Temple
17 Jade Buddha Temple
18 Longhua Temple
19 Shanghai Dongling Temple
20 Eaglewood Pavilion
21 Dongyue Temple

complete destruction during the Cultural Revolution by quick-thinking believers who posted images of Mao on it, and a poster of Mao kept watch over the building until the first decade of the 2000s. On February 15, 1994, the building was recognized as a city-level cultural relic preservation unit while still serving as a private club. The loft was reconsecrated and weekly services resumed during Expo Shanghai 2010.[27] Services can now be performed under special authorization for Orthodox feast days. Attendees originate mainly from Greece, Kazakhstan, Romania, Russia, Slovakia, Ukraine, and the United States. There are some Chinese attendees from Harbin or adjacent districts and a handful who converted to Orthodoxy in Hong Kong, abroad, or through marriage. During the rest of the year, weekly services are held in the sterile surroundings of the visa office waiting room in the Russian consulate; it was also the case for a good part of 2016, including for the Easter service, when the church was being renovated (plate 9).

On December 4, 2013, Deacon Papiy Fu Xiliang, a Chinese national raised in a Beijing Orthodox orphanage who received his clerical education in Russia, sets up the sacred space with two attendants. Two large suitcases with wheels contain liturgical equipment. Within thirty minutes, the three men have unpacked an altar with icon imagery and a side table with books and candles. Sixty people make up the congregation for Communion, including a small number of Chinese. About a month later, on January 7, the day of the Orthodox Feast of the Nativity, attendance rises dramatically, even though it is a workday. The St. Nicolas Church stands at the center of the Orthodox community's spatial consciousness. The former Orthodox Cathedral, now an exhibition space,[28] and the alternate liturgical space offered by the Russian consulate constitute two other points of spatialization. A few favorite restaurants complete the mental map of a community on the religious outskirts, even though most of its members and landmarks are positioned in central Shanghai.

On Orthodox Easter Day 2014 (April 4 that year), the picture is anything but usual. The street and alleyway outside St. Nicolas Church has been brightened by tables piled high with Russian Easter cakes and eggs for sale. "We normally parade around the church," said Pavel, an attendant from Romania, "but we cannot do that in China, as the Orthodox Church is not recognized here." The Orthodox reconstruction in Shanghai, encouraged by the cooperative climate between China and Russia, is moving step by step.

Many other religious spaces could be cited as showcases for the complexity of local memories, the interactions between international and Chinese communities, and the importance of landmarks that build a web of sacred spaces that resonate differently across a shared geography. At the same time, the frontiers and functions of religious spaces can be porous and evolving.

A religious place is very rarely only a landmark. It can serve concurrently as a compound and even a place where religious intimacies can be lived and expressed.[29]

A NETWORK OF WORSHIP

The area surrounding Shanghai's City God Temple is generally called "Yu Garden." Yu Garden has been linked to major episodes of Shanghai's history and assertive merchant class from the sixteenth century onward. The City God Temple and Yu Garden are linked by collective memories and by a cyclical, seemingly never-ending process of construction and reconstruction.

> The garden was first created between 1559 and 1577 by the Ming dynasty official Pan Yunduan (1526–1601) for his elderly father Pan En (1496–1582), who had supervised the building of the city walls to defend against marauding pirates. The descendants of the Pan family, having fallen on hard times, sold the garden in 1760 to associations of rich merchants. After extensive restoration and rebuilding, the garden was donated to the adjoining City-God Temple complex and became the headquarters for trade guilds and societies of various sorts. In the late nineteenth century, the garden was made into an administrative center for commerce and industry, and at the same time became a crowded public bazaar, with teahouses, taverns, and vendors. . . . The garden was also severely damaged after being commandeered on multiple occasions to headquarter and bivouac European, Chinese, and Japanese troops. . . . It is words — the garden's name, couplets, poems, titles, and inscriptions — that link the Yu Yuan with its past, and despite countless changes in physical shape and form, these words and the memory they evoke allow the present-day architecture to be perceived as the authentic original.[30]

From the mid-nineteenth century to 1949, the northeastern part of the former walled city was home to a network of sites of worship (Christian churches were for the most part excluded) that groomed the collective psyche.[31] The city god was first a god of the soil, whom the Shanghainese call by the familiar name Tudi Gonggong, or Grandfather of the Soil. This expression, still very much in use, can refer to the official city god, the God of the Soil of any local temple, or the general category of a spirit of the soil. The city god cult could be seen "as a point of transformation between the official and the popular religions,"[32] conciliating popular aspirations with state requirements through the combination of official rituals and popular processions. The city god's role in calling on all wandering ghosts, ensuring their rest, and thus bringing order to a city where untimely deaths were a too-frequent occurrence is particularly noteworthy. The city god temple was both the point of departure and the return destination of the three annual processions of wandering ghosts.[33]

Traditionally, popular temples were not only places one visited; they were the sites from which the gods departed on their inspections of the neighborhood. The expression *yingshen saihui* (lit., "a festive meeting for welcoming the gods") refers to processions in which the statue of a god was carried around in order to mark its territory. *Sai* has taken on the meaning of (festive) competition, but the classical expression *saishen* was used in ancient times for an offering or thanksgiving sacrifice. The processions that started from the city god temple and similar, often much smaller places were journeys through a marked geography that occurred three times a year.[34] The residents served by the temple, rather than clerics or officials, organized the ritual (though imperial officials were more involved in city god temple processions than they were for other deities).[35] In Shanghai, some of these processions took place on the city's waterways. The choreography of the procession followed a common pattern: opening rites, dances, interventions by penitents, and transportation of the gods' palanquins. Between 1912 and 1949, there were approximately two hundred processions every year in the territories that today constitute Shanghai.[36] The board of Shanghai's City God Temple managed the procession circuits through which the god manifested its spiritual protectorate of adjacent territories.[37]

A fire that destroyed much of the City God Temple in 1924 led to major building projects from 1926 to 1927. In those troubled times, the empowered citizens association was supervising donated funds, substituting for a failing government. A highly structured committee was entrusted with governance of the temple, overseeing the upkeep of popular religious practices, the organization of charitable works, and the provision of a sustainable financial base. Such temples were becoming both political and religious landmarks, signifying the rise of a civil society organized around its traditional institutions but empowered through new legal and managerial practices as they entered modernity.

The Han dynasty's powerful chancellor Huo Guang (d. 68 BCE), whose statue sill occupies the anterior hall of the temple, became Shanghai's first city god because of his alleged role in flood control; however, evidence of his accomplishments is meager.[38] Later, Emperor Hongwu, who founded the Ming dynasty, elevated Qin Yubo (1295–1373), an official from Shanghai, to the status of city god, and his statue presides over the posterior hall. Having two figures for one city god temple is already rather exceptional, but during the anti-Japanese war, a statue of Chen Huacheng (1776–1842), a Qing dynasty

PLATE 1. Foot massage workshop, St. Francis Xavier Church, 2015. A Swiss missionary priest stationed in Taiwan pioneered contemporary techniques of foot massage in Asia. In St. Francis Xavier Church, Catholic parishioners teach the craft to one another and to migrant workers.

PLATE 2. Thai Buddhist shrine, Super Brand Mall, Lujiazui area, Pudong, 2016. Super Brand Mall is one of the largest shopping centers in Asia. Chai Tai Group, a major Thai company, which developed the mall, set up a Buddhist shrine outside the front door. Passersby perform rituals at the shrine, and these are believed to have improved the mall's business.

PLATE 3. Multifaith event, Songjiang Experimental High School basketball hall, 2013. On September 28, 2013, the Songjiang District government organized a multifaith event in the high school's basketball court for the five state-recognized religions and ethnic minorities.

PLATE 4. Longhua Revolutionary Martyrs' Memorial, 2015. The Longhua Revolutionary Martyrs' Cemetery commemorates the Party members and other activists who died during the revolutionary struggles of 1928–37. Located near the Buddhist Longhua Temple, it is part of the "sacred geography" of Shanghai.

PLATE 5. Memorial Hall of the First National Congress of the Chinese Communist Party, Xintiandi area, 2015. Shanghai is a locus of revolutionary history. In 1921, the Chinese Communist Party was founded in the Xintiandi area of Shanghai. A memorial hall preserving and reconstituting memories of the event now stands on the spot.

PLATE 6. Fushouyuan Cemetery Park, Qingpu District, 2015. Fushouyuan is a luxury cemetery park. During the Tomb Sweeping Festival and at other times, families visit the deceased. In addition to grave sites in the park, a tall pagoda in the center of the cemetery houses rooms of cabinets that serve as ash containers and contain a photographic portrait and/or other marks for remembrance of the deceased.

PLATE 7. Ancestor worship, Chinese New Year, Chuansha New Town, Pudong, 2013. On New Year's Eve, the Jiang family set a table in their kitchen with food and wine for the ancestors. After burning three incense sticks, leaving time for the ancestors to eat, they perform the ancestor worship (*jizu*) ceremony by burning handmade tin-leaf ingots (*xibo*).

PLATE 8.   Eid al-Adha, outside Huxi Mosque, Changde Road, Shanghai, 2014. For the celebration of Eid al-Adha, city authorities close the street next to Huxi Mosque and allow the pavement to be covered with white cloth so that the large crowd can pray outside.

PLATE 9.   Orthodox Easter service, Russian consulate, 2016. Orthodox Christianity is not one of the five recognized religions in China. The 2016 Easter service, which was held in the Russian consulate, was the first one that both foreigners and Chinese were allowed to attend.

PLATE 10. White Clouds Monastery, 2014. White Clouds Monastery, built in the 1880s just outside the walled city, was the center of the Daoist Quanzhen tradition in Shanghai. In 2004, the temple was moved slightly to the northeast and is now located inside the former walled city.

PLATE 11.   After the Christmas Eve service, Zhangjialou Church, 2014. Worshippers threw banknotes onto the manger after the Christmas Eve service at the Catholic Zhangjialou Church. Many city dwellers attend Christmas services and performances put on by Protestant and Catholic churches throughout the city.

PLATE 12. Xu Guangqi Memorial Hall, 2016. A memorial to the Chinese scholar, statesman, and Catholic convert Xu Guangqi (1562–1633) is located in a small park named after him. Xujiahui, the site of the former properties of the Xu family, was a Catholic and Jesuit enclave from the 1840s until the 1950s.

PLATE 13.   Sheshan Seminary Chapel, 2013. Since the 1870s, the Sheshan Basilica has been the major Catholic pilgrimage site in China. It is located on one of the few hills in Shanghai, with the Sheshan Seminary situated at its foot. At the time this photograph was taken, the seminary chapel was closed to visitors due to the resignation of Bishop Ma Daqin from the Patriotic Catholic Association.

PLATE 14. Jade Buddha Temple, 2015. The Jade Buddha Temple was founded in 1882 by Master Huigen. The temple, which hosts the Buddhist Research Institute of Shanghai, also aims to promote Buddhist doctrine and social influence nationwide, with several cultural and media outlets on its premises.

PLATE 15. Construction of Guangfulin Relics Park, Songjiang District, 2014. The city government funded the construction of Guangfulin Relics Park, a recreational and cultural complex in western Shanghai. A museum of local culture, a Buddhist temple, and a Daoist temple are among the attractions.

PLATE 16. Jing'an Temple, 2016. Shanghai's modern high-rises surround Jing'an Temple. The temple was built during the thirteenth century and redesigned during the Qing dynasty. It has been renovated and further embellished from the 1980s onward.

general responsible for the defense of Shanghai during the First Opium War, joined the other two by popular acclamation. The three statues remained in the temple until the Cultural Revolution.[39] However, when the City God Temple was restored, Chen Huacheng's statue did not return with those of the two other deities. The only city god that had been selected by the people is the one that the new regime did not confirm in this function.

From 1951 onward, the temple's management was entrusted to the Shanghai branch of the Daoist National Association (the lay committee was disbanded in 1956), which meant that religious orthodoxy was enforced by the removal of statues that embodied "feudal" beliefs. Daoism was a particular target during the Cultural Revolution and the period that preceded it. The temple was destroyed in 1966 and was not restored to its former state until 1994. Since then, it has become a beacon of Shanghai's renaissance, and additional restoration in 2005–6 has augmented the site's original splendor.

It is now difficult to distinguish the City God Temple from its built-up surroundings. Locals generally designate the larger area by the name of the temple itself, while residents who are not Shanghai locals call it "Yu Garden." The restoration and reorganization of the historic district has created a dizzying labyrinth of partially covered walkways. Yu Garden, the City God Temple, the Fuyou Mosque (an ancient and tiny building decorated in Chinese style), and the Chenxiang Buddhist Pavilion intermingle with shops and stores in a way that recalls the atmosphere of old Shanghai. Horizontal architecture balances the vertical contemporary metropolis. Religious enclosures are scattered throughout the maze, representing the anchored sacredness reminiscent of Shanghai's past.

HALF-HIDDEN SACREDNESS: EAGLEWOOD PAVILION

Landmarks serve a variety of functions, some public and some of a more intimate nature. The Eaglewood Pavilion (Chenxiang Ge), served by a community of nuns and home to the women's annex of the Buddhist Studies Institute of Shanghai, has been a main center for the worship of Guanyin since the Qing dynasty.[40] At the time of the foreign concessions, the other recognized center was the neighboring Red Temple (Hongmiao). The Red Temple was located in a district dedicated to nightlife, so courtesans and prostitutes imploring Guanyin, the Goddess of Mercy, constituted a sizable proportion of devotees. Here, offerings brought by the faithful were not only vegetarian, as Buddhist orthodoxy requires, but also animal products, a sign of the popular appropriation of Guanyin.[41]

The Eaglewood Pavilion links the legend of the gilded statue of Avalokitesvara (Guanyin) to the figure of Pan Yunduan, the founder of Yu Garden. Pan discovered the eaglewood statue by dredging the Huai River under divine instruction. Wishing to respond to his mother's Buddhist devotion, Pan erected the pavilion (which later became a monastery) in front of the family's ancestral temple, a sign of his Confucian filial piety.[42] In 1997, a replica of the Guanyin statue, made from eaglewood timber bought in Thailand, was placed in the temple. Sacredness thus emanates from the ancestral energy that the temple and its artifacts evoke and re-create.

On March 10, 2015, Eaglewood Pavilion held a ceremony for Medicine Buddha (Yaoshifo), the first major event in the temple after Chinese New Year. Two weeks after welcoming the Year of the Sheep, shops around the temple were still stocked with lanterns and stuffed toy sheep. The chanting began at 8:30 a.m. and ran until 4:00 p.m., with a two-and-a-half-hour midday break. Twenty resident nuns, fifty women participants, and one rather lonely man moved from the main hall to a conference room. Older local residents made up the majority of volunteers.

With six cooks at work, the kitchen was a hive of activity. Participants lined up to receive their large bowls of vegetarian food. Most of the attendees joined in the chanting every Saturday, and on this particular day, some had invited friends. Everyone seemed to enjoy taking part in the group event. In the dining hall, the canteen benches were marked with pink stickers inscribed with the names of the nuns. At each marked seat, there were stacks of cartons, often brought by family members, containing food specialties from different provinces.

In the Medicine Hall, small Buddha figurines and lamps lined the walls, marked with the names of people who were the subjects of prayers for their health. Lotus-shaped lanterns and ancestral tablets for the dead, the "reborn" ones, were located in Dizang Hall. Emplacements in both halls are rented for one year. For the living, name cards can also be placed in the outstretched hands of the thousand-armed statue of Guanyin. On this particular day, near the Medicine Buddha, a woman tried to find a space close to one she had rented for other family members; her daughter and husband already had a lamp lit in their names. Most of the high rows, closer to Heaven, had no more slots available.

Only upon inquiry can one find the eaglewood statue of Guanyin. A sign on the far side of the courtyard invites visitors to take a small staircase up to an antechamber. After paying a supplementary fee, one enters a splendidly decorated room where the statue stands inside a glass case. The room does not suggest a ritual setting. The atmosphere varies between that of a museum and a meditation center. The few visitors show special devotion and are silent. Everything about the setting nurtures a sense of mystery (*shenmi*). The focal point from which energy radiates, permeating the whole compound, is situated at the margins, rather than exhibited at the center.

White Clouds Monastery (Baiyun Guan) (plate 10), established as a small cloister in 1874 by Wang Mingzhen (d. ca. 1880), lies a ten-minute walk west of the City God Temple.[43] His successor, Xu Zhicheng (1835–1890), took up building of the premises and converted the cloister to a Quanzhen "universal monastery" (*shifang conglin*) and acquired a prized copy of the Daoist Canon.[44]

Thus, the City God Temple dominated by the Zhengyi Daoist tradition and White Clouds Monastery, a bastion of the Quanzhen lineage, occupy the same part of the city. However, unlike the City God Temple, White Clouds Monastery was originally located just outside the walls of the old city. Founded later than most other famous temples, the monastery was not marked with the aura of civic sacredness associated with the religious buildings inside the old city. In 2004, amid the frenzy of urban restructuring that seized Shanghai before the Expo Shanghai 2010, the temple was moved slightly to the northeast, closer to the City God Temple and near the much smaller temple to Guandi Temple (Guandi Miao). The temple, now located inside the former walled city, next to the only remnant of the wall, duplicates the function of the City God Temple as a sacred place that epitomizes the local ethos.[45]

A gigantic statue of the Jade Emperor (Yuhuang Dadi) is in the main hall, flanked by the statues of the sixty avatars of the calendrical god Taisui.[46] Two other spaces on the first floor are used for smaller rituals. Some of the worship rooms located on the second floor contain the seven Ming statues that greatly contributed to the temple's reputation after 1894 after their attribution to the temple by the customs administration. The statues had been confiscated before they were smuggled abroad. The main deities of the Daoist pantheon are all represented in the White Clouds Monastery.

On March 10, 2015, a number of volunteers vigorously hose down the doors and walls of the monastery, and another group addresses thousands of letters reminding people of upcoming activities for the Tomb Sweeping Festival. In the aftermath of Chinese New Year, two ceremonies are being held. One, in the main hall, a ritual for Taisui, has been requested and paid for by a family, all of whom — grandmother, grandfather, daughter, granddaughter, and grandson — are present. In a smaller side hall, the same ceremony takes place for the benefit of a woman born in the Year of the Sheep, who watches the ritual from the side. Her sign conflicts with the Taisui avatar of the year, and the masters devise the appropriate ritual based on her Chinese zodiac. In present-day China, the cult of Taisui symbolizes a new stress on individual destiny (or that of the nuclear family), rather than communal destiny.[47] Rituals to Taisui are one of the most frequent occurrences we witnessed in Shanghai's Daoist temples, not only in White Clouds Monastery and the

City God Temple, but also in less fashionable temples such as Chongfu Temple in the popular neighborhood of Sanlin, in southwestern Pudong.

On top of their blue and black Daoist vestments, the ritual performers wear vibrant, detailed robes from a factory in Suzhou. Eight traditional Chinese instruments are used in the ceremony. Shanghai Daoist masters learn to play musical instruments from teachers at the Shanghai Conservatory of Music. The authenticity of its musical tradition is one of the main ritual markers of White Clouds Monastery. The local connection is reinforced by the requirement that all monks must graduate from the Shanghai Daoist Academy and serve internships at the temple during their training.

There are currently around twelve Daoist masters (*daoshi*) at White Clouds Monastery (thirty-two serve at the City God Temple).[48] The temple was forced to close in 1966, which also ended its connection to the Quanzhen monastic tradition. After it reopened in 1983, married Zhengyi masters were put in charge of the compound and asked to perform all rituals in the temple rather than celebrating them at people's homes and organizing street processions, as had been the case in the past. White Clouds Monastery also served as the training center for the new generation of married Daoist masters until the Daoist Academy moved into its new premises in Songjiang District. As a sign of its origins, White Clouds Monastery continues to offer gracious hospitality to traveling Quanzhen monks when they pass through Shanghai. The Zhengyi masters are now requested to come to the temple every day and adhere strictly to their working schedule. Besides performing the rituals asked and paid for by the faithful, they recite two daily offices. During the daytime, at least, they form a community of sorts, erasing the earlier distinction between Quanzhen Daoist monks and masters who live at home.

GRACING PEOPLE'S SQUARE

The large Moore Memorial Church (MMC) (Mu'en Tang), adorned with a neon cross, occupies a privileged site facing People's Square, a central part of Shanghai. Large crowds gather in all seasons, and at Christmastime, the church offers the "official" celebration of the Nativity.

The church was founded in 1887 as the Central Methodist Church. Fifteen years later, it was renamed for the Moores, a family of benefactors in Kansas City, Missouri. Foreign and Chinese pastors have been worshipping together there from 1906 onward. Two American pastors, Sid and Oliver Anderson, were the church's dominant figures from the 1920s to 1949. There were strong connections between Moore Memorial Church and the Soong family (the three Soong daughters attended Sunday school there), although tensions were known to exist between the two parties. The church's prominent role in the community soon led to its involvement in city politics.[49] The

Social Gospel, a Christian social-reform movement, was the norm, rather than evangelism. Through its network of kindergartens, schools, and sports clubs, as well as health and charity endeavors, the church became known as Shanghai's "social club" (*shejiao huitang*).[50]

The building testifies to Shanghai's ebullient construction history at the time of the foreign concessions. In 1931, a new church was built next to the original site, making it the largest Protestant church in the Far East. The church was designed by the famous architect László Hudec, making it even more of a landmark, which it remains to this day. The five-meter-high neon cross atop the bell tower was set in place in 1936. During the 1950s, after united worship was established, the Chinese name of the church was changed from its original Mu'er (the phonetic approximation of "Moore") to Mu'en (Bathing in Grace).[51] Other churches modified their names in a similar way so as to avoid associations with missionaries and donors. Little of the church's material history survived the Cultural Revolution, as most objects were destroyed and burned. The building served as a high school until it reopened on September 2, 1979, one of the first churches to be reassigned to its original function nationwide.

Initially, a period of extreme caution followed the Cultural Revolution. Since then, the congregation's growth has been continuous and steady, much like the local and international reputation of the church itself. Services accommodate a variety of styles in devotion, music, and traditions. Under the cover of Moore Memorial Church, Anglican and other denominations have maintained their individual character. An Anglican-style service with more formal liturgy is held once a month and is the only service that offers Communion at the altar. At other times, specially dressed staff distribute bread and grape juice, served in small plastic cups, to the seated congregation.

During the 2014 Christmas season, Christmas trees lined the entranceway of the church, shielding it from the bustling, pedestrian-packed People's Square. A large painted model of Santa's sleigh, embellished with golden reindeer, was placed over the baptismal pool. The church was decorated with a large Christmas tree and festive wreaths. Plastic dolls with heavy eye makeup and cardboard wings dangled from the ceiling, and clouds made of cotton wool hung under their feet, completing the angel imagery.

Moore Memorial Church is a well-run organization with a huge team of volunteers. At each service, a crew of smiling people wearing official T-shirts greets worshippers and onlookers. On the evening of December 25, a Christmas performance narrated the gospel parables through songs and dance. An overflow crowd watched and photographed the performance on a television screen that hung above the golden reindeer. In the dressing room, Iris, the Chinese woman leading the dance team, commented, "Lots of people come on Christmas to take photos and upload them on WeChat. Christmas is seen as fashionable because it's Western. It's important that we put on a good show." One of the performers, a fifteen-year-old middle school student, donned a long curly wig and fake beard for his role of the obedient son in the parable of the prodigal son. He stated proudly that his family has been part of the church for more than one hundred years. The performance, he stressed, was "a Christian thing to do."

Afterward, over coffee at a Starbucks next door, Wendy, a Singaporean who leads youth group activities, commented on the Christmas gift designed by the chief pastor, a cross-shaped key holder and a religious pamphlet, agreeing that it was particularly "evangelical" this year. "We're aware of the significance of the church being located in People's Square, and Christmas is a time to spread the Christian message to people who don't come to the church at other times." Wendy and her friends were sharing pictures on WeChat (Weixin), the popular Chinese social network. The photographs were of members of a migrant workers' church (located in an old factory on the outskirts of Shanghai) wearing Santa hats and singing Christmas carols in a Pudong mall.[52] Some people who attend Moore Memorial Church have connections to this congregation, an example of the porous line between "official" and "unofficial" churches. No official church could perform carols in such public places, someone commented, but Mu'en Church leads caroling events in old people's homes and orphanages.

Moore Memorial Church is thus part of a network of churches, alliances, and affiliations that determines the Protestant landscape of Shanghai. John Keating, a keen observer of the city, aptly characterized this web of rather complex relationships:

> People I interviewed at other churches across Shanghai and indeed across China often expressed a mixture of envy and awe towards MMC. When I spoke with people at other churches in Shanghai with fairly basic facilities, such as Zhabeitang and Huai'entang, they seemed a little jealous of MMC's more attractive appearance and prominent location. One pastor conceded that some people were drawn away from his church to MMC because of this. Conversely, another felt that large prominent churches such as MMC may attract people initially, but then they move off to their local church. One elderly lady at the small shed temporarily housing the church in Pudong spoke of MMC in reverent tones as their "mother church."[53]

In contrast to its Social Gospel roots, Moore Memorial Church, nowadays a flagship downtown parish, harbors political caution and doctrinal conservatism. In Pastor Jiang Xili's homily on the third Sunday of Advent 2015, she reminded parishioners to behave during Christmas celebrations and to be content with the pew (or the absence of pew) they might find. What followed was even clearer:

> In any case, we should always be content with what we are given. The rich person must use his money wisely and generously, and must remember that he has been established steward of the goods of the earth. If he starts to use his fortune just as he pleases, God can always find another Christian to whom he will entrust the goods he had first given to the rich person. And the poor should consider that God made him so and live his condition in hope and faith.

If the nearby Bund enshrines the symbols of Shanghai's civic sacredness, Moore Memorial Church offers a threshold located between the city's secularity and sacredness, even at the cost of infringing on the latter.

It should be added that the congregation is entangled in a sort of polarity with another prominent Shanghai church, Hengshan Community Church (Shanghai Guoji Libaitang) in Xuhui District. This parish is known for serving the foreign community, but that does not mean that the church building is reserved for foreigners. The first Sunday service in Chinese takes place at 7:00 a.m., with loudspeakers from the parish heard in the neighborhood shortly after six. The Chinese congregation is proud of the parish's international outlook. If Moore Memorial Church epitomizes the national spirit of the Chinese Protestant Church, Hengshan Community Church symbolizes its transnational, universal fellowship. This sentiment dates back to its origins. Built in 1925 and located in the French Concession, Hengshan Community Church held its nondenominational services exclusively in English.[54]

Even with official separations established, the foreign and native communities of Hengshan Church interact in many ways. Spiritual musical events are open to both nationals and foreigners,[55] and following the success of the Alpha course for foreign worshippers, an Alpha course for Chinese nationals was launched in March 2013.[56] Each group is structured the same way: twelve people, consisting of two leaders, two helpers, a host, a cook, and eight participants. In other words, through very different channels, both Hengshan Community Church and Moore Memorial Church play leading roles in the structuring of Shanghai's Protestant landscape. At the same time, the style and background of each is so ingrained that the transfer of pastors between congregations has sometimes caused uneasiness.[57]

THE CATHOLIC DIAGONAL

Though its population remains modest in size, Shanghai Catholicism is composed of a variety of layers and social groups. Such diversity is a product of its long history. The faithful from Pudong and Chongming were from a rural, long-established population. Catholics living in the areas bordering the ancient city and the Bund were often boat owners and compradors. Later, they turned to banking and manufacturing. To the west, Xujiahui was populated by descendants from the Xu clan and their relatives, as well as from families formed through the marriage of orphans raised in Catholic institutions, men trained at the Jesuit arts and craft school of Tushanwan ("T'ou-se-we" in the local dialect), and women at the Good Shepherd orphanage. Farther to the west were the rivers and lakes where Catholic fishermen made their living. In the north, the county town of Jiading had an ancient, well-established community. Such lineages are still apparent today, and local memories shape parochial practices and imagined boundaries.

A northeast-southwest diagonal organizes the three main Catholic landmarks of Shanghai: the St. Francis Xavier Church, still considered the diocese's cathedral by the Church's central authorities; St. Ignatius Church; and the Marian pilgrimage site of Sheshan Basilica. Such a scheme does not give a full picture of Shanghai's Catholic landscape, as the contrasts between the Pudong and Chongming parishes, on the one hand, and the communities on the west side of the Huangpu River, on the other, are also significant.

The following excerpt from *A Guide to Catholic Shanghai*, published in 1937, illuminates the role played by St. Francis Xavier Church:

> St Francis Xavier Church, the cathedral of Shanghai, is situated in the Chinese city near the east end of the Bund. The land was given by the Chinese authorities in exchange for other pieces of property confiscated during times of persecution. . . . Its opening in 1853 was a veritable international festival. In the following years, when roving bands of Tai-Pings were pillaging the country, many Christians settled around this church so as to enjoy the protection of a French gunboat anchored in the river close by. These Christians organized a little city of their own and, until recent years, had their own police force and fire brigade. The parish of St. Francis Xavier contains a fervent group of 6,700 Christians under the direction of the Chinese secular clergy. Besides the eight schools with over 3,000 pupils, the flourishing Sodalities for men and women and a St. Vincent de Paul Society, the parish has a remarkable Catholic Action Society.[58]

In locating St. Francis Xavier Church within the Chinese city, the booklet was slightly misleading. At the time of its construction, it was indeed located outside the foreign settlements, but it was also outside the Chinese walled city proper. Its familiar name, Dongjiadu Cathedral, speaks volumes.

Dongjiadu was the first landing on the Huangpu River, a shipping hub that grew to become Shanghai's economic engine until the Japanese occupation. From the time of the Qing dynasty onward, merchants developed the land between the Huangpu River and the city wall. Dongjiadu "was a compact metropolis of stores, warehouses, inns, boat-building yards and workshops. . . . [Its] intricate web of lanes and surviving architecture [remain] a physical index of every era of the port's history."[59] However, its remnants are now being cleared for an extensive urban renewal project.

The walled city was the interior (*nei*), the sacred civic space, so to speak, while the docks were the exterior (*wai*), the space where commercial and missionary activities were allowed to develop. This explains why, after the Treaty of Nanjing, Chinese authorities flatly rejected the Jesuits' request for the return of their former church inside the walled city. Built in 1553, the little wooden building to the east of the City God Temple had been converted into a church in 1640. It was subsequently confiscated under the edicts prohibiting Christianity and became a temple dedicated to Guandi. The symbolic importance of this location was so great that the magistrate compensated the Jesuits with three pieces of land, two of which are now the sites of St. Francis Xavier and St. Joseph's Churches. However, in 1862, another request could not be turned down, and Jingyi Church (Jingyi Tang) regained its status as a Catholic worship place.[60] After a tumultuous history, it was closed in 1959. In 2014, the former church was converted into a local painting and calligraphy academy. As of today, despite being listed as a cultural relic, there is no written mention of its former religious use.

St. Francis Xavier Church, built in early Spanish baroque style, has been well preserved and tastefully restored. Initial plans for the church were much grander, but in the 1860s, the lack of money led the apostolic vicar to compromise with a smaller cathedral. The church originally stood on a pier where leading Catholic fishermen clans gathered, welcoming poor newcomers at the time of the Taiping Rebellion.[61] Several of these clans made their fortune in trade and banking, and St. Francis Xavier Church became the parish where affluent Chinese Catholics congregated. Much of its identity was lost after the Japanese invasion, when wealthy Chinese took refuge in the French Concession.[62] In 1960, it lost its position as the seat of a diocesan bishop, which, even though the move was not canonically sanctioned, further diminished its status. The church has gradually regained its place as a hub for laity-inspired activities, with regular meetings of groups of Catholic artists or social activists. St. Francis Xavier's unique tradition and welcoming premises, as well as its location some distance away from the political center of St. Ignatius Church (or Cathedral, as its canonical status remains unclear), have distinguished it as a place where people can launch new initiatives.

St. Ignatius Church, a prominent landmark in the Xujiahui District, is often called the "Xujiahui Cathedral." Completed in 1910, six years after construction began, the cathedral is located in the center of Xujiahui's former Jesuit complex and is large enough to accommodate three thousand worshippers. The impressive structure, with its two fifty-six-meter-high towers, was certainly conceived to be a landmark, and its significance extends far beyond Shanghai. Today, St Ignatius's status is evident at the English-language Sunday mass, which is attended by foreigners, overseas Chinese, and locals with connections abroad. St. Ignatius is also a popular setting for wedding photography.

As with Shanghai's City God Temple, St. Ignatius Cathedral cannot be separated from its surroundings. The French Jesuits, whose land bordered the French Concession, had built up the western part of Shanghai in response to the walled city to the east. After 1949, the concession's institutions were dismantled; however, the urban planning that has taken place over the past twenty years has been reviving the symbols and memories of this Catholic neighborhood. Xu Guangqi Memorial Park (plate 12) contains several items related to the veneration of the Catholic statesman, including a replica of the cross and the Latin-Chinese inscription erected in 1903 for the three hundredth anniversary of his baptism. The colonial-style former Jesuit residence has been restored, and its library of Western books is now open to the public. The exterior and interior of the former seminary, built in 1928, have been carefully restored.[63] The Tushanwan Museum simultaneously encapsulates three different historical sequences: the arts and crafts school that existed on the site for a century, the Jesuit enclave, and the history of Xuhui District.

Located on the western outskirts of the city, atop one of the region's rare hills, Sheshan Basilica is the third landmark of Catholic Shanghai. The basilica originated as a small Marian shrine containing a reproduction of the Parisian image of Our Lady of Victories. In 1870, after anti-Christian riots in the northern city of Tianjin, the interim superior of the Jesuit Jiangnan mission vowed to build a large church if the territory he held sanction over was spared. The sanctuary was opened in 1873 and soon became a pilgrimage site of special devotion for the Catholic mariners and fishermen who were active on the large network of waterways.

In November 1935, more than 3,500 Catholics gathered for the consecration of a larger basilica adorned with a new Marian symbol featuring a dragon pinned under Mary's feet, representative of both the missionary fervor of the time and Shanghai's aesthetic modernity.

Fr. Léonard, a French Jesuit based in Shanghai, designed the statue, which was known as Our Lady of Sheshan and weighed 1,200 kilograms. . . . The Sheshan Mary is not especially Chinese-looking in either the garment she wears or in her visual features. . . . Mary holds the infant Jesus up above her head in outstretched arms, proudly displaying him to the regions all around, thereby symbolically claiming these lands for her son. The church was twenty-two metres high overall; thirty-eight metres high from the base of the church to the foot of the statue. The statue itself was four metres, eighty centimetres high.[64]

The statue was destroyed during the Cultural Revolution and replaced with a replica in 2000, its majesty a stark contrast to the present situation of Shanghai Catholics.[65] Still, Sheshan remains the place where this community's networks and memories coalesce.

From the 1870s onward, the site has been developed as the major Roman Catholic pilgrimage site in China. Today, buses flock to the Sheshan Basilica from all the parishes in Shanghai and the surrounding region, sometimes from as far away as Inner Mongolia.[66] Most pilgrimage activities take place in May, culminating on May 24, the feast day of Our Lady Help of Christians. Even on weekdays, the basilica is busy with visitors, small groups of women singing in the church and devotees grouped around the statues on the hill. The basilica is also part of the Catholic Church's organizational structure, and a large seminary on the grounds (plate 13). Although most of the functions of the Sheshan Seminary have been suspended since Bishop Ma Daqin resigned from the Patriotic Catholic Association in July 2012, the popular fervor surrounding the sanctuary remains undiminished.[67] Liturgical service is offered in the basilica proper only on Christmas Day and Easter, while masses are celebrated in the nearby Zhongshan Church, a two-story gray building with a small backyard.

Thus, the Sheshan Basilica fulfills three functions: it is one of the main public spaces in which the story of the city is narrated and represented; it epitomizes Catholic Shanghai in the face of adversity brought on by political conflict; it is the grand theater of Chinese Catholic devotional life at designated times of the year and is shared by both official and underground communities.[68] The basilica struggles, however, to meet the neighborhood's liturgical and devotional needs, which require a sense of privacy, and the Zhongshan Church fulfills this fourth function by providing a substitute space within a space.

There are two west entrances at the base of Sheshan that visitors can ascend. Locals call a third entrance, at No. 3, Huanshan Road, "the door of the Catholics," as it allows direct access to the basilica. On May 21, 2014, three days before the Feast Day of Our Lady of Sheshan (or "Zose" in Shanghai dialect), the road leading to the site is blocked for miles, and the final leg of the journey must be completed on foot. "The door of the Catholics" is guarded by security staff in casual clothes and Catholic volunteers wearing green waistcoats. Along the hill, groups of devoted Catholics recite the Rosary, kneeling before the shrines to the Sacred Heart, the Virgin Mary, and St. Joseph, and stop at each of the fourteen Stations of the Cross. The crowd also includes the curious and tourists. The two publics willingly mix and interact. An old volunteer stands among the curious, perched on a foldable chair and speaking to them with great passion. "Do you know how much it has cost to build this church? You can't imagine how many silver dollars [*yinyuan*], just like these"—and he pulls two ancient silver dollars out of his pocket—"were spent to build our church. So, this church is a priceless treasure!" He proceeds to sing canticles and show everyone how to gesture and to pray when following the Via Dolorosa. His audience obligingly follows his instructions.

Other activities also take place in October, the Month of the Rosary, among them, a small students' pilgrimage, which has been organized every year since 2006. On the evening of October 25, 2014, around forty people, divided into four groups, all in their twenties, gathered at Sheshan after walking about thirty-five kilometers, mainly along highways and metro lines. During the strenuous walk, pilgrims had the opportunity to exchange WeChat messages with Catholic friends.[69] After a celebratory meal in the seminary's canteen, twenty-three people stayed overnight, and the others returned home by metro. The next morning, a Sunday, the group awoke at 6:00 a.m. and went up from the seminary to the church for the 8:00 a.m. mass. By the time the celebration was finished, the hill at Sheshan was bustling with people praying at shrines and eating ice cream, immersed in the atmosphere of a family outing. One couple had brought plastic chairs to sit on as they recited the Rosary. Others were tomb sweeping at family graves (some Catholic families maintain illegal burial sites under the trees that cover the hill). If the basilica, with its imposing statue of Our Lady of Sheshan, lays claim to the surrounding land, the hill is appropriated by the pilgrims and other visitors who maintain their discreet practices and sketch countless wandering lines across the land along their way.

BUILDING UP NEW LANDMARKS

Any urban landscape may experience a surge of new landmarks. In Songjiang District, a gigantic cultural park in the Guangfulin area has been under development since 2010 (plate 14). The Zhiye Temple opened inside the park in 2013, although the surrounding area was still far from ready to welcome visitors. It took two years and more than ¥200 million to build the Tang dynasty–style building. Four *luohan* trees (*Podocarpus macrophyllus*), more than two hundred years old and exceeding ¥600,000 each in cost, were placed at the front of the temple. By January 2014, five monks were living in the large, aesthetically pleasing complex. They complained that it was not really designed for Buddhist practice but was more of an art piece and tourist attraction.

On a second visit, in January 2015, the site was still surrounded by temporary construction walls. However, holes had started to appear in the walls, enabling easier access at regular intervals, whereas the official opening was scheduled for the end of 2017. The head monk was constantly traveling and very busy when on-site. The entire complex is a mix of architectural styles replicating various historical periods, including a cave construction serving as a toilet, enormous terra-cotta-colored Romanesque pillars near the river, and two modern-looking pyramidal structures floating on the lake described on signs as a library and a museum. The complex also includes a Daoist temple, scenic gardens, and three-dimensional wall murals, with convincingly "ancient" details, depicting the life of the Buddha. The substantial number of people milling around the park indicates its potential popularity once it officially opens, even with a planned entrance fee of ¥100.

Guangfulin is laden with history. Songjiang was the seat of Huating County, erected in 751, and became a full-fledged prefecture (*fu*) in the Yuan dynasty. The cultural relics of present-day Songjiang District — a Yuan dynasty mosque, a Song dynasty pagoda, and a Ming dynasty carved wall — are unique to Greater Shanghai. Songjiang District was also the birthplace of an impressive number of Chinese literati. Songjiang was gradually integrated into the administrative limits of Shanghai from the Republican period onward. Its present administrative status and territory were fixed in 1998. Shortly after, "New Towns," resembling Western-style suburbs, and large-scale university campuses were planned and constructed. Once this was done, urban planners started to prioritize the recovery of local pride and a cultural heritage weakened by repeated administrative mergers. Successful archaeological excavations gave the Guangfulin project the necessary impetus, yet the buildings in Relics Park are only remotely linked to the New Stone Age and Zhou dynasty artifacts found in the area. However, the inclusion of active Buddhist and Daoist temples within the complex is intriguing. Living religious practices contribute to the sacredness of the place; symbols of civic religion and congregational devotions unite in a form of ancestral worship that combines praying and playing.

THE BUDDHIST CURVE AND A MAUSOLEUM

The Jade Buddha Temple (Yufo Si), Jing'an Temple, and Longhua Temple are at the core of the city's network of Buddhist institutions. They are located on a curve that runs roughly from southwestern to northeastern Puxi.

At the southwestern end of the curve, in Xuhui District, is Longhua Temple, a remarkable religious landmark and by far the most ancient of the three temples. Built in the third century, the temple's name testifies to its founders' devotion to Maitreya, the Buddha of the Future, who is supposed to awaken and teach the law under a *longhua* tree. The temple's history, with its cycles of aggrandizement and destruction, is similar to that of many Chinese Buddhist temples. Longhua Temple flourished during the Ming and Qing dynasties, until the Republican army seized it in 1912. After the Cultural Revolution, the temple was the first religious edifice allowed to resume operations. Its layout is typical of a Song dynasty temple of the Chan School, with a magnificent pagoda more than forty meters high. The temple's antiquity and historical lineage contribute to its exalted position. Local residents sometimes asked why we were wasting our time visiting small neighborhood temples, when Longhua, the oldest temple in Shanghai, was their own preferred place of worship.

Another remarkable feature is linked to the temple's geographic location, which places it between the tormented history and achievements of modern China. Just opposite the temple stands the Longhua Revolutionary Martyrs' Cemetery, a park that serves as a major civil memorial site. In 1927, on the grounds of the temple (then the headquarters of the Songhu Garrison), the Nationalists carried out a purge of suspected Communists. The memorial rooms focus on the suffering of Communists and other revolutionaries who were martyred between 1928 and 1937. In the years that followed, the Japanese army operated a large civilian internment camp nearby, and mass executions and internment took place on the temple grounds. The edifices that fill the park's nineteen hectares were part of a wave of construction of revolutionary memorial sites in the post-Mao era.[70] Between 1950 and 1963, projects for making the site a memorial were proposed, but none was completed. In 1983, the widow of a former revolutionary submitted a petition in support of erecting a memorial, and in 1997 the structure was complete.[71] The cemetery now includes spaces for public worship, a hall for storing the urns of senior cadres, and an area for funerary tablets. The statue at the end of the park represents the body of a dead martyr whose raised arm is meant to symbolize a torch. The combination of Confucian and Christlike elements in the Longhua Revolutionary Martyrs' Cemetery locates its aesthetic almost at the opposite end of a Buddhist ethos. Taken together, the temple and the park compose a landscape in which the sacredness of each is enhanced and confirmed by that of the other.

Literary scholar Kirk Denton has characterized the aesthetics of the cemetery as follows:

The aesthetic is a strange brew of modernist grandiosity with the social-ist realist heroic. The exhibition hall, which is the centrepiece of a large park filled with artwork and other forms of memorial, is a large glass pyramid in a modernist mode. Its glass and stone style is radically dif-ferent from the heavy and ponderous style of, say, the classic socialist realist Military Museum in Beijing. Yet, though the style of the building speaks of the modern and the global, the exhibitions inside are devoted to martyrs, the vast majority of whom died fighting for the revolution or leftist revolutionary causes. . . . Regardless of the content or narra-tive structure of the exhibition, the modernist aesthetic of the building speaks volumes. First, it marks an explicit rejection of the socialist aes-thetic and suggests that the meaning of the exhibition within its walls moves away from standard socialist narratives. The modernist aesthetic also explicitly marks a joining with the world and an implicit rejection of Chinese cultural essentialism.[72]

Yet there is not necessarily a basic discrepancy between the socialist real-ism that inspired the remarkable statues and the architectural style of the memorial monuments. It seems rather that a layer of significance has been added to, but has not negated, those that were already present. The whole complex, with its alleys and main building, is designed as a mausoleum; the statues and artifacts manifest meaning and dimension, enhanced by the void and resonances organized by the mausoleum's structure. Revolutionary his-tory has been inserted into China's national history. Most interestingly, the choice of a pyramid structure for the main building works as a contrast or complement to the temple's pagoda. Pagoda and pyramid embody forms of sacredness that may be seen as both conflicting and cooperating. More gen-erally, the architectural choices institute a sacred place marked by tensions that reflect the complexity of history and a desire to harmonize diverging memories into a unified whole.

Moving northeast from Longhua, the curve leads to the heart of the com-mercial and business center of Puxi: Jing'an Temple, the only religious edi-fice in Shanghai that lends its name to a district.[73] The temple itself, which has occupied the site since the Song dynasty, is extremely large (seventeen thousand square meters after large-scale additions made from the 1980s to the first decade of the 2000s) and remains subject to frequent embellishment works. It can be accessed from a number of entrances on different streets (plate 16). It adjoins a busy shopping center and several cultural institutions, a location that makes it one of the city's main tourist attractions. With its main entrance on West Nanjing Road, the temple is often perceived as part of the area's commercial culture. This is not a new phenomenon. The temple fairs (*miaohui*) that were once held here are remembered as the liveliest in Shanghai. The ornate material exuberance of the temple impresses some visitors, while others see the gold, jade, and camphor statues, each weighing several tons, as typifying the excesses of present-day Chinese Buddhism, as does the high cost of tickets for events such as those occurring around Chinese New Year. We asked a number of people what places they associate with sacredness in Shanghai, and were sometimes told, "Not the temples . . . not temples like Jing'an." Others, however, are attracted by the Tantric Buddhist (Mizong) tradition that Jing'an has developed along with the Pure Land (Jingtu) Buddhist School and, more generally, by the esoteric nature of its relics and practices, which offer sophisticated "technologies of salvation," as anthropologist Francesca Tarroco has termed them.[74] One of the temple's former abbots, Master Chi Song (1894–1972), renewed the Zhenyan tradition ("Shingon" in Japanese) after studying in Japan, at Koyasan. He set up a Zhenyan place of worship (*mitan*) in 1953; the Cultural Revolution brought it to a stop; and the temple revived the Zhenyan tradition in 1985, when it received liturgical instruments brought by a delegation from Koyasan.

The atmosphere at Jing'an Temple is defined by a number of local customs. A tripod located in front of the Mahavira Hall attracts many visitors who throw coins into it in order to secure blessings or simply for fun. On the first and fifteenth days of the lunar month, a volunteer collects the fallen coins and puts them into the donation box. "It would be better if visitors just put the coins into the donation box respectfully," he declares. Another volunteer performs the same task near a large Hotan jade (*hetianyu*), a stone that has magnetic properties on which people try to balance coins.

Jing'an Temple is also closely associated with the history of humanistic Buddhism. The first meeting of the General Buddhist Assembly of China was held there in 1913. In the same year, the reformist monk Taixu delivered a famous programmatic discourse at the temple. Taixu was also the inspiration and moral leader of the Buddhist Studies Institute, founded at Jing'an in 1946, a year before his death. Venerable Zhenchan revived the tradition when he was elected prior in 1992, setting up funds for handicapped children and to support rescue efforts during natural disasters.

Compared to Longhua and Jing'an Temples, the Jade Buddha Temple (plate 15) is relatively new. It was founded in 1882 to house two jade statues brought from Myanmar by its founder, Master Huigen. The present structure was inaugurated in 1928. Inscribed into both the Pure Land and Chan Schools, the temple soon became an important center of Buddhist studies, influenced by the humanistic Buddhism tradition. The Buddhist Research Institute of Shanghai was founded at the temple in 1942. Since being revived in 1983, it has asserted itself as a leading institution for training monks and propagating Buddhist culture in society at large. A library, magazine, and media center contribute to the role of the Jade Buddha Temple in promoting Buddhist doctrine and social influence in Shanghai and nationwide.[75] Unlike Longhua and Jing'an Temples, the Jade Buddha Temple declares its position as a center of Buddhist orthodoxy and teaching.

The three temples are part of a collective mental geography. Informants are almost unanimous in their definitions of each temple's specialty: The Jade Buddha Temple is the place to go when praying for health and peace; both the luxurious aspect and the location of Jing'an make it the perfect place for requests related to financial matters; and Longhua is the best site for petitioning for job promotions (officials and cadres are supposed to particularly favor this temple).

At the same time, a lack of physical (and psychological) distance from one of these temples is often said to be potentially harmful. We were told, for example, the story of a bank manager whose office window offered a direct view into the courtyard of Jing'an Temple and whose business ultimately failed. There are also tales of devout Buddhists who bought apartments in the residence opposite the Jade Buddha Temple, and when their relationship with the temple turned sour, the rumor goes, these faithful eventually fell ill.[76] Obtaining favors from places of worship requires finding the appropriate spatial and psychological positioning, the former often determining the latter.

◆ ◆ ◆

Landmarks are not isolated; they draw polarities, lines, and constellations. For instance, Mu'en Church orients a hierarchy of communities, the connection between the Longhua Temple and the Longhua Revolutionary Martyrs' Cemetery shapes the way Shanghai's history is told, while the Longhua, Jing'an, and Jade Buddha Temples are located on a diagonal of decreasing antiquity and increasing focus on spreading the doctrine. Centers of sacredness collaborate and compete in shaping the city's religious consciousness. St. Francis Xavier Church and St. Ignatius Cathedral are both cathedrals, although of conflicting significance; Moore Memorial Church represents the public face of the Chinese Protestant Church, while, in a district with an important expatriate population, Hengshan Community Church stresses the universality of its style, music, and message. From one public or even one person to another, these patterns are visualized, understood, and lived with varying intensity. Comprehending Shanghai requires figuring out a collective religious geography organized around a constellation of landmarks, which we just sketched.

We now need to go from the general to the particular. Some city dwellers may locate landmarks mentally without much emotional involvement.

Others identify themselves with a local congregation, which automatically affects their entire urban geography. They envision the sacred landscape of the city from the vantage point provided by a religious compound. Having mapped the religious landscape of Shanghai from the top, we can experience it from the perspective of the local communities that make it a living, continuously changing reality.

CHAPTER 3

The Wall and the Door

PLACES OF WORSHIP FASHION A WAY OF COMMUNING AND INTERACTING that enables local attendees to live and experience them as "compounds"— enclosed places that serve a variety of needs. Temples, parishes, and mosques operate at the frontier of the public and the intimate. They regulate the relationship between a community of believers and its immediate environment by means of doors and enclosures that are both symbolic and material. In China, the tradition of surrounding buildings with walled courtyards extends to religious edifices. This is true not only of Buddhist and Daoist temples but also of Christian churches, which are similarly separated from nearby buildings.[1]

Although the focus here is on what happens inside the compounds, for city dwellers, the structures themselves are charged with varying levels of meaning and intensity at different points of space-time. Compounds are both incubators and cells of a larger urban ethos through which microcultures live and develop interdependently.

CROSSING THE THRESHOLD

A tiny room adjacent to the gate separates the surrounding neighborhood from the Sacred Heart of Jesus Catholic Church in Pudong (often called the "Zhangjialou Church") and functions as a breakroom for the parish's receptionists, parishioners, and volunteers. When a new visitor arrives, the receptionist suggests, "If you're interested in the Catholic doctrine, or if you just want to talk, you can come to our course of religious instruction which is held every Sunday." These are effective words, as almost all catechumens preparing for baptism mention them when recalling how they became involved in the process.[2]

The Chinese religious compound is an autonomous entity that asserts and protects its existence through fences. In almost all cases, buildings are composed of areas for worship and spaces for meeting and living, with a kitchen and other dependencies. Religious compounds could comprise an even greater variety of buildings in the past. This is obvious enough for Daoist and Buddhist temples, considering the communal function they have always played. This is also the case for churches in Shanghai, which was a center for nationwide missionary efforts, so that a church commonly shared a site with a school.[3] Clinics, sports clubs, and other institutions exist within religious compounds, and among two hundred rooms at St. Francis Xavier Church were once used for pastoral activities, school, hospital, residence, shops, and charity services.[4]

The word "compound" refers not only to a fenced or walled-in area but also to a chemical or lexical combination. The compound's congregation is likewise marked by diversity. Today's Protestant churches amalgamate different congregational lineages; Buddhist and Daoist temples accommodate layers of ritual and canonical traditions. Local worshippers and those from afar share the same space, in sometimes uneasy combinations. As religious buildings are scarcer in China than in the West, a greater social mix is very often the norm. Compounds also accommodate blends of Mandarin, Shanghai dialect, English, and sometimes sacred languages, while balancing liturgical and devotional parlance with the political lingua franca expected from officially recognized enclosures. Even compounds that nurture an extremely unified religious culture need to combine a number of factors in order to effectively gather communities and organize rituals. St. Joseph's Church, a haven of traditional Catholic practice, regularly organizes masses according to the Tridentine ritual. For its celebration, the faithful receive a booklet that includes the Latin text, the Chinese and Shanghai-dialect alliterations necessary for reading the same text aloud, and a semiclassical Chinese translation of the original text.

The term *daochang* originally referred to any area prepared for the performance of an ad hoc ritual. In some ethnic minority areas (especially in southwestern China), one can still observe how a ritual field is delineated through a series of symbolic markers and recovers its original function after the ceremony is over. Chinese Buddhism designates both the place where the Buddha reached enlightenment and the space where the Law is taught by the term. In 1926, the founders of the new compound of the World Buddhist Householder Grove (Shijie Fojiao Jushilin), a Shanghai-based association despite its name, officially described it as a *daochang*. The compound was a mix of ritual halls, meeting places, and lodgings (and later housed a school for orphans) but was managed exclusively by Buddhist lay volunteers, not monks. It combined many of the traditional characteristics of a Buddhist temple with the "modern" culture of Republican Shanghai.[5]

Today, Shanghai's religious culture is more clerical in scope than it was in the 1930s. While laypeople during the Republican era were both able and willing to take charge of their congregation's destiny, the Reform and Opening policies of the 1980s re-created a legally circumscribed religious space. This entailed reconstituting and controlling the clergy while, until today, laypeople intervene through patriotic associations that convey the state's directives. Still, a religious compound today fulfills functions consistent with the meanings of the word *daochang*: it is an area where rituals are performed, it is an enclosure that aims to be a place of practice and meeting where clerics, volunteers, and ordinary believers form a worshipping community, and it is part of an urban culture that it helps shape and enrich.

NURTURING DEVOTION IN CHUANSHA

Any place can serve as a landmark of sorts for a close-knit community. Defining a center from which other spaces are seen as peripheral enables a neighborhood to assert itself against a larger urban background. Traditional communities are now scarce, as Shanghai has been entirely remodeled through expansion and urban planning. Nevertheless, the continuity and resilience of specific local cultures can be striking. Chuansha New Town (Chuansha Xinzheng), a former fishermen's village that has retained its local flavor, is located in southeast Pudong, near the sea. Until recently, the word "Shanghai" applied only to the city's central districts, and the villagers of Chuansha did not define themselves as Shanghainese. Things have been changing quickly, however, especially since 2010, when the Chuansha metro station began operations. Religious communities traditionally played an important role in village life. Chuansha has been home to a Buddhist temple since at least 1189, and Catholicism reached Chuansha at the very beginning of the seventeenth century. A large church was built there in 1865–72 and was enlarged and remodeled in 1927.[6]

Changren Temple (Changren Chansi) and the Sacred Heart Church are symbols of what remains of ancient Chuansha. Both congregations depend on core groups of women over the age of sixty, many of whom worked as farmers or in the textile industry. The local dialect is widely used, including in the recitation of scriptures. On feast days, when the two congregations are larger, the leading role of the women's group becomes apparent. This illustrates a common phenomenon, older women carving out a space of their own and transforming their assets into moral capital through religious activities.[7] At the same time, Buddhist vegetarian sisterhoods of cotton weavers were a fixture of the social landscape and at times organized social protests:

> Vegetarian communities were relatively egalitarian. Rank within Vege-
> tarian circles was not generally determined by gender. Men and women
> regularly prayed and ate their meals in each other's company. Unlike
> Confucianism, Buddhist-Vegetarian customs did not exclude women
> from the important ritual life of their community. Women could and
> did become prominent spiritual and community leaders as managers of
> temples and residences. . . . When members of the sect mobilized for col-
> lective political action, they relied heavily on the communication chan-
> nels and leadership provided by the temple associations. In addition, the
> Vegetarian centers functioned as a cultural focal point for individuals,
> including many non-Vegetarians, who combined their knowledge of the
> occult with the practice of medicine.[8]

These women-based Buddhist vegetarian traditions are layered with an industrial culture that has been developing in this area from the end of the nineteenth century. In cotton mills, the creation of a sisterhood (*jiemeihui*) providing mutual support for a few women workers involved pledging loyalty and, often, visiting a Buddhist temple where the women burned incense together. Workers' sisterhoods may have been adapted from traditional associations of women, which were often linked to lay Buddhist sects. In Chuansha, sisterhoods included a number of young widows who refused to remarry.[9]

Several features of this local tradition, which transcends religious distinctions, are discernible today. In the Buddhist temple, cooking vegetarian meals in the temple's kitchen is one of the most popular ways of "gaining merit." This benefit can be extended to the whole family when, for example, auspicious noodles are taken home. Health is the main subject of conversations heard around the compound, along with stories of miraculous healing, and volunteering is said to increase the frequency of such miracles. Visits to Sacred Heart Catholic Church reveal similar topics of discussion and concerns. In addition, religious sisters are sometimes allowed to preach at mass in this particular parish (as was the case at the Easter Vigil in 2013), an occurrence we did not record in downtown parishes.

Peripheral to Shanghai's social dynamics and geography, Chuansha keeps local memories alive. Its two religious communities contribute to the way it defines its surroundings rather than being integrated by default into a larger urban space. Furthermore, these communities assign a central role to women positioned at the margins of the socioeconomic organization.

Religion here reasserts orders that are different from those inscribed on official maps of the city.

THE ONE AND THE MANY: ISLAMIC COMPOUNDS

Muslim merchants have been present in the greater Shanghai area since at least the Song dynasty, particularly in Songjiang District. A comparative study of their worship places shows the way Muslim communities in today's Shanghai carefully position themselves within the urban space as a whole (map 5).

Fuyou Road Mosque (or North Mosque) is adjacent to the City God Temple (plate 17). The smallest of the city mosques, constructed in Chinese style during the Qing dynasty and renovated several times, it was home to the first Islamic school in Shanghai's modern history and to the Shanghai Islamic Board of Directors, founded in 1909. Today, its architecture and delicate ornamentation continue to attract visitors. Though there is no separate prayer hall for women (some usually sit at the back of the men's prayer hall), the prayer hall is divided on major festival days, and men and women sit separately. For Eid al-Fitr, the celebration marking the end of Ramadan, on August 8, 2013, the mosque was packed by 7:00 a.m. Two women handed out generous bowls of porridge prepared in the mosque kitchen. Hui people from Jiangsu are often said to be at the core of the mosque's congregation and management,[10] but attendees for Eid al-Fitr were from many provinces. Zhaona is Hui and moved from Henan to Shanghai in 1989. She works as a cleaner and is married to a Shanghainese man. The mosque is a twenty-minute scooter ride from her home. She used to visit the mosque regularly with her mother, but attends only for this holiday after her mother passed away.

Xiao Taoyuan Mosque (or West Mosque), also located in the central Huangpu District, is home to the Shanghai Islamic Association, established in 1962. Constructed in 1917, the mosque was rebuilt in 1925 in the West Asia Islamic style, with a three-story Chinese-style building on the east side of the courtyard, containing a lecture room, offices, and ablution facilities. Next to the men's building stands the women's mosque, built in 1920 and renovated in 1994 (plate 19). There were four women's mosques before the Cultural Revolution,[11] but this is presently the only women's mosque in Shanghai. During the Republican period, mosques for both men and women served Muslim people from all over China who stopped in Shanghai on their way to Mecca for the hajj.

Early in the morning of October 15, 2013, the day of Eid al-Adha, food sellers set up their stands outside the two buildings. A parade of around twenty men, all in matching dark jackets, proceed down the street and chant

MAP 5. Muslim Fieldwork Sites

1 Fuyou Road Mosque
2 Songjiang Mosque
3 Xiao Taoyuan Mosque
4 Xiao Taoyuan Women's Mosque
5 Pudong Mosque
6 Huxi Mosque
7 Jiangwan Mosque
8 Jinshan Mosque

Note: Private or unofficial places of meeting and worship are not listed.

in front of the women's mosque before entering the men's mosque. In the packed prayer room of the women's mosque, participants watch the imam's sermon broadcast live from the men's mosque on a large screen. In addition to local women, a number of African women and children are among the attendees. After the prayer, a group of men drag a recently slaughtered sheep down the street from the men's to the women's mosque. A group of women spend more than thirty minutes hacking it to pieces on an old cardboard box. Everyone is invited to eat the spiritually sustaining soup they make from it. On a main street nearby, two sheep are tied up outside a halal restaurant, attracting the curiosity of passersby who eagerly photograph the festivities. Frequent communication between inner and outer spaces exemplifies the way the Xiao Taoyuan Mosque integrates the community into the life of the city.

The Songjiang Mosque, the most ancient of all, is more secluded. This historic compound has a small local museum and a graveyard for Muslim leaders who lived in Songjiang. A small shop at the entrance sells mainly clocks and head scarves. According to Imam Mi, who officiates at the mosque, the majority of worshippers are immigrants from western China. The mosque runs Arabic classes three times a week for about forty people. Outsiders are not encouraged to join in the Friday service. The compound cares for the needs of a close-knit congregation while asserting the role of the Muslim community against the backdrop of the history of Greater Shanghai. These tasks are not easily harmonized.

The small mosque in Jinshan District (an area in southwest Shanghai that can be reached only by train or car) serves a population of migrants. Opened in 2010, the mosque is recognized only as a "fixed establishment," not a full-fledged place of worship. Factories located in the district employ a number of Hui from Ningxia, Henan, or Gansu. A modest bungalow painted green, the mosque would look just like one of the small plants or workshops in the neighborhood except for the moon and stars affixed to the top of its metal gate. Before it became a place of worship, the building was a storehouse for the Jinshi Medical Company. It has two entrances, the main one with space for taking off one's shoes, a donation box bearing a quotation from the Koran, and a list of the neighborhood's halal restaurants. The adjacent bungalow serves as the residence of Imam Ma Jinliang, a native of Ningxia who arrived in Shanghai in 2009 and served for a while at the Xiao Taoyuan Mosque.

On a Friday in March 2016, slightly before 1:00 p.m., forty to fifty men, most of them riding mopeds, arrive at the small compound. Almost all of them are Hui. A young Uighur entrepreneur who rarely attends prayer service arrives with his girlfriend, also a Uighur from Xinjiang, who is studying at Shanghai University of Science and Technology. As there is no separate setting for women, the young student waits patiently in the courtyard. She rarely attends worship services and says that she goes to the Huxi Mosque mainly for the delicious snacks sold in the vicinity. "Ritual isn't important, but everyone should have a faith. I think people should fear something. If people don't fear anything, . . . I don't know [what might happen]." At the end of the prayers, people gather in the courtyard. The atmosphere is welcoming, quiet, and subdued. After chatting for a while, people return to work.

The Pudong Mosque, located on Yuanshen Road, tells a different story. In 1995, support and funding from the district government made it possible to move the building to its current location and rebuild it over a larger area. The government has given this very large and well-advertised religious compound the status of "model space." It offers year-round educational activities, even for the very young, and a Koran-study school during the school holidays. The main prayer room on the second floor accommodates five hundred worshippers, the back prayer room holds three hundred, and the women's prayer room accommodates fifty. In the kitchen, women in matching chef uniforms prepare the daily meals offered in the mosque canteen. Catering mainly to a migrant population, the Pudong Mosque contrasts with the unofficial places of worship that have been mushrooming in peripheral areas of the city. According to the Shanghai Islamic Association, the number of Muslim migrants living in Shanghai exceeds 100,000, while the 2010 census estimates Muslims with Shanghai resident permits at around 85,000, more than 78,000 being Hui.[12] It is impossible to get an accurate estimate of the ethnic composition of the Muslim migrant population, but the migrants come predominantly from the northwest. They generally work in small ramen shops and, as various constraints make it difficult to attend one of the official places of worship,[13] often establish makeshift places of worship (most of the time with the tacit consent of local authorities), where migrants from the same locality gather.

Uighurs generally worship in one of the official mosques.[14] In the bustling and ethnically diverse Huxi Mosque located on Changde Road, a youth engaging in business observed,

> At the mosque, there are courses about Islamic history and the contribution of Islam to the world, also courses on Arabic, world economy, martial arts classes, and so on. It gives a common religious platform to people of different ethnic backgrounds. It links together the traditional functions of the mosque and modern society. Most mosques in Xinjiang do not have similar conditions and outlook. The imam at Huxi Mosque has a doctorate in philosophy. Imams in Xinjiang or other landlocked provinces do not have such a degree of formal education, and their vision is rather narrow. The situation at Huxi Mosque is a good omen.

A Uighur student who attends Jiangwan Mosque on Zhengfu Road, northeast of Puxi, explained,

> Often, during the Friday preaching, a few Muslim believers who work overnight fall asleep while listening to the imam preach. The imam won't blame them, because he knows they have to work hard, and he won't wake them up. In Xinjiang, the imam would treat them rigorously. Shanghai has a more humane side, but for beliefs and practices, I think it's somehow loose and weak.

A fellow attendee, also a student from Xinjiang, was less hesitant in his appreciation:

> Shanghai mosques provide positive help for women. They can enter the mosque and worship. In Xinjiang, women believers are not allowed to enter the mosque. I think that women, if they can listen to the preaching, will have a better understanding of their faith. Also, in Shanghai, you can see a lot of believers from different countries in the mosques. Their behavior and thinking are different from ours. Sharing with them makes us more open. In Xinjiang, such opportunities are very few. Besides, you often visit the same mosque all your life, and the imam's influence on believers is enormous. In Shanghai, believers may float from one place to another; the mosque is just a place where they go to worship.[15]

For migrants, integration means redrawing the boundaries between sacred and secular. The extent of such redrawing may vary according to the compound in which they choose to worship.

ENTERING THROUGH THE DOOR: CATHOLIC PARISHES

When considering Catholicism in contemporary China, scholars tend to privilege a strategic analysis of Church-and-state relationships centered on institutional issues and political concerns, with the division between open and underground churches continuing to draw special attention.[16] Important as such issues may be, observation shows that communities worship and grow by focusing on the tasks at hand and ignoring underlying institutional challenges. This may be especially true in large cities and among new converts. Rural Catholic communities have been said to nurture "a collective passion for history,"[17] and, in a city like Shanghai, long considered the Rome of Chinese Catholicism, the local Church still struggles with heavily loaded memories. Nevertheless, these memories vary slightly from one parish to another and foster different relationships within the neighborhood (map 6).

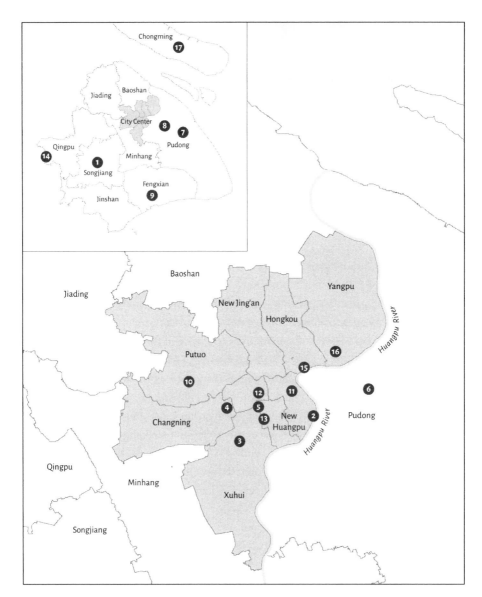

MAP 6. Catholic Fieldwork Sites

1 Sheshan Basilica of Our Lady Help of Christians

2 St. Francis Xavier Church (Dongjiadu Church)

3 St. Ignatius Cathedral (Xujiahui Church)

4 St. Michael's Church

5 Christ the King Church

6 Sacred Heart of Jesus Church (Zhangjialou)

7 Sacred Heart of Jesus Church

8 Our Lady of Lourdes Basilica

9 St. Peter's Catholic Church of Nanqiao New Town

10 Sacred Heart of Our Lady Church

11 Saint Joseph's Church

12 St. Teresa's Church

13 St. Peter's Church

14 Catholic Prayer Hall of Huaxin

15 Sacred Heart of Jesus Church

16 Our Lady of Peace Church

17 Sacred Heart Church of Chongming Island

Note: Private or unofficial places of meeting and worship are not listed.

The Zhangjialou Sacred Heart of Jesus Church,[18] considered one of the oldest parishes east of the Huangpu River, traces its history back to 1744. The community's origin precedes those of the church proper; according to the *Chuansha County Chronicle*, a certain Zhang Jingqiao was baptized under the influence of Matteo Ricci.[19] Later, he followed Xu Guangqi from Beijing to Shanghai and took care of Xu's properties in Pudong as an assistant. Before the Qing dynasty, the Zhang family prospered, building more and more houses for new family members and forming a village in the area that bore the family name. This story is very similar to those of other Chinese villages, except that around 1744, members of the fourth generation commemorated the centenary of their ancestor's death by erecting a building called "The Holy Church of the True Cross."[20] Catholicism, like the family's roots in the land, was embedded in the family's collective memory.

After Shanghai opened to foreign trade, the Zhang family's descendants twice renovated the old church. During the second renovation, the church was enlarged to accommodate more than a thousand people and was placed under the patronage of the Sacred Heart of Jesus. The church building, at the center of the village (on present-day Hongfeng Road), was a main place of worship for several generations of the Zhang family; around twenty men were ordained as priests, one man became a bishop, and more than thirty women became nuns.

The church weathered many historical events, including the Cultural Revolution, but was demolished toward the end of the 1990s as part of the municipal urban plan. In 2003, it was rebuilt on its current site in the Jinqiao Free Trade Development Zone in Pudong, located in the poetically named Jade Cloud (Bi Yun) International Community, a neighborhood in the Jinqiao section of the Shanghai Free-Trade Zone. This community is attractive not only to expats whose companies have set up their operations in the free-trade zone but also to locals, for its wealth of facilities, including schools, medical service providers, sports centers, a big shopping mall, and many restaurants. The community appears tranquil and pleasant, an impression that may be enhanced by the neighboring Catholic church and Protestant church.

The exterior of the Catholic church is of a pseudo-Gothic style, while the interior is of a sober, contemporary design. The church's relocation triggered a process that mixed tradition with innovation. The congregation of the old church had to adapt to a new setting, while acting as guardian of the traditions, memories, and practices of the worshipping community. At the same time, newcomers, many of them migrants of diverse backgrounds, started to appear in the church's compound, bringing their own ideas and ways of proceeding. The Zhangjialou parish has a mixed parish culture composed of its local community and a variety of newcomers.

Eighty to eighty-three priests serve the approximately 110 church buildings presently managed by the Shanghai diocese, though a few of them are principally busy with administrative or teaching activities. Parishes may present sharply different outlooks, as the following comparison between two church compounds illustrates.

St. Joseph's Church, on South Sichuan Road, was deeply involved in the struggle against the diocese and the government from 1950 to 1955. Until 1955, it was the financial headquarters of the Church (at that time, rich with institutions and properties), and Bishop Gong Pinmei was arrested on its premises. Surrounded by convents and Catholic schools, St. Joseph's was the center of Shanghai's Catholic life in the French Concession. The church shares its door with a primary school, and visitors have to walk through the school's basketball court to enter. The inner space includes two little chapels, one of which holds the remains of the daughter of the first consul of France. Everything in the church's arrangement reflects deep respect for the Catholic architectural and liturgical traditions, a feeling reinforced by the decorum of the celebrations. St. Joseph's is the only church in Shanghai that celebrates some masses according to the Tridentine ritual, something a visitor noted as "giving you the inexplicable flavor of old Shanghai." St. Joseph's Church anchors its parishioners in both the traditionalist variety of global Catholicism and local commemoration of things past, enforcing strict separation between the sacred and the mundane.

In contrast, Our Lady of Lourdes Basilica in Tang Town, Pudong, is infused with the collective memory of the district's Catholic communities, which date back to the seventeenth century. A large church modeled on the Lourdes sanctuary was constructed in 1898 in order to serve a congregation of more than three thousand faithful. The church is located in front of the district's government building and connected to the road by a small white bridge. Second in importance to Sheshan Basilica for pilgrimages to Shanghai, it experiences a similar influx of pilgrims during May. The church is a large-scale compound with living quarters, meeting rooms, a kitchen, and a garden.

On August 31, 2013, the compound was filled with youth from around Shanghai gathered for Catholic Singles Day. The day's events combined Catholic teaching, prayers, games, and a cooking contest. When it began to rain, some attendees retreated to the shelter of the garden's Marian shrine to eat their dumplings. The same shrine was put to playful use in the afternoon, when participants were asked to kneel in front of the statue while balancing a book on their heads. The compound and the activities it hosts act as bridges between the congregation and its surroundings, between devotional traditions and urban culture. For example, in Zhangjialou, after the 2014 Christmas Eve mass, the manger was covered with banknotes (plate 11).

This practice is reminiscent of Chinese popular religion and is absent from downtown parishes, like St. Joseph's, that enshrine past struggles to preserve Catholic doctrine and maintain their integrity.

Parishes are not islands. Congregations tend to know about the liturgical trends that others promote or incarnate. For instance, some Shanghai Catholics, notably the younger ones, see the use of Latin hymns as a way of nurturing a "sacred" atmosphere during celebrations. This trend, which is far from supported by all priests, has gradually influenced parish choir repertoires. Thus, during the 2015 Christmas Eve mass, the Zhangjialou parish choir sang in Latin, intending to deliver special solemnity to the occasion. Instead, the faithful were confused, and the choir itself was sometimes at a loss. The improvisational feeling triggered by the change in language eventually reinforced the character and style proper to the congregation. Trends and practices that are supposed to unify a cluster of congregations are lived and interpreted differently from one place to another.

Regardless, the frontiers between parishes are much more porous than they were in the past. One pastor noted that people used to be firmly anchored to one parish, but the transportation system had made moving to another parish much easier. However, in the course of the conversation, the priest qualified his remarks:

> When I was moved from one parish to another, some people followed me at first, migrating from one congregation to another. However, after some time, you get tired of the ride, you get used to your new parish priest, and so on. . . . Besides, in the Catholic Church, priests are solidly attached to one particular place; they can't wander around and get their own following as many Buddhist masters do. . . . So there's probably more local anchorage, more stability in Catholic parishes than is the case for other denominations.[21]

Do these observations apply to Shanghai's underground Catholic communities? To a remarkable degree, the answer is affirmative. Underground Catholics have reconstituted the traditional parish culture, meeting only in rented spaces rather than in church buildings. In Shanghai, they are solidly organized, with around fifteen places of worship, forty priests, and an elder cleric playing the role of an Episcopal vicar. One such place is located between the Qufu Road and Baoshan Road metro stations, toward northeastern Puxi. An office space in a nondescript building has been converted into a parish compound. The congregation pays around ¥10,000 per month for renting the facility. In the main room, a crucifix and a veil representing Our Lady of Guadalupe hangs over a poster depicting scenic nature. The space is in use daily, with each day of the week dedicated to a specific activity: instruction, prayer, chanting, or service to the sick. On a Saturday evening, from around eight o'clock onward, about seventy people (mainly young couples congregated to recite the Rosary, with children gathered at the back of the room. The mass started about forty minutes later. As there was no Sunday service, the evening mass was the main gathering.

Most attendees came from outside Shanghai, from families and counties with a traditional Catholic background in which the underground Church is considered the only legitimate authority. Men and women sat on different sides of the room, a tradition that is very rarely observed in official, urban congregations. This particular community attracts mainly Catholics from Wenzhou. A certain Mr. Qin (pseud.), who owns a small printing plant, attended with his two children. Asked why this congregation chooses to worship underground, when its devotional style is so strikingly similar to that seen in official parishes, Mr. Qin immediately answered, "Once you start to give a finger to the Patriotic Association, you'll have to give your whole arm!" Historical memories and political diffidence can explain the continuing separation between the two communities. Otherwise, the importance given to the Church's hierarchical structure, the devotional tradition and the congregation's pursuits testify to a shared ethos, even if they are echoed and translated by many compound cultures.

A NETWORK OF CONGREGATIONS

Not all religious communities offer the immediate solace of a close-knit group in which sharing develops intimacy and solidarity. The highly structured Protestant Hongde Church, in Hongkou District, may even seem to represent the opposite of such a model.[22] The large building, erected in 1928, is located on Duolun Street, a "culture street" dedicated to the Shanghai of the Republican era. It is renowned for its mix of Chinese and Western architectural styles and especially for its Chinese-style bell tower. Hongde Church, named after the Presbyterian minister George Field Fitch (Fei Qihong), has a large and solemn worship hall on its second floor and additional tribunes on the third floor. The present arrangement dates from 1998, when American Presbyterians funded and directed the building's renovation. Massive choir stalls face the congregation from behind the pulpit. The hall soon proved to be too small, and additional worship space was created on the first floor, with seating for another one hundred people and a giant screen that shows the service being celebrated upstairs. Smaller services can also be celebrated here. The decorative style of the first floor, done in 2000 by a local pastor, differs from the strict Presbyterian style of the second floor. Here, two pulpits are located along the aisles, allowing space for the Communion service. On the wall facing the congregation hangs the inscription "The True

Source of All Beings" (*Wanyou zhenyuan*), written by the Kangxi emperor (r. 1661–1722), who at one time was reputedly close to Christianity. The same inscription adorns the external wall of the Immaculate Conception Church in Fengxian District. An illustrated Via Dolorosa, also in a recognizable Catholic style, decorates the lateral walls. Thus, different Christian cultures coexist in the same Protestant building, and the faithful do not seem to take much notice. According to one of the pastors, young people occasionally wish to celebrate weddings on the first floor because they prefer the atmosphere.

Its governance structure testifies further to the fact that Hongde Church works as an organization and is in no way an informal group. Conforming with the model followed by the Three-Self Church (Sanzi Jiaozi) in Shanghai,[23] the congregation is part of a network of three churches located in the same area, with a head pastor and three other pastors serving as its leadership and responding collectively to a lay elder (map 7). Though no official census has taken place, there might be close to two thousand people attending the three Sunday services at Hongde and almost ten thousand for the Sunday services celebrated in the network of three churches. Whatever the exact figures, it is clear that the church's attractiveness is a product of its mobilization capacity and organizational strength. In Hongde, forty lay monitors are in charge of the Sunday school and are supervised by volunteers recruited from certified teachers in public schools.

Hongde Church functions as an organization rather than a grassroots gathering because of the social diversity of its congregation. Some congregation members are extremely well off, while others live on municipal subsidies, and members with different backgrounds do not mix. There are no meals or other gatherings after Sunday services. Alms are collected four times a year, ensuring some kind of aid within the community and for the less fortunate outside the church, who have been identified by the city's street committees.

Yet this is not to say that the church does not provide an environment for close contact, a sense of intimacy, and small-group encounters. First, there are regular meetings for youth and adult Bible study. A young woman pastor indicated that she has intentionally grouped members from different backgrounds for gatherings as small as ten and as large as thirty. Participants are also linked through social networks, although, the pastor noted, groups associated with the underground Protestant Church in the same area network more intensely. More important may be the division of labor that exists between the faithful and the church's official leaders. For instance, despite the general preference for marriages between members of the congregation, the church does not organize any activities to that end. Instead, matchmaking gatherings are organized within WeChat groups and take place at the

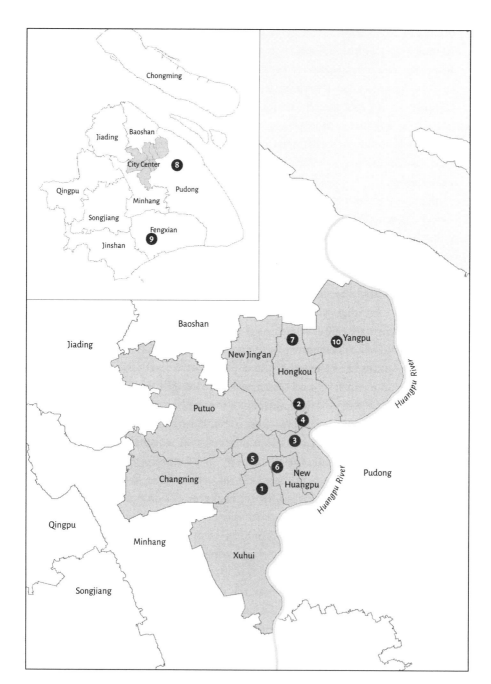

MAP 7. Protestant Fieldwork Sites

1 Hengshan Shanghai Community Church
2 Hongde Church
3 Moore Memorial Church
4 Young John Allen Memorial Church
5 Grace Church

6 All Saints Church
7 Jiangwan Church
8 Abundant Grace Church
9 Protestant Church of Nanqiao New Town
10 East Shanghai Church

Note: Private or unofficial places of meeting and worship are not listed.

homes of some members. Families also organize meals, at home or in restaurants, for personal events that they feel justify the giving of thanks. In other words, the church functions as a kind of umbrella that provides organizational strength, respectability, and both political and religious orthodoxy.

Since the beginning of the 2000s, Chinese social scientists have been arguing that civil society expresses and defines itself in China in a process governed less by competition than by cooperation with the state.[24] Civic organizations that would stress their independence from the state in the West try to cooperate closely with it and thereby enlarge their sphere of influence in China.[25] Chinese authors therefore often discern in the "participative growth of Chinese civil society" China's way of gradually creating a new type of sociopolitical space.[26] Official religious associations are similar to professional organizations (such as chambers of commerce): participation in civic tasks prioritized by the government reinforces their agency as the state progressively trusts them more and grants them more space for initiative. This institutional growth gradually allows the faithful to engineer modes of action and gathering that are flexible enough to answer their spiritual and communal needs.

At the same time, underground religious communities challenge the participative model espoused by the official Church by exchanging the safety offered by the institutional umbrella for more rapid and less restricted growth. This may be understood less as a political statement than as an expression of psychological and spiritual needs that prioritizes immediacy and spontaneity. Such groups rely heavily on new media, and the younger clergy are especially prone to resent the stress and constraints of the participative model. At Hongde Church, for example, a young pastor, recruited in 2006 from the official Nanjing seminary, decided to join the underground Church after a few years of ministry.

Young John Allen Memorial Church (Jingling Tang) (plate 27), which was the congregation of the Soong family, is in the same pastoral network as Hongde Church. It reinforces the impression that official churches suffer paradoxically from a wealth of organizational resources that are detrimental to grassroots spontaneity.

On the evening of February 26, 2014, a devotional gathering began at 6:30 p.m., with a charismatic male leader directing the singing. Slowly, a congregation of mixed ages gathered, averaging forty to fifty years old. At 7:00 p.m., a choir of thirteen people in their early twenties started singing with warm smiles. At 7:30, a pastor and lecturer from East China Theology College (Huadong Shenxueyuan), established on North Shaanxi Road in 1985 and now based in Qingpu District, showed a video of the college choir and shared extensive information about the college proper. He spoke about the four-year bachelor's degree and ordination training offered for men and women from four provinces following high school graduation. By July 2013, a total of 1,116 students had attended the college, with 155 students enrolled at a time. When the talk finished, participants broke up into eight groups. A woman with a loudspeaker directed each group to take a prayer card. The group that got the angel card prayed for world peace and for countries suffering from earthquakes or war, while other groups prayed for church personnel or for more people to join the church. Participants were asked to use other cards to write personal prayers that would be forwarded to other people who would recite the prayers on their behalf. On the backs of the cards, they wrote their names and contact information, the most important appearing to be their social network user IDs. The whole evening was overtly "educational."

The third church in the same pastoral network, Jiangwan Church, was named for the neighborhood it serves. It was built in 2008 on Shuidian Road, a lower-middle-class area.

On May 24, 2015, the Feast of the Pentecost, the building is filled to capacity. Its internal architecture is similar to that of Hongde Church. The service will last for an hour. In this "ordinary" church, the choir is not as impressive as those of some landmark congregations, but everyone joyfully sings simple songs. The leaders of the service are all women. The assembly leader adopts an evangelical way of speaking. A few attendees try to respond to her with "Amen," but she speaks so fast that they cannot keep up with her. Songs, prayers, and short Bible excerpts read by the whole assembly quickly follow. Jing Jianmei, the young woman pastor from Hongde Church, delivers the homily, insisting that the highest charisma given by the Spirit is not a "spectacular" gift, such as speaking in tongues, but rather sharing in the humility of Christ. Baptisms follow. In these three parishes, 130 baptisms take place on this day, but only around 20 of them are performed in Jiangwan Church. The service concludes with the Lord's Prayer. Some attendees stay for parish activities. The people who attend this church come from a more modest social background compared to those who attend the other two, but the dominant feeling is the same: the congregation relies on a solid institutional structure that also links it with the authorities, and the level of commitment varies greatly among individuals.

This official network of three churches shares not only pastors but also volunteers and social initiatives. Two hundred volunteers from the three churches visit about one thousand old or disabled parishioners who are too incapacitated to go to church. Each pastor participates in the visits at least twice a year and sometimes performs baptisms at home. Such initiatives illustrate the multilayered functioning of the official Protestant churches in Shanghai. They need to respond to pressure from the authorities but also to the desire of the faithful for a freer, more spontaneous Christian testimony while managing sustainable growth of their organizational structures. The current dominant position of women in the Church (the majority of Shanghai's official pastors are women) may contribute to this "organic" growth model: communities need to be brought to maturity slowly and cautiously by tending to everyday needs. The tactics of these official parishes and their leadership fit well within the "growth by participation" model.

COURTYARDS AND ALTARS

Parishes and mosques nurture their own compound cultures, which are noticeably different at times from those experienced in affiliated communities. Affinity grouping reinforces the characteristics proper to each compound, and differences can generally be ascribed to variances in the flexibility with which sacredness is defined, enclosed, and distributed. Some rarefy sacredness, limiting its access to a core congregation, while others manage it as a diffused and more accessible commodity, trying to balance between (exclusive) compound culture and (inclusive) social ethos.

Our fieldwork suggests that the situation may be different for Buddhist temples, or at least for the most important among them (map 8). Each compound provides a large variety of religious activities, the nature and extent of which are defined by the feast days. Xilin Temple is the biggest Buddhist temple in Songjiang District (plate 18). The seven-story, 46.5-meter-high pagoda, made of brick and wood, stands out within the large complex. The compound is home to twenty resident monks, a large administrative department, a vegetarian restaurant, and a shop with religious objects for sale. A media department produces a daily newsletter on WeChat consisting of speeches from masters, Buddhist stories, recipes for vegetarian dishes, and attractive pictures.

A visit to the temple on January 2014 with two wealthy Shanghai entrepreneurs and the family of one of them confirms the variety of the temple's spiritual offerings. The son of one of the businessmen plans to participate in the annual weeklong course the temple runs for young entrepreneurs.[27] The head monk (described as "busier than most politicians" by the whole party) receives the guests. He lived for two years in an Australian temple serving immigrant Chinese, and before his current post (which he has already held for ten years), he was the second in command at another Shanghai temple.

The temple is smaller than it used to be, as the people living at the back of the site refused to move so that the temple could be rebuilt to its original size after the Cultural Revolution. The argument with the residents continues, and as the rapid increase in the price of the land makes it unlikely

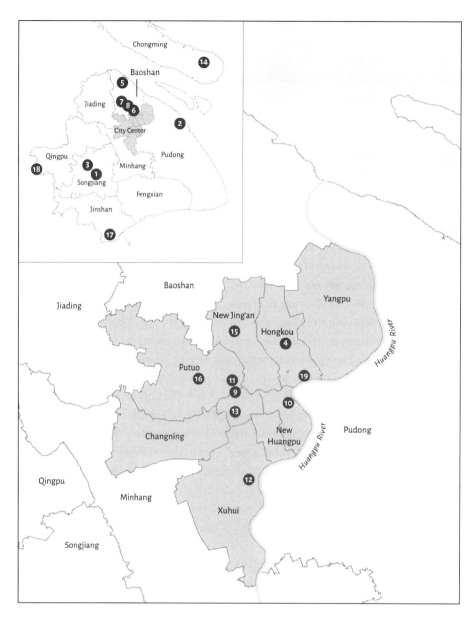

MAP 8. Buddhist Fieldwork Sites

1 Xilin Temple
2 Changren Temple
3 Zhiye Temple
4 Sanguan Temple
5 Baoshan Temple
6 Yongfu An
7 Jinhuang Temple
8 Guangfu Temple
9 Chan Yi Club House
10 Eaglewood Pavilion
11 Jade Buddha Temple
12 Longhua Temple
13 Jing'an Temple
14 Qingjing Temple
15 Baohua Temple
16 Zhenru Temple
17 Jinshan Wanshou Temple
18 Yihao Temple
19 Xiahai Temple

that the temple will regain the lost space. There is, however, a kind of synergy between the temple and the recalcitrant residents, who have established stalls behind the temple where they sell paper money and elaborate objects.

The most solemn Water and Land Dharma Service illustrates the ritual and social function reclaimed by Buddhist urban temples throughout China. One such service is usually held at the end of the seventh month of the Chinese lunar calendar and was celebrated September 4–10 in 2013. At Xilin Temple, 108 monks participate in the opening ritual on the evening of September 3. The crowd is mixed, a majority of them irregular practitioners. A week later, eight masters from different temples are present for the last day of the ritual. Local women have prepared a large elaborate paper structure to be burned. A list of benefactors hangs at the entrance to the temple. After lunch, groups form in various areas of the temple. When the ceremony finally begins, the long line parades twice outside the temple. As the chanting of Buddhist sutras proceeds, passersby contribute approving remarks, "Chanting is more useful than burning boats for the ancestors!"

Just nine days later, the Mid-Autumn Festival Offering (held on September 19 in 2013) is marked by yet another kind of atmosphere. Before the event, the temple website stated the religious purpose of the ceremony: respect would be shown to the elements (the moon in this case) and love to human beings. The bodhisattva reconnects separated people, makes sick people strong, helps confused people get out of trouble, and makes happy people even happier. In the evening, many families gather in the temple complex in front of the monks who stand on either side of a large table laden with food. A monk rings the temple's large bronze bell twice, chanting in between. The head monk flicks holy water on attendees, who bow and chant. They all participate eagerly, seemingly more familiar and comfortable with the ceremony than with the Water and Land Dharma Service. The monks then distribute vegetables and low-sugar vegetarian moon cakes made in the temple. Overall, the ceremony is much shorter than the strictly Buddhist ones.

This ritual flexibility is even more obvious on the first day of Chinese New Year, when most Shanghai temples are inundated with visitors, each conducting devotions as they please. Buddhist and Daoist compounds dispense sacredness to a larger population and in more varied ways than Christian and Islamic places of worship do.

Xilin Temple testifies to the multipurpose character of Buddhist centers in today's China. It serves as a liturgical and educational compound and also as a community center that links social life with Buddhist-inspired doctrine and ways of life. It is indeed a compound, a place where some degree of autarky can be achieved, albeit in a most public space—in which a community goes beyond strict denominational boundaries and can express a communal identity, shared concerns, and even collective transformation.

This corresponds to the traditional character of Chinese Buddhist temples. As a liturgical place, the temple acts as a collective intercessor for the community of believers. As a place of learning, the temple made it possible to translate the Buddhist canon into Chinese and to multiply its interpretations through several centuries. A place of power, the temple knows how to negotiate its relationship with both local and imperial rulers. The reconstruction of Chinese Buddhism after the turmoil of the Cultural Revolution relied on the monastic institution, and the vitality of the monasteries bears witness to the vigor of Buddhist practices and beliefs nationwide.

TEMPLES IN BAOSHAN DISTRICT

A closer look at the way different Buddhist temples manage their territorial and communal bases may highlight the diversity inherent to the Shanghai Buddhist ethos. Baoshan District lies in the northern, industrial part of Shanghai, home to the BaoSteel conglomerate. Baoshan Temple has always been central to the life and collective consciousness of the area. A new Buddhist complex opened nearby in 2010. Its wall runs alongside a canal.

On November 15, 2014, as our party proceeded along the wall toward the entrance door, we encountered numerous fortune-tellers. A Mr. Chen handed out his name card and started a conversation on the wisdom enshrined in traditional divination. After a while, gesturing toward the walls of the temple, he said, "We're very different from them." He continued to compare the down-to-earth Daoist and popular wisdom, transmitted from master to master, to the abstract teachings of Buddhists and intellectuals.

The new complex collected modest entry fees. On that day, a large crowd filled the main square. Baoshan Temple holds a Water and Land Dharma Service twice a year, and in 2014, the second took place from November 9 to 15 (the seventeenth to twenty-third days of the ninth month of the lunar calendar). Around eighty monks were divided among seven altars. Visitors had to pay ¥150 to participate. In the square in front of Baoshan Temple, worshippers had displayed vegetarian offerings. Paper houses and paper money were ready to be burned as oblations to ancestors and the deceased. In front of the offerings, there were also paper and fabric representations of the judges of the five divisions of the underworld riding horses. At 1:00 p.m., a long procession of monks and donors set out from the other end of the temple, near the monks' quarters and the vegetarian restaurant. After a long pause at the main hall and continuous chanting, the procession traveled to the courtyard, where oblations were burned. The festival was recast and restarted around ten years earlier, and the new space has encouraged the reenacting of a specific ritual that strikes a chord in the collective spiritual memory of a neighborhood, akin to a community revival.

Three smaller temples in the same district convey entirely different impressions. The Yongfu An (the term *an* is applied to small temples) is located near the East Gate of Shanghai University. On Saturdays and Sundays, various groups meet on the premises. In January 2014, regular participants in an Animal Release (Fang Sheng [lit., "Releasing Lives"]) community (see chap. 5) gathered there for scripture readings. The group does not always meet here but alternates between different locations. "We do this twice per month," explains Tim, a young Buddhist convert. "For good! One time at the beginning of the month, another time in the middle of the lunar calendar. We wear special clothes during the chanting. The inner piece of clothing is called *haiqing* and the outer one *manyi*." Before the event begins, he elaborates, "It's the highest level of practice, and some people think it's too much for them. It varies in length between an hour and an hour and a half, because people read the book at different speeds. I read it fluently because I've been reading it for two years twice a month. If you feel like it, you can take the higher level immediately. Some people find it hard, but I think one can go directly to this level. It's the best thing for you, as it will stay with you for the rest of your life."

Six women and seven men sit on opposite sides of the third-floor conference room. A small Buddha statue has been placed on an impressive wooden table. A woman who works in the financial department of a company in Pudong takes devotional books she bought in Taiwan out of her bag. She joined in April 2012 after a friend introduced her to the group. In addition to this twice-monthly activity, she attends an all-day prayer at Sanguan Temple, in Jiangwan subdistrict in Hongkou District, twice a month and weekly Animal Release rituals. "That's quite a lot," she admits. At 7:30 p.m., they all move into the corridor to dress in their ritual clothes. The temple provides them with the decorum and solemnity necessary for celebrating the ritual. At the same time, the group is able to create its own rules when needed. On that particular night, after a debate among the members and the intervention of a monk passing by, they decide that no external observer can stay in the room when the chanting begins.

In the same small temple, on October 10, 2015, another group invited a monk from Fagushan (a monastery in northern Taiwan famous for the progressive spirit of its founder, Master Shengyan) for a day of doctrinal training. And the following day, a Sunday, yet another group of around eighty people gathered for the chanting of sutras from 7:45 to 10:00 a.m. Middle-aged and older women made up the majority of attendees, most wearing Buddhist robes, and six nuns led the chanting. Next, the chief nun delivered a long lecture on the importance of concentrating and persevering in the chanting of scriptures. Participants, stressed the orator, were still lacking in focus and effort. The close-knit community makes extensive use of WeChat to spread news about ritual events and other religious happenings. A man had been hired to photograph the gathering, as photography was obviously very much part of the ritual process, as was its propagation through WeChat.

Located not very far from Yongfu An and bordering a canal, the Jinhuang Temple houses a small monastic community. Its long history has been centered on the propagation of the esoteric Vajrayana Buddhist tradition, as it is the only temple in Shanghai dedicated to this particular school. The temple posts its annual budget in the courtyard for all to see, the yearly donations of the faithful being estimated at more than ¥1 million. A small number of elderly volunteers are busy cleaning the premises and bringing offerings to the altars. On the green that borders the temple, small sticks of bamboo with tiny images of boats made of aluminum paper have been fixed below the trees in memory of loved ones who passed away over the year. The temple mixes a strong local flavor with a particular worship tradition that the monastic community takes care to perpetuate.

Northwest of Baoshan, in a dilapidated former industrial zone that borders Jiading District, Guangfu Temple is home to both the ruins of an older temple and the slow, painstaking attempt to build a new one. A team of volunteers gathers there every weekend for worship and construction work. Among them, people from the neighborhood insist that tens of thousands of people died in and around this compound during the war of resistance against Japan. For years, they have been praying here for all the dead, "without making distinctions," they stress, so as to spiritually cleanse the premises. They intend to dig farther and hope to find historical remains, as the site, which was originally part of the harbor, dates to the end of the thirteenth century. Others, particularly from Jiading District, have joined the locals to aid with the rehabilitation of the temple. All the participants now follow the teachings of a Buddhist master in Yunnan and plan to transform Guangfu Temple into a meeting place for his nationwide followers. While they are dedicated to restoring the temple, they have so far succeeded only in building dormitories for worshippers who stay over the weekend and a few prayer rooms where people can chant scriptures on their own. The prayer hall is not completed yet. On one of its walls, two artists have depicted the Eighteen Arhats (the original followers of the Buddha), representing the members of the small community. The temple's relationship with the local government is unclear. Members are confident that local authorities "do not oppose" (bu fandui) the project and may even support it. Nevertheless, they repeatedly stress that funds for their project come solely from private donations.

If larger temples, homes to a sizable monastic community, cater to the diversity of a neighborhood's spiritual needs, then smaller places of worship can easily become sacred ground for informal networks gathered around a specific tradition or mission. In that respect, some of the less conspicuous

Buddhist sites nurture an atmosphere similar to that of house churches (discussed in chap. 4). Charismatic local leaders, constant networking, and insistence on scripture readings are features common to the two. In both cases, the avowed respect for clerical leadership may come with relative independence from it, or at least with a sense of initiative ingrained in the laypersons responsible for the group's sustainability. The difference might lie in the importance given to the "sacred ground" of the compound for Buddhists; sacredness seems to be less geographically localized when it comes to Christian house churches.

VOLUNTEERING IN THE COMPOUND

In addition to Buddhist neighborhood culture, centered on large-scale rituals led by a monastic community and to the use of some temples as a fluid space in which lay leaders often play a prominent role, a third model associates monks and the faithful in a novel way.

From the 1980s onward, temples have been able to make use of volunteers' service. Traditionally, volunteers were elderly people from the surrounding area. Most local temples still function on that model. In Baohua Temple (Baohua Si), located in the former Zhabei District, a seventy-year-old volunteer is in charge of gathering donations made by the faithful and writing down the subject of each petition paired with an offering. He believes petitions should be of a spiritual nature, such as praying for peace or enlightenment, so if petitioners submit requests related to wealth or health, he asks them to write them themselves, refusing to have anything to do with such earthly demands.

In recent years, the numerical growth of volunteers may be the most significant change to Chinese Buddhism. The trend is especially pronounced in Shanghai, often described as a *jūshi* (lay householder who has vowed to follow the Buddhist Five Precepts and other rules) stronghold. In Taiwan, where the trend arose, lay volunteers have long been a driving force behind Buddhism and its impact on civil society at large. There are still marked differences between the island and the mainland. For example, Taiwanese Buddhist volunteers very quickly expanded their outreach beyond the temple walls, while volunteers in China still operate mainly within the compounds. In addition, if the *jūshi* tradition is indeed a feature of Shanghai's Buddhism, in the first half of the twentieth century, its main representatives were mostly independent from (and often critical of) the monastic community, which is generally not the case today.

Longhua Temple decided to recruit volunteers around 2007. Having large teams of volunteers helps the temple reduce costs, enhances the temple's influence and aura, and creates more bridges to society at large. Sun Weiqiao, who volunteered at the temple between 2014 and 2015, reports that the number of volunteers has grown from fifteen to more than two thousand since the new system was established.[28] A young monk organizes volunteers on behalf of the temple and is their direct manager. Volunteers clean the worship halls, stand in attendance near the altars, arrange tables and chairs, and make dumplings for the monks or tea for visitors. They typically contribute one day or more, from very early in the morning until four or five in the afternoon. They also meet outside the temple to dine, play games, and celebrate birthdays or weddings together. Socializing outside the temple is a trend fueled by the widespread use of social media. According to Sun, one volunteer had one hundred subscribers to his WeChat group, and thirty could be considered core members. Within a year, ten of those thirty volunteers had undergone the ceremony elevating them to the status of *jūshi*. In other words, interacting outside the temple and identifying with the temple might be mutually reinforcing. However, jokes about the temple's monastic leadership or expressions of dissatisfaction are also results of the volunteers' use of social media.

Sun divides the volunteers into three groups. The first, which he calls "homemakers," comprises around a hundred people, 70 percent of whom are women and all approaching or at retirement age, but this small group takes on nearly half the tasks. The temple gives them a home where they can practice the altruistic values they were taught to uphold since their childhood in Mao's China. Some arrive at the temple as early as four in the morning and immediately begin cleaning. They are strongly attached to their positions, to the specific hall where they perform their duties, and adapt only very painfully to the policy of rotating responsibilities now enforced by the monk in charge of volunteer affairs. Sun labels the second group, the vast majority of volunteers, "helpers." For them, the temple is a place where they offer service and accumulate merit. Many of these volunteers are office workers, often dissatisfied with the environment and behavior they experience at work. Although they do not consider the temple to be theirs, they are grateful for the network and the sense of peace and fulfillment it provides. The third group is composed of "marginal people" who come at irregular intervals but see themselves as apprentices and relish the opportunity to learn new things.

Observation at other sites confirms that the number of people signing up at recruiting temples exceeds the tasks available. This may trigger an adaptation crisis and the need to expand work beyond the compound, while political limitations will make it difficult to respond. However, the present success of the model confirms that Buddhist temples are compounds that are, as in the past, flexible enough to fill a variety of needs.

Foreign expatriates often live in actual compounds — villas or apartment blocks protected by walls. These places may also become religious compounds, blurring the separation between home and compound. In pre-1949 Shanghai, both the Jewish and Sikh communities worshipped in religious compounds. Although the buildings have disappeared or been converted to other uses, the religious geography of these communities is still shaped by recollections of older compounds, which in turn triggers specific ways of relating to Shanghai's spiritual space as a whole.

Mapping Judaism in Shanghai

The Shanghai Jewish community traces its roots back to settlers, mainly Jews from Bombay, who called themselves "Baghdadis" on the basis of their genealogy. They began arriving in 1848, and the most successful among them built many of the city's greatest corporations and landmark buildings.[29] From the 1870s onward, they rented space for worship, and in 1897, the Baghdadis organized a synagogue before opening the Ohel Rachel Synagogue, built to accommodate seven hundred people, on North Shaanxi Road in 1920. Of the seven synagogues established in Shanghai, only two — Ohel Rachel and Ohel Moishe Synagogue, located in Hongkou District and now a museum dedicated to the history of Jewish refugees in Shanghai — are still standing. After 1920, thousands of Russian Jews migrated to Shanghai through northeastern China. From 1938 onward, stateless refugees from Europe took refuge in the city, the only place in the world that did not require visas; twenty thousand refugees came from Germany and Austria and two thousand from Poland. Japanese occupying forces relocated the European refugees to a Hongkou ghetto between 1941 and 1945. Almost all of the twenty-four thousand Jews residing in Shanghai migrated to Australia, Hong Kong, Israel, and the United States immediately after the end of World War II.[30]

Today, that history has been reclaimed and kept alive by the Jewish expatriate community. Chabad in China, a branch of the Hasidic movement, is the main support for Shanghai's Jewish revival. The Intown Jewish Center manages a mini-market, a Jewish library, Shabbat meals, prayers, and adult education. The Chabad Jewish Center of Pudong has a Hebrew school (four classes on Sundays for children ages two to nine), as well as community and children's activities (plate 21). The third Chabad Center, located in Hongqiao, in southwestern Shanghai, hosts the Beit Menachem Synagogue and provides all the services offered by the two other centers. Founded in 1995, the Hongqiao center serves more than 500 families, and the Pudong center around 120 families. The Intown Jewish Center was founded after the Ohel

Rachel Synagogue reopened during Expo Shanghai 2010. The synagogue is permitted to open for services a few times per year on major holidays. Chabad manages the centers, but the community maintains a variety of traditions, with the more orthodox Sephardic community based primarily in Hongqiao, and the Kehiliat liberal community active mainly in eastern Puxi.

The Jewish Center of Pudong is the smallest of the three Chabad Jewish centers in Shanghai. Rabbi Avraham Greenberg, brother of Rabbi Shalom Greenberg, who set up the Shanghai Jewish Center in Hongqiao in 1999, established the Pudong center in a villa complex, which is also home to his wife and six children, around 2005. The rabbi's wife comments, "We're living off the fruits of the hard labor of the past years. It wasn't easy back then to establish the community and negotiate with the government about the building." The community is made up primarily of American families from different areas in Pudong District. In December 2014, the center held a pre-Hanukkah party one week before the holiday, with numerous festival activities for children, such as Hanukkah candle painting. In the basement, which normally serves as the synagogue, the rabbi demonstrated how to make olive oil by crushing olives. Around sixty people attended the event. In this close-knit community, families regularly meet socially outside the center.

Other organizations testify to the growing diversity and assertiveness of the Shanghai Jewish community. Moishe House, established in January 2014 by three young professionals, is a branch of an international nonprofit organization that manages homes throughout the world that serve as hubs for the young adult Jewish community.[31] The Jewish museum in Hongkou is run by the city government and benefits from the keen involvement of the American Jewish Joint Distribution Committee, a worldwide Jewish relief organization. A young representative of the committee has been positioned in Shanghai since 2010. The representative is responsible for organizing community events for the younger members of the Jewish community who may not be practicing but want to maintain and cultivate their Jewish identity and culture. The first representative, Jeanine Buzali, is from Mexico and still lives in the city. Maytal Kuperard, of English origin, succeeded her in 2013. Buzali says that Kuperard faces a much harder task than she did, as the Jewish community of Shanghai is now swamped with events: "When I first organized an event, two hundred people came, which was a huge surprise, but there was nothing else back then. Now when Maytal organizes an event, there are often three other Jewish community events at the same time!"

In 2000, the Hongqiao Center opened a preschool run by the rabbi's wife. The school follows a US curriculum with Hebrew- and Chinese-language integration, and employs Israeli and international teachers. Each class has a special session devoted to Chinese language, and all teaching assistants are Chinese. All of the children (fifteen months to six years of age) are Jewish, and four have Chinese mothers. Every Friday, the children knead and braid challah. The bread is then baked for them to take home. After lunch, the Shabbat party begins with a candle-lighting ceremony, followed by challah and grape juice distributed by the mother and father of Shabbat. After that, the children dance to songs from *Shabbat for Children*. School finishes at 1:30 p.m. on Fridays, so the children can return home in time for Shabbat.

The community is pursuing an active communication policy within the city itself. For instance, the Hanukkah celebration of 2008 was the subject of a cover story in *Shanghai Daily*, which reported the attendance of city officials.[32] Another article in the same newspaper described the activities of the three centers at length.[33] The return of Jewish refugees for a memorial trip was another cover story.[34] This global community localizes its past and sense of belonging in a way that significantly contributes to the reshaping of the historical and spiritual landscape of contemporary Shanghai.

Shanghai's *Sikh* Gurdwara

The Sikh presence in today's Shanghai opens up altogether different perspectives. Their history reaches far back into Shanghai's semicolonial history.

> After Shanghai was opened as a treaty port in 1843, the infrastructure of the small and initially solely British-run settlement was overseen by a Committee of Roads and Jetties. In 1854 this was reformed as a Municipal Council, and in the same year for the first time a police force was established. Chinese were recruited to the force from 1864, and the idea of recruiting Sikhs was first seriously mooted by the Shanghai Municipal Council in 1883, as part of a major re-organization and increase to the size of the Shanghai Municipal Police. . . . The first Sikhs engaged by the Shanghai Municipal Police were recruited locally: Sikhs were already employed in Shanghai as private watchmen, as they would continue to be in increasing numbers throughout the existence of the foreign concessions, forming with the Sikh branch of the Shanghai Municipal Police a sizeable Sikh community.[35]

This enlarged Sikh community soon found ways of satisfying its spiritual needs. The Sikh *gurdwara* was known among the locals as Yindu Miao (Indian Temple) and encompassed a space of 1,500 square meters.

> Although the Shanghai Municipal Police paid little attention to the religious needs of its early Sikh recruits, as their numbers grew the men successfully petitioned for a place of worship: a Gurdwara. In 1905 plans for the building were obtained from Hong Kong and subscriptions worth $8,000 were raised from the Sikh community (both Sikhs

employed by the Shanghai Municipal Police and those employed privately as watchmen), demonstrating their desire for a place of worship. The Gurdwara opened in 1908 and became a place to meet as a community, to observe the rituals they were accustomed to practicing in Punjab, and, when one could be obtained, receive guidance from the Granthi, the religious leader (lit., "reader of the Granth").[36]

Internal conflicts cast a shadow on the Sikh community's spiritual landscape. From 1916 onward, a *gurdwara* was open solely to meet the needs of the Shanghai Municipal Police. The end of the concessions system brought the exile of almost all members of a community that was, for the most part, loathed by locals. Sikhs returned to Shanghai when the new policy reopened the city to international exchanges.

The functioning Sikh *gurdwara* in Shanghai is located in a luxurious complex of villas in Hongqiao (plate 23). From the security gate, a tree-lined path leads from the busy, gray city into a calm, green park enlivened by birdsong. Every Sunday, the Chinese housekeeper opens the villa door to around twenty Indian Sikh families. On the second floor, facing the top of the stairs, doors open into a large room arranged in the standard layout of any *gurdwara*. Guru Granth Sahib sits on top of a bed that is covered by an awning. Images of Sikh gurus and holy sites hang on the walls, and rich carpets on the floor create comfortable seating.

The prayer meeting takes place from 11:30 a.m. until 1:00 p.m., when participants break for lunch. Men, women, and children take turns reading, singing, and playing musical instruments during prayers and hymns. An English-language translation of the liturgical texts scrolls on a large TV screen at the right side of the room, controlled by a participant's iPad. Slowly more people join, all in family groups, each bowing in front of Guru Granth Sahib before sitting at the back of the hall. At 1:00 p.m., after the prayers are complete, participants go downstairs for a potluck lunch. The large circular table bears a plentiful mix of Indian dishes, chapati made by the Chinese house helpers and take-out pizza. "We never know what will be on offer. Each family brings what they want to share," says Bethal, the father of the family who hosts the event in their home.

Is this specific Sikh community affected by the secular context of Shanghai? To this question, Bethal replies, "It's the same everywhere. As religion is in our hearts and heads, it's only 1 percent localized. Only we don't do prayer events at five in the morning as they would in a standard *gurdwara*." Having a landmark communal meeting place is clearly important though. The family established the *gurdwara* in their home in 2005. "We wanted our children to have the chance to worship every Sunday. . . . We brought all the decorations as well as Guru Granth Sahib over on the airplane. Thanks to my sons' technical knowledge, we can read the hymns and prayers on the screen, which is connected to their iPhones and iPads. It's very convenient," concludes Bethal.

Shanghai is home for Bethal. His family's relationship with the city goes back generations. His father lived as a trader in Shanghai and remained in the city until 1961 (which is exceptional). Bethal himself has been trading with Shanghai from India since 1984. He moved to Shanghai in 2000 with his wife and three sons, who all work in the family business. Bethal's family has visited the two former *gurdwara* and the waxwork Sikh policeman exhibited in Shanghai's public security museum on Ruijin Road.

◆　◆　◆

Religious compounds in Shanghai provide an environment that replicates several of the functions played in the socialist period by the work unit (*danwei*). Support is based on mutual trust, and connections strengthen the response when illness or other life events arise. Additionally, the compounds managed by communities offer opportunities for recreation. As a recreational space, the compound remains a sacred place; it is sanctified by the regular performance of common rituals and is often marked by the sharing of meals. Compounds have also proved to be remarkably elastic. The variety in size, modes of management, and geographic positioning makes way for creative and differentiated uses among subcommunities. In time, each compound acquires a personality of its own.

Foreigners cannot but nurture a different relationship to Shanghai's religious geography. However, some do make use of existing religious compounds, as Protestant and Catholic communities of various linguistic backgrounds are allowed to celebrate services in specially designated parishes and many Asian expatriates visit Buddhist sites for private prayer. Furthermore, religious groups with different historical backgrounds contribute, even if modestly, to keeping the memory of earlier religious compounds alive and to spiritually enlivening their environment.

The compound model does not encompass the whole of Shanghai's religious life and geography. It imposes a number of administrative and political constraints on religious expression, and other limitations arise from the necessity of accommodating groups that share a common space with different expectations. Homes provide other forms of spiritual experiences, as do networks that are partly detached from clear territorial affiliations. They, along with landmarks and compounds, ultimately align on the same continuum.

CHAPTER 4

A Shrine of One's Own

FEELING AT HOME WHILE WORSHIPPING DOES NOT IMPLY BEING AT home. Deeply personal religious practices can take place at public sites, the imagery of which permeates private, even intimate spaces.[1] In a similar vein, compound cultures can legitimately be termed "home cultures"; when a kitchen is located on its premises (as is generally the case in Shanghai), the religious compound is even more homelike. The feeling of being at home is informed by the way life experiences shape the perception of "home." This last point is important with regard to China in general and to Shanghai in particular, as the scarcity of housing that prevailed from the 1950s until the 1990s was followed by a surge in relocation and construction.

Although the distinction between public and private spheres has been rightly challenged,[2] home remains the privileged place for private worship. What is worn, how one sits (or lies down) while meditating or reading, the images on the walls, and ways of delineating and decorating what is considered the sacred space are all part of how one lives religion (plate 24). Of interest here are private religious spaces in present-day Shanghai and how the home paradigm informs the totality of the religious domain, including the practices and spatial arrangements of worship and prayer in the places where people live, as well as what it is like to feel homeless in the religious realm and, more generally, to experience spiritual displacement.

WORSHIPPING AT HOME

Landmarks and compounds define and enclose sacredness, and they facilitate varying degrees of connection between the religious realm sensu stricto and the public/secular space. In global cities, however, sacredness is as easily found enshrined in the realm of the private. No doubt, Chinese rural society gives a prominent role to altars and rituals performed at home. In Chinese, the term "home" (*jia*) does not necessarily convey the idea of privacy understood as the capacity to seclude oneself. Anthropologist Jie Li has stressed the shift from family compounds to nestlike homes that occurred in Shanghai's concessions at the beginning of the twentieth century with the development of the *lilong* (alleyways) compound system:

> Both as clan and as architecture, the traditional neo-Confucian *jia* is like a tree that grows over time to accommodate multiple generations, from venerated ancestors as its roots to unborn descendants, or leaves, on its branches. . . . With migration and fragmentation, homes, or *jia*, were no longer trees but nests, and each individual sojourner resembled not so much a leaf fixed to a branch, but a bird that flew about daily for its livelihood. The Shanghainese term for "home" is *wo*, *woli*, or *wolixiang*. . . . The compound *wolixiang* can evoke for Shanghainese speakers the following meanings: "towards the inside of the nest/room" or "room nestled in the wing of a house" or "room nestled inside an alleyway." . . . The Shanghainese term is more intimate and inward looking, lacking the sense of the traditional family as a corporate lineage or as a microcosm of the state that reinforces Confucian hierarchies. Its spatial focus is on the individual room and a side wing, evoking a more private feminine boudoir or nest than a more public masculine ancestral hall.[3]

Shanghai's recent urban transformations have deepened and amplified the sense of privacy fostered by colonial architecture. The practical and ideological denial of privacy from the mid-1950s to the mid-1980s has exacerbated the trend. Since then, and as a reaction to earlier periods, urban dwellers have entangled their ways of living and constructing privacy with the sacredness of their spatial environments. Jie Li describes an informant reveling in the privacy of the apartment where she lives alone after years of enduring life in a crowded *lilong*: "I decided to put an end to our cold, stale relationship by sending [my mother] to a nursing home, where she found another society among other retirees, so that I could enjoy my own apartment on the nineteenth floor with a view of the Huangpu River, the river that symbolizes the city of Shanghai. I like to spend my evenings by the balcony, read a book, and I look out onto the shimmering waters, knowing that my room is adding another glimmer to the panorama of lights."[4]

Likewise, in January 2015, a woman in her late forties who moved to Shanghai in 2009 after living in southwestern China for most of her life, described the changes she had experienced:

When I go out of my apartment, I look at the high-rise buildings around me, and there's the moon, or the sun, or some fog. . . . Sometimes, there's only one lit window in a building, and this fills me with awe. When I was traveling in the highlands of southwestern China, as I did for so many years, sometimes the clouds were below me, and then I was feeling very proud. . . . But here everything seems to stand tall — everything is like beyond me. I know friends in Shanghai who come from an ethnic minority group or from a small local community, and when they arrive, they are very vain about the place they come from, proud of their origins and traditions. But here, they start to realize that they cannot judge things from the viewpoint of their place of origin; they sometimes even start to apologize, asking people not to make fun of them. . . . Of course, there's also the solitude that you can experience in Shanghai, and this makes people look for solace in a religious community, sometimes also in an art group or some other community.

Mrs. Wang Zhen (pseud.), a devout Buddhist from Zhabei, whom we met in the first section of our second chapter, has deserted her local temple and now follows a master residing at a temple in Wuxi, where she goes for important rituals. She has set up a core group of friends who meet at her apartment weekly to recite scriptures. When they enter her apartment, these elderly women exchange their shoes for the slippers they have brought along with them (usually handmade) and bow in front of an altar where a medium-size statue of the Buddha is surrounded with pictures of spiritual masters and bodhisattvas and a few devotional objects. Mrs. Wang is on friendly terms with the "door gods" (*menshen*) and Tudi Gong, deities whom she collectively calls *jiatang* (in this context, "the ancestors of our family"). She offers them fruit on the first and fifteenth days of the first lunar month. Nowadays, most people put couplets on the apartment threshold, not images of the door gods, she laments, and the couplets sometimes stay there forever, with nobody renewing them at the beginning of the year.

Mrs. Wang has devoted a lot of thought to the relationship between the home and the temple. In the past, many rituals took place at home, she notes. Nowadays, everyone goes to the temple, which is indeed a more proper ritual setting. Participating in a temple ritual allows the deceased to listen to the chanting of scriptures and the teaching of the doctrine, which is more helpful for their posthumous fate than giving them food. However, this does not mean that home practice has no significance. Home is where one prepares for the important rituals performed for the Tomb Sweeping Festival, the ghost month, and the winter solstice, notably by folding spirit money and "tin-leaf ingots" (*xibo*). Next, one goes to the temple to hear the doctrine, participate in chanting scriptures, and listen to the names of ritual participants. After all this, Mrs. Wang adds, one must redirect the merits one has just earned toward those for whom one has been praying. Though she does not explicitly link this last step to "coming home," Mrs. Wang has described a process that moves from the internal (*nei*) to the external (*wai*) and then back to the internal. In practice, the center of her spiritual life is her home, and it extends outward to the little neighborhood where she recruits fellow practitioners and invites them to visit a temple and a master that amplify their beliefs and practices. Alternating between the internal and the external governs the rhythm of Mrs. Wang's religious life.

There are similar features in the life of Zoe, a single woman slightly over thirty. She lives in an old apartment in Xujiahui with a former classmate with whom she was baptized. Zoe converted to Christianity after a difficult struggle with illness. She lived for two years in Sweden, where Christianity became a part of her life. She has made a number of artistic short films about her religious experience and earns a living teaching tea ceremony and calligraphy. She attends a family church, led by a female pastor, with a congregation of about sixty people who meet in a rented apartment. With friends, Zoe organizes weekly Bible readings and cooking sessions in participants' homes. Clearly, homes are the spiritual focus of her life and of the network to which she belongs.

Home-centered religiosity often stresses the centrality of reading habits. Zoe's Bible is very important to her; she reads it daily and has marked passages in different colors that she rereads according to her moods and needs (plate 22). This stress on Bible reading is found throughout China. Since 1987, Amity Press, based in Nanjing, has produced more than 70 million Bibles for Chinese Christians.[5] The books are handled by seventy-seven distribution centers that deliver to fifty-seven thousand grassroots churches and meeting places.

Born in 1918, Pastor Dai Lizhen is the oldest woman pastor in Shanghai and the first to be ordained in the city, in 1981. Pastor Dai's father was the pastor of Jingling Church. He died in 1990 at the age of 104. Pastor Dai's one-room home is inside Hongde Church (plate 26). This simple room is a haven where her helper organizes meals for guests. Jing Jianmei, the young female pastor, often visits. Pastor Dai's moral standing makes her room a focal point, a much needed home within a compound that does not fit the model of a close-knit community. The room, permeated with memories and the presence of the old pastor, has become a secret shrine for a community that delineates and reclaims its space and genealogy within the city.

Though often associated with underground Protestantism, the home is central to many religious landscapes. Sammi is approximately forty years old and comes from a wealthy Shanghainese family. Her husband, Niketa, of similar age, is also from a well-to-do Chinese family; he grew up in Russia and studied in Germany. They have their own interior design company with offices in the former French Concession. Sammi discovered Tibetan Buddhism in her thirties, and Niketa followed. They have built a shrine in the storage room of a lane house. The couple spent some time finding the right place. A guru came to offer advice on every potential residence they visited, and once the place had been approved, they held a blessing ceremony in every room. Sammi spent the months of her pregnancy putting the elaborate temple together. It consists of two altars, one for Sammi and one for Niketa. They bought the majority of the statues and decorations in Thailand. A few photos on the wall recall retreats they undertook with other wealthy Tibetan Buddhists from around the world.

For Zhou Lin (pseud.), a woman in her fifties, her workshop serves not only as a spiritual home but also as a shared sacred space. It is strategically located near the Bamboo Carving Museum in Jiading District. Technically, the place is the office of the antique-furniture business that Zhou Lin established after she left her job in the army. However, she now works as an intermediary and conducts all her transactions through WeChat, which has enabled her to convert the large, elegant space for dual purposes. On weekends, she teaches painting and bamboo carving to a group of young girls and women, whom she treats as her protégées. She has organized a little collection of artworks around an ancient statue of Guanyin, in front of which incense and a teakettle continuously produce a thin veil of smoke. This is where Zhou Lin spends her time and instructs her pupils in both art and wisdom.

Home-centered religion may be seen as a withdrawal from the public space, yet it also actively inserts the domestic space into a network of alternative ritual and study. It confers a sacred quality on practices of ordinary life such as reading, cooking, and making tea. "Sacredness within ordinariness" is expressed through specific spatial arrangements and by experiencing special, ritualized moments at home. The home becomes a sanctuary from which a larger space is shaped and oriented.

DEALING WITH DISPLACEMENT

If being at home generally means feeling secure, moving house, having no home, or being away from home is associated with a sense of estrangement. This is reflected in the way spiritual itineraries and practices are lived and retold. Though diverse in nature, the three cases that follow deal with both material and spiritual displacement.

Moving House

Moving is a familiar experience for Shanghai dwellers and has been occurring at an unheard-of rate in the past three decades (plate 25). This is due in part to upward social mobility, often the result of somewhat "voluntary" relocation from the city center to the urban periphery. In this respect, the simple ritual prescriptions described by an older Zhabei resident are not treated as mere traditional remnants but are inscribed into an ever-changing urban environment.

> Two days before moving into the new house, before the furniture has been taken away, the thing to do is to stand on an empty spot near the door of the new apartment building. There, you need to report to the door god and the God of the Soil, saying something like "Grandfather of the Soil, Mistress of the Soil, Ancestors![6] Here we come, moving into this new house [and then mention the address of the new location]. Here we come — please protect us!" Having said this, you need to burn some tin-foil ingots and three sticks of incense.

Shortly afterward, the same informant specified:

> Outside, you report to Tudi Gong. Upstairs, in the apartment, you report to his wife. Each year, at winter solstice time, when you burn paper money, you'll need to dedicate some to them. You'll also need to dedicate some to "the neighbors" [the ghosts]. After entering the apartment, holding a basin in which some paper is still burning, you first go to the living room, asking for blessings. Afterward, you go around the bedroom and the kitchen (the bathroom does not matter). Today, you can also go to a temple and get a jingle bell from a monk that you'll shake around the apartment. This is also a way of attracting blessings. And you have to put some fruits and incense everywhere in the apartment, and bow. On the very day you move in, you'll need to explode some firecrackers. This is a way of telling the gods of the soil and the door: "We have arrived!" You also need to arrive in the new apartment with bamboo and steamed bread. It means, "Let us rise higher!"[7]

As furtive as these customs may be, as fragmented and changeable as they may appear, they order the paths on which Shanghai residents migrate throughout their own city.

Whispering on City Roads

During the nineteenth century, missionaries noted the importance of home-focused religiosity in the lives of fishermen working on the waterways surrounding Shanghai. "Sand boat people have always been attracted by pious images: each boat contains, at the center of the cabin, a domestic oratory, where, in front of the indulgenced crucifix, of paintings of the Sacred Heart, the Virgin and the saints, and of the blessed Palms adorned with naive figures in paper, the family meets several times daily for prayers."[8]

The story that follows is alien to the spatial arrangement described above but is still about a peripatetic home. A sense of displacement and exhilaration may arise from being "on the road," both physically and spiritually. On Christmas Eve 2014, Liz and Liang are lucky enough to find a taxi in congested downtown Shanghai. After ten minutes of being stuck in a blocked tunnel, Liang voiced a polite "Merry Christmas!" to the taxi driver. Little did she know it would elicit an extended response.

"Many people know about God but do not understand God. They do not read the Bible," he began.

"So, you read the Bible?"

"I read the Bible, and not only the Bible. I read a lot of books."

"Are you a Christian?"

"I'm not. And I don't go to the church. But there are many good things in the Bible. It teaches men to be kind to one another. And there is the precept in Matthew, which is so important for Westerners: Love thy neighbor like thyself. But I think that there are many things that may be even better in our Eastern tradition. Westerners entrust everything to God. Can God really solve everything? Well, God will die of exhaustion! Our Daoist tradition is amazing: Man must rely on himself. Make yourself stronger — this is the way ahead!"

"Do some people in your family believe in Jesus?"

"None. I read books by myself. I read the Bible. It's full of little stories, interesting ones, not the boring kind. It moves me, sometimes to tears. I feel like I'm flying in the air."

"Do you read in your car?"

"I work one day, and I rest the other one. I read on the day I rest. The Bible gives me strength; it really makes me stronger. God taught me to be imaginative. Imagination is very important for people. When I feel bored at work, I start to think about a few good things."

"And . . . what do you believe in after all?"

The taxi driver laughs aloud.

"I don't go to church, but I study the Bible. I also read Buddhist Classics; I take what is good in them. I want to become stronger. I believe that God can teach me how to get rich. I believe one day I'll be able to buy a house like this for my daughter."

He points to the luxury villas the car is passing in the neighborhood of Biyun International Community, Pudong. The car stops at the door of Zhangjialou Church. The taxi driver tells Liz and Liang that his family name is Nie. The character *nie* means "whispering in the ear."

Such a mix of spiritual eagerness and insulation is widespread in Shanghai, though most people connect with a community at some point. Isolating occupations may engender spiritual loners. On that particular Christmas Eve, Mr. Nie's cab might have become a transient sacred place.

Feeling Homeless

Privacy remains a luxury. On January 24, 2015, a group of deaf Chinese Christians meets at a Kentucky Fried Chicken, and its leader repeatedly asks for help in finding an empty room in Shanghai where they can gather to pray and read the Bible.

The meeting grew out of a chance encounter. Not far from a large Korean community church, a much smaller Korean congregation found a welcome in a dental office. The congregation consists of Korean and Chinese believers. English translation is offered, when English speakers are present. On January 11, 2015, a service is being shown on the screen broadcast live from Korea. Once a small crowd has gathered, the home service begins. It lasts for only fifty minutes, including a thirty-minute homily and some expressive group prayer.

The Korean pastor in charge was a businessman before enrolling in a missionary school in Korea at the age of forty-nine. He then spent eleven years in Taiwan. After a short stint in Beijing, he arrived in Shanghai ten years ago to create a church for the locals. He began holding services for Chinese worshippers, with attendees numbering around fifty for the two Sunday services. A few deaf Chinese people began to attend, aided by someone who could communicate in sign language. The pastor has since learned sign language himself. However, the mix of both deaf and non-deaf people at the services became difficult, and most non-deaf worshippers stopped attending. Now he leads two small services every Sunday, one for Koreans and one for deaf Chinese. In his new role as a CEO, he has a privileged position for spreading the Gospel in the business sector, he explains. He leads prayers before business lunches and comments, "Everyone, Christian or not, likes to receive a blessing!" He sees the business mission as his most important work now and says he is motivated by the example of the Apostle Paul, who found his disciples through his work as a tent maker.

The sign-language service is run by a small network of about ten people who attend the weekly service. Zhan Hua (pseud.) is the unofficial leader of the group. He probably comes from northeastern China, though he introduces himself as Shanghainese. His first contact with Christianity came from his aunt and cousins, who had migrated to Canada. He notes approvingly that the Korean pastor generally takes attendees to lunch afterward but criticizes the financial management of the church. He likes the setting of the church, he explains, not the pastor. The frustration expressed by this small group of deaf Christians certainly has to do with their precarious situation and the lack of a place where they can meet regularly.

Zhan Hua stresses that they are not members of any cult. He writes the name "Jehovah's Witnesses" and asserts that they are not members and know well that it is a prohibited group. Group members enthusiastically demonstrate their use of sign language to express key Christian words, discussing their faith and sharing details of their practice. They pose on a bench in People's Square, hands outstretched to signify "reading the Bible." Even though their relationship with the Korean pastor is an uneasy one, they stay in contact with the other Koreans, teaching them sign language with computers and projectors.

Aspiring apostles and recent converts join together through itinerancies that are far from linear. Expectations on both sides may be blurred and evolving, so that agents adapt to each other uneasily. At the same time, this crossroads of destiny creates a dynamic fostered by the world of potentialities made available by the urban space. The shared journey transforms the outlook and prospects of all persons involved, the preachers arriving in the city to spread their faith and the converts entering into a new community. The difficulty for all sides is finding a stable place to anchor, the lack of which creates a sense of continuous displacement that can generate feelings of loss and grievance.

CAN CHURCHES BE HOMES?

Can churches or other worship places substitute for homes? In China, the question is far from rhetorical. The expression "house church" (*jiating jiaohui* [lit., "family church"]) has entered the everyday vocabulary, expressing a deep concern about interpersonal relationships. In a society in which trust among strangers or even casual acquaintances is not a given, one expects to find another style of sociability on entering a religious community. The congregation has the potential to become the place where neighbors can be trusted as much as or sometimes even more than family members. A house church is almost beyond the realm of the private, bordering on the intimate.[9]

Home and Faith in the City

Consciously differentiating themselves from official Protestant churches, house churches emphasize their peripheral or marginal character. At the same time, in Shanghai, many members of such groups now refer to themselves as members of a "city church" (*chengshi jiaohui*). A city church is simply a house church in urban context, but the preferential use of the expression constitutes a way of recognizing that, contrary to the situation that predominates in the countryside, these particular congregations are rich in resources, able to meet in houses or offices and sometimes even rent apartments and hotel rooms. Members paint an intricate picture of these religious networks. Space here is defined less by locations than by trajectories. Several interviewees stressed the role played by the Alpha course. A leader gathers a group of usually twelve people who meet weekly for two to three months, possibly at the workplace, with the expectation a new church unit will be established after they have completed the course. Food is a central part of the Alpha course, and someone is in charge of cooking for the group at every meeting.

However, the city church, which is often associated with middle-class status, is not the sole model of house church in Shanghai. Migrant groups meet at regular locations, sometimes on the basis of regional affiliations. On the outskirts of the city, Christian bosses sometimes organize services for their workers. Such is the case in a factory owned by a family from Wenzhou, near the Anting metro station, one of the last stops on line 11, on the northwestern edge of Shanghai. This particular congregation meets every Sunday at 6:30 p.m. in a room near the head offices. The leader of the service normally comes from Shanghai. Once a month, the owners invite a pastor from Wenzhou, their hometown. One Sunday in August 2013, thirty people from the factory arrive for the service, women seated on one side, and men on the other. As they enter, most women put on black caps, though this is not compulsory. During the forty minutes of singing, accompanied by a young woman playing music on a computer keyboard, more people continue to enter and sit down. Spontaneous and group prayers follow, along with more singing and then Communion. A large white plate is passed around, and everyone breaks off a piece of the round yellow Communion wafer; a small glass of sweet yellow wine is also shared. After more singing, the young leader gives a forty-five-minute sermon. As the preacher speaks, the young woman writes and projects notes on the screen above, while a few attendees play on their cell phones. More group prayer, one song, and then fifteen more minutes of spontaneous individual prayers close the service at 8:45 p.m. The meeting room then returns to its secular usage. The house church is again a factory plant.

Another family church meets regularly in Jing'an District. Almost all members are students or young alumni from the same university, reinforcing the family-like character of the small congregation. They are aware that another family church also meets regularly in the office building where they hold their services. Opposite the elevator, a roughly painted acronym directs the visitor to the group's meeting place, a room full of seated worshippers. Only one service is held on this weekend, the last in January 2014, rather than the two that usually take place, because it is the Chinese New Year season.

As a consequence, the congregation is larger. Tinsel still hangs on the walls in the shape of Christmas trees. The words "I love Jesus," sprayed in white, appear on the window overlooking the inner city high-rises below.

After ten minutes of singing, accompanied by a keyboard, a female leader gives an hour-long sermon followed by prayers. The congregation is invited to take a five-minute break, with coffee, tea, and sweets offered on a little table at the side of the room. The service resumes with the monthly Communion celebration. Grape juice is dispensed in little plastic cups from a silver tray. After Communion, new attendees are asked to stand and introduce themselves, as well as say whether or not they are Christian. After the folding chairs have been put away and the floor mopped, some members of the congregation stay for lunch.

The male leader, around forty-five years old, established the church ten years ago. The congregation has been meeting in this location for only six months, as they sometimes shift from one apartment to another in order to avoid unwanted attention. The difficulty of securing a permanent location does not seem to hinder the church's growth; several small Bible study groups meet elsewhere during the week. "The church caters mainly to students, and it is not always convenient for them to travel to get here," says the leader. "We want to plant many more churches in the suburbs of Shanghai."

On December 21, 2014, the same congregation gathers for a Christmas party. This particular event is open to outsiders, and about half the attendees are seen as potential believers. The tinsel Christmas trees still hang on the walls. The only liturgical items are a piano and guitars for the band as well as a new-looking wooden lectern propped against a well-worn white board. The meeting starts with a game of charades; all attendees are required to take part in the icebreaker, which generates the expected outbursts of laughter. Next, eight young people sing carols, followed by a drama, accompanied by American Christian music, in which the lead character acts out God's relations with humankind. A student's speech and more carols close the show, after which everyone is invited to break into small groups for discussion. Snacks and pamphlets with discussion points are distributed. The groups mix Christians and potential believers, the latter questioning the existence of the soul or wondering if humans invented God, while Christian members respond by affirming the reality and individual character of the soul.

The home dimension of the worshippers' cell is even more apparent on the Saturday before Easter in 2016, in a villa in Hongqiao that a family church has rented for the day. Around twenty-five people are gathered in the spacious living room, preparing for baptisms by chanting hymns and listening to the preaching leaders of the youth group. Young and middle-aged couples, some with their children, compose the vast majority of this middle-class Shanghainese group. Many participants did not know much about Christianity until recently. At least one of the catechumens, a first-year university student brought to the church by his girlfriend, is going to be baptized after only one month of instruction. A wave of excitement sweeps through the villa as the six catechumens are ushered up the spiral staircase and separated by gender into two rooms. Cameras are raised in anticipation as they emerge, wearing white robes marked with a cross. The full-immersion baptism takes place in the third-floor bathroom. Towels are laid out like a red carpet leading from the adjacent bedroom to the bath. The bare room is filled with the eagerness of relatives and church members as the plastic bathtub becomes a transformative vessel for forty-five minutes. Once immersed, each catechumen lies silent for a moment before answering the three ritual questions, receiving the sacrament, and being welcomed into the community by a refrain. Once the newly baptized are fully dressed, the rest of the day is spent chatting, relaxing, and sharing a celebratory dinner.

Can these congregations become home to their members? They do provide a less formal environment than that of most institutional churches. They also satisfy a need for intimacy and homogeneity within the group, while facilitating external interactions, as their informality encourages members to invite friends and acquaintances. Snacks, meals, and plays also contribute to a homelike feeling, which may be especially appealing during solitary weekends. More important, the leadership figures seem to play a paternal or maternal role, more so than do pastors at official churches. Although the young Christians at the three Hongkou District churches and those belonging to these groups are similar in profile and outlook, the house churches are characterized by a more evangelical style and the desire to avoid any kind of governmental pressure in expressing and sharing their faith. Unofficial worship groups are *home* indeed for people who are even more closely united by the desire to avoid state interference.

A MIGRANTS' CHURCH

Unofficial Protestant movements are especially prone to identify and approach specific conversion targets. Still, according to our observations, in Shanghai most conversions to Christianity happen not through well-devised strategies but rather in an informal, unpremeditated way. People who often only recently had joined a small-size prayer or Bible study group would invite friends to attend with them. The autonomy of small groups based on expanding mutual connections is a strong factor in the organic growth of unofficial Protestant movements. Questions remain on the way networking is developing among these groups, the channels that generate a consistent supply of religious literature and doctrine, and the crises and readjustments the growth of such groups may provoke.

In 2015, Easter Day coincided with the Tomb Sweeping Festival, and the metro was crowded with families clutching flowers and packages on their way to visit the graves of their ancestors on the outskirts of Shanghai. The Shanghai representative of a missionary society and Liz are driven forty minutes to an industrial area of Pudong. There are around sixty thousand migrant workers in the area, and a large unofficial church is there to serve them. Shanghai-born Wang Qinfu (pseud.), the founder, was a factory owner who embarked on theological self-study and trained herself for the ministry before taking on a full-time job as a pastor. In six years, the congregation grew to more than fifty people, and the church moved to a former factory that accommodates three hundred worshippers. Almost all attendees are migrant factory workers, and the congregation is transient. From the beginning, the church was supported by a wider network. Allan, a Malaysian factory manager working for a US company, was involved in founding the church and continues to preach there once a month. The representative of the missionary society says that some bank employees also volunteer by offering training to the faithful. The missionary society donated one hundred Bibles in 2014 and plans to donate another hundred in 2015.

The car weaves along narrow lanes between old industrial buildings and then stops at a warehouse. Clotheslines and meat hung out to dry overhead indicate that many migrants are living in the old factory. The church consists of a pastor's administration room, canteen and kitchen, children's room, and the main worship hall, which is located on the second floor. At 9:30 a.m., when the service begins, attendees are few, but within two hours, a mixed crowd fills the donated chairs. Around thirty children attend Sunday school in a separate room. Two men and a woman lead the singing at the start of the service, while the whipping and crucifixion scenes from Mel Gibson's *The Passion of Christ* are projected on a screen behind them. A prayer is read, and the congregation sings a series of cheerful songs with arms raised; during the chanting, those at the front wave colorful flags. The homily, given by Allan and aided by a PowerPoint presentation, focuses on the pain Jesus endured and on the example this sacrifice offers to Christians. The preacher highlights the contrast between the Tomb Sweeping Festival, which is about death, and Easter Day, a celebration of new life. During the prayer session, he thanks attendees for coming to church rather than going to their ancestors' graves for tomb sweeping. After Communion, newcomers are encouraged to stand up. Each receives a pink towel with the word "Emmanuel" sewn on it in English and Chinese characters, as well as a slip of paper on which to write down contact information. The service concludes with the children dancing and performing an Easter song before handing out hard-boiled eggs to the congregation. The church empties quickly as attendees rush to the adjacent room for the free lunch of rice and vegetables.

Over lunch, the leaders express their concern that the church's building may be destroyed to make way for the new Shanghai Disney Resort complex, which is being built close by. One of the leaders, the coordinator of an overseas Methodist church and a businesspeople's fellowship, speaks of his two current projects: establishing an international church in Jiading on the model of the one on Hengshan Road and building a health center on Chongming Island (halted a few months later due to government intervention).

The missionary society representative and Liz revisited the church on January 24, 2016, the coldest day in Shanghai for more than forty years. The society sent ninety-five Bibles as Christmas presents in December, and the representative carries another five in his bag, "for those who converted at Christmas." It is 8:30 a.m. and minus eight degrees Celsius when Liz and the representative arrive at the designated meeting point, where a member of the church's team ushers them into a battered old brown car. As they drive through the makeshift migrant-worker village, he informs them that the local town-planning bureau has slated the whole area for demolition in order to make way for construction around the Disney resort. The church and the workers have yet to find new locations.

On each floor along the stairs leading up to the worship place, we saw rooms containing home furnishings, mainly beds, and the red crosses that decorate the calendars handed out by the church on the walls. From a room known as the DJ's room, poorly heated by a wall-mounted hot-and-cold air conditioner, a worship team member sets up a computer that projects the lyrics of the chosen hymns onto the front wall. The congregation begins to assemble on the sunny side of the freezing-cold hall. Attendance has been reduced to around sixty people because most migrant workers take four to six weeks off for Chinese New Year, traveling back to their hometowns, with many resigning from their factory jobs. At 9:30 a.m., the worship team kicks off with cheerful songs, encouraging attendees to warm up by swaying to the music. Despite the cold, the church's female pastor speaks for fifty minutes, her nose running, until a member of the worship team pleads with her to stop. After encouraging the assembly again to place all worries and fears in God's hands, she concludes, "I don't feel the cold when the word of God is in my mouth!" Immediately, the congregation bursts into a song, as if released from captivity. After a few quick announcements, attendees file out into the canteen where steaming bowls of egg, pork, vegetable, and noodle soup await them (plate 28). No one lingers after the meal today. The worship team and the pastor eat in a separate, well-heated room. Afterward, the missionary society representative interviews the five new converts who received the Bibles. "It's important to collect individual testimonies and stories to feed back to donors," he explains.

In this networked conversion endeavor, the apostles play the prominent role, bringing in a fairly well-rehearsed evangelical outlook and doctrinal content. The spatial dimension of the endeavor is striking. Evangelists focus on peripheral sections of the city, where the characteristics and needs are well analyzed (Jiading is not Chongming Island, is not an industrial outskirt of Pudong). Within a given neighborhood, a multifunctional evangelizing space is then conceived and constructed that combines a setting for worship with specific services. This networked endeavor does integrate a home dimension. The migrants' church gathers people at the margins, who are in many ways homeless; the converted church compound offers a meeting place, a few meals, and temporary lodgings. This home model is both protective and hierarchical, where seemingly rather passive settlers find a dwelling, however provisional the arrangement may prove to be.

DEEP RIVER: HINDUISM IN PUDONG

In Shanghai, foreign communities may experience a privileged relationship with a specific territory. In the Shimao Riviera Garden compound in Pudong live approximately fifty Indian families, attracted by the active community life. On the evening of Diwali, the festival of lights, November 3, 2013, the Kshirsagar family, a couple and their adult son, share a prayer around a small shrine decorated with fresh flowers. From 7:30 until 10:00 p.m., a steady flow of Indian families comes and goes, totaling around fifty people, mostly couples over fifty and a few others with young children. Indian dishes are laid out on a large table. Families take turns hosting the community in their apartments for major festivals (plate 29).

Mala Katare, who lives in the same compound, had recently shaved her head, a customary practice in her Hindu family for women who give birth to boys. In support, her husband Ravikumar did the same. The couple keeps a family shrine in a large Chinese-style cabinet in the front room of their apartment. They had the portable shrine handmade during the fifteen years they lived in Japan. They have been in Shanghai for three years. On Saturday mornings, Ravi cleans every statue and picture in the shrine, an activity he finds both inspirational and enjoyable. After he has finished reapplying sandalwood and bindi dust, he lights oil lamps and incense, and he and Mala pray to the shrine. Mala comments, "It takes him only about thirty minutes, as the shrine is not so big, but some people have a full room of items to clean, and that can take a whole day. We have a small one because we have to keep moving for work. It keeps growing in size when relatives die and we add pictures, and then when we buy objects on our travels."

Mala also takes pride in her bindi collection. She keeps a bindi fixed to the center of her forehead, even painting one on in the evening, so it is still there at night. It is not of great significance to them that there is no Hindu

PLATE 17. Eid al-Adha at Fuyou Road Mosque, 2013. Fuyou Road Mosque is the smallest of Shanghai's mosques, constructed during the Qing dynasty (1644–1911). It is located near the City God Temple. There is no separate prayer hall for women; however, on major festival days, a curtain divides the prayer hall, with men sitting on one side and women on the other.

PLATE 18. Renovations at Xilin Temple, 2013. Xilin Temple is the biggest Buddhist temple in Songjiang District, Shanghai. It is an active temple with twenty resident monks, a large administrative department, a vegetarian restaurant, and a shop. The temple complex was rebuilt in the 1980s following the Cultural Revolution, and renovations continue to this day.

PLATE 19. Collecting donations at the Xiao Taoyuan Women's Mosque, 2014. The Xiao Taoyuan Mosque, located in central Shanghai, is the headquarters of the Shanghai branch of the Islamic Association of China. Next to the mosque is the Xiao Taoyuan Women's Mosque, built in 1920. The donations collected by the mosque are used to support poor Muslim communities within and outside of Shanghai.

PLATE 20. Kehilat Jewish seder, Renaissance Shanghai Yangtze Hotel, 2014. The Kehilat Jewish community holds Passover events at this Renaissance hotel in Shanghai, which has become renowned for its kosher cuisine.

PLATE 21. Rabbi Avraham Greenberg and his children, Chabad Jewish Center of Pudong, 2015. The vitality of the expatriate Jewish community in Shanghai comes with its strong organizational structure. Rabbi Avraham Greenberg, brother of Rabbi Shalom Greenberg, who set up the Shanghai Jewish Center in 1999, established the Pudong center in his family's home villa.

PLATE 22. Zoe's Bible reading, 2013. Zoe, a teacher of tea ceremony and calligraphy, became a Christian during an extended stay in Sweden. She organizes weekly Bible readings and cooking sessions at friends' homes and attends a family church in a rented apartment. Zoe reads from her Bible daily and highlights passages in different colors to be reread according to her moods and needs.

PLATE 23. Home *gurdwara*, Hongqiao, 2015. Sikhs first came to Shanghai during the 1880s to serve as policemen for the British colonial government. Today, although Sikhism is not officially recognized by the state, one family has set up a functioning *gurdwara* within a complex of villas in the residential Hongqiao area.

PLATE 24. Deacon Fu at home, 2015. Deacon Papiy Fu Xiliang, a Chinese national raised in a Beijing Orthodox orphanage, received his clerical education in Russia. He decorated his home with photographs of his one granddaughter.

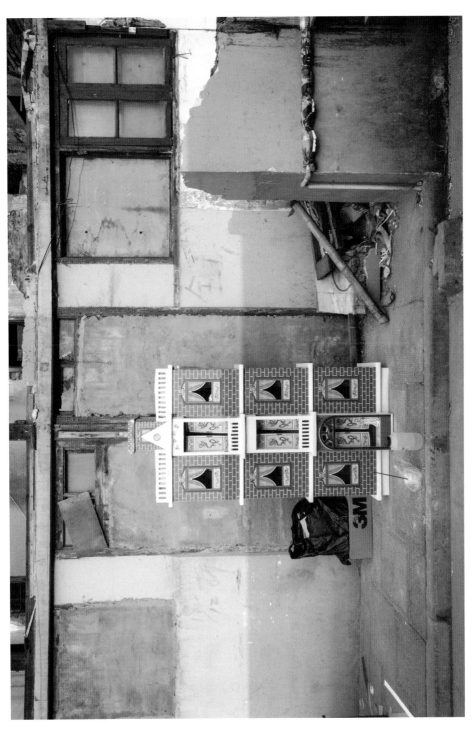

PLATE 25. Joss paper house, Shanghai Old City (former Nanshi District), 2015. Elaborate items made out of paper not only serve as offerings for the dead but also reflect the values of the living. The omnipresence of joss paper houses speaks of both the housing shortage that Shanghai experienced in the past and the rapid pace of urban transformation it has undergone since the 1990s.

PLATE 26.   Pastor Dai in her room, Hongde Church compound, 2014. Pastor Dai Lizhen (b. 1918) is the oldest woman pastor in Shanghai and the first woman to be ordained in the city, in 1981. She trained as a pastor before the Cultural Revolution and retrained afterward to serve a flourishing church. Pastor Dai lives within one room in the church compound, where she regularly greets visitors.

PLATE 27. Youth Choir of Young John Allen Memorial Church, Hongkou, 2014. Young John Allen Memorial Church, like other official Protestant congregations, organizes activities tailored to different groups, which fosters the parish's organizational growth.

PLATE 28. Migrant workers' church, Pudong, January 24, 2016. After the Sunday service, migrant workers share a lunch offered by the Protestant church organization on the coldest day in Shanghai in more than forty years. The church is located in an old factory near the new Disney resort site and would soon have to move to make way for construction.

PLATE 29. Diwali festival, Shimao Riviera Garden, Pudong, 2013. Around fifty Hindu expatriate families live in the Shimao Riviera Garden compound, in Pudong. The community chose this compound because it is close to the Huangpu River, mirroring the pivotal role of holy waterways for Indians. Lacking a Hindu temple, some families also attend Buddhist temples to pray on special personal occasions such as birthdays.

PLATE 30.   Halal meat shop, Zhejiang Road, Shanghai, 2016. The first mosque in Shanghai was built on Zhijiang Road, which is now a bustling street lined with halal food shops. At least 23 million people in China eat halal foods. Although both central and local governments regulate the industry, supervision is absent in some areas.

PLATE 31.   GGJ (Guanguanji) halal restaurant, Shanghai, 2016. A young man from Gansu eats a meal offered to workers before their twelve-hour night shift at GGJ. The building was once a significant mosque for the city, with a provisional structure, built in 1855, giving way to a full-fledged place of worship in 1870, and many famous Hui imams were trained within its walls. It still offers a prayer space for Muslim restaurant workers.

PLATE 32.   Catholic couple, St. Michael's Church, 2013. A couple practices singing before a Taizé prayer evening. Taizé services were introduced to Shanghai Catholic churches by a young Shanghai-born man who was inspired by the musical prayers of the Taizé community he visited in France. The events have become popular among young Catholics.

shrine in Shanghai. Instead, they go to the Buddhist Jing'an Temple on major Hindu religious festivals or for wedding anniversaries and birthdays.

In December 2014, in another apartment in the same compound, two men lead a scriptures class, chanting and then analyzing the scriptures in the book *Bhagavad-Gita for All*. The men sit in front of a huge living-room window looking out onto the Huangpu River. Aparna, the wife and mother of the host family, admits that the apartment is above the couple's budget, but says that they cannot bear to give up the view. The host family provides dinner after three hours of reading. The careful preparation of food for others is a source of pride.

The majestic view of the Huangpu River is part of the religious landscape of this particular Indian community, and the city's Buddhist temples may serve as substitutes for Hindu places of worship, although such public spaces generally are not required. A room with a view inserts itself into a larger mental geography, reflecting and furthering a spiritual experience that flows from both the Indian psyche and the lived landscape of Shanghai.

FOOD, HEALTH, AND CLUBS

Eating together, at home or at a favorite place, solidifies spiritual intimacy, while the ritual or quasi-ritual character of the event may inform and transcend its apparent informality. Jewish organizations in Shanghai attach great importance to holding Shabbat dinners and organize larger community events (plate 20), aimed notably at keeping young people attuned to the faith and the community. Some members of the Jewish community also organize more informal culinary events. Ice Cream for Breakfast takes place every year on the first Saturday of February. Started by a Jewish family in the United States, the custom was adopted by a family member who moved to Shanghai and married a Chinese man. Their daughter is the first fully Orthodox Jewish person of mixed Chinese and Western background. The small family has been running the Ice Cream for Breakfast holiday in the Shanghai typewriter museum since 2009, with kosher ice cream and a combination of Chinese and Western-style toppings. Sixty to one hundred people usually attend, connecting the event with the Chinese Lantern Festival that happens at around the same time. Accordingly, the family makes ice cream cones shaped like lanterns.

Lucky Veg and Happy Zen

On February 12, 2015, Tim has organized a lunch at his favorite Buddhist restaurant, Lucky Veg (Jixiang Cao), near Xintiandi. Jessica, one of the attendees, is visiting Shanghai over the Chinese New Year holiday; she is a Shanghainese who moved to Los Angeles three years ago with her daughter and husband, a wealthy businessman. She studied English and business in the United States with the aim of establishing a chain of vegan Buddhist restaurants in Los Angeles. Tim similarly chose a major, computer programming, that complements his Buddhist practices, with the aim of promoting Buddhism in English online. The Lucky Veg restaurant is a spacious environment in downtown Shanghai. Grass, auspicious to Buddhists, is planted in pots on every wooden table, and soft chanting music plays in the background. At the entrance, Tim points out a bookcase stocked with free books on Buddhist teachings. On the second floor opposite the restaurant, a shop sells books about Buddhism, spirituality, and creativity, as well as beautifully crafted wooden incense holders, calligraphy brushes, and paper.

A Taiwanese Buddhist founded Lucky Veg restaurant in the 1990s. Buddhist vegan restaurants began developing over the past twenty years in China, but the trend started earlier in Taiwan. Temple restaurants are more authentically Buddhist, insist Jessica and Tim. Jessica stresses that she wants to keep her religious practices separate from her Buddhist restaurant enterprise, commenting, "Business and Buddhism should not go together." She wants to establish a vegan restaurant in Los Angeles that would be for everyone, not just Buddhists. Jessica attends a temple established by a Taiwanese monk in Los Angeles and goes to the Jade Buddha Temple when she is in Shanghai.

The young female manager of Lucky Veg is herself a practicing Buddhist and a member of Ciji (transcribed as "Tzu Chi" in Taiwan), a Buddhist charitable organization founded by the Taiwanese nun Zhengyan.[10] She studied customer relations in her home province of Yunnan before coming to Shanghai five years ago, in search of better work prospects. She began volunteering in a Buddhist temple restaurant and met the owner of the Lucky Veg restaurant through Ciji. The owner offered her a job three years ago. For Tim, the strain of Buddhism followed by Jessica and the one promoted by Ciji are too focused on daily life; this is not "professional" Buddhism, he points out.

Lucky Veg is a restaurant and a public space, even if regulars feel that it is like home, with the right food, atmosphere, and conversations. However, it is far from being as homelike as the Zen One Clubhouse (Chan'yi Jingguan Tang). This club is not the most exclusive Zen-centered club in Shanghai, but it is focused on intimacy, with a distinctive, meticulously designed and executed interior decor. The club's founder deals in real estate. An art collector with a predilection for ivory sculptures and African wood artworks, he exhibits the pieces he has bought at the club. He has translated his passion for art and architecture into the club's design, with the aim of shaping a specifically Zen atmosphere. A wooden Buddha statue opens one eye while closing the other, expressing what it means to follow the way of Happy Zen (Kuaile Chan) in daily life. The clubhouse boasts an eleven-meter-long rosewood table and a piece of Suzhou embroidery three meters square made (so it is claimed) by the oldest and most famous female embroiderer in China.

At first, the clubhouse was used solely for welcoming the founder's friends, but it was later opened to club members. Lectures held on the premises address the practical and spiritual aspects of traditional Chinese medicine and include exercises for club members. They illustrate the specific understanding of Zen propounded in this place, that Zen is all about practice (*chanxiu*) in order to obtain internal peace and physical health. When the clubhouse was established, it also served as a small Buddhism school: the manager required all waiters and waitresses to undergo one year of in-house training about Buddhist traditions and practices. Li Xing (pseud.), a waitress, testifies that they were asked to practice Zen and study the "Duties of the Disciple" in the morning. In the afternoon, the practice was about drinking a cup of tea while keeping silent and giving up all expectations in regards to taste but concentrating on the tea proper. The trainer was a Buddhist believer who had sold his two apartments in Shenzhen and made enough money to travel to China's famous teahouses, studying tea ceremony. After a year, he left to continue his journey, and since then, there has been no training for workers.

Bowl Therapy

The spiritual club model has become popular among Shanghai's upper middle class, fostering the development of niche markets. Jasmine, a Chinese woman who introduces herself as an explorer (rather than a follower) of the Tibetan Buddhist tradition, has been specializing in therapy based on Tibetan singing bowls. Now living in Pudong with her German boyfriend, Frederic, Jasmine trained in Western medicine in Dalian before coming to Shanghai to work in a second-tier hospital. This is when she became interested in spiritual medicine. "I found the surgery I was doing was too engaged with suffering, and I wanted to earn more money," she explains frankly.

In her kitchen, Jasmine points out a display of photographs on the side of her refrigerator portraying people she met on meditation retreats around the world. She averages four such spiritual trips a year. "It's about discovering yourself. You meet wonderful people in these seminars, and you share life experiences with them." Jasmine met her boyfriend, a dealer in Chinese art, at one of these meditation retreats. He seems more intrigued by the trading value of the singing bowls than by the idea of playing them. He defines himself as decidedly Christian. "Christianity is our history."

Jasmine's spiritual-medicine training includes spiritual dancing and hypnosis through singing-bowl therapy. At a Tibetan Buddhist school in Kathmandu she learned how to enter a trancelike state by playing the bowls. As of February 2015, Jasmine has been offering Tibetan singing-bowl therapy for three years, mostly to Chinese clients. The sessions take place at a members' club on Xingfu Road in the center of Shanghai. Jasmine's thirty-nine singing bowls are laid out on soft rugs in a small room that used to be her daughter's bedroom. Framed Tibetan Buddhist artworks are propped against the walls, decorated with teddy-bear-theme wallpaper. Sometimes, trusted clients come to receive therapy sessions in her living room. Jasmine's practice is part of a wider trend. She estimates the number of Tibetan monks currently living in the homes of wealthy people in Shanghai at around a thousand. They run programs from these homes and organize Animal Release events around Shanghai. For Jasmine, a designated space for religious practice is superfluous. "The temple is just a surface." Spirituality is entwined with all aspects of daily life, from making money to leisure activities.

In front of the club on Xingfu Road where Jasmine practices her art, swathes of Tibetan flags hang loosely between an unremarkable building and a tree on the pavement. The interior is vibrant and luxurious, with a shrine, conference rooms, restaurant, and tearoom where a cup of tea costs ¥80. On March 29, 2015, in a room at the back of the club, shoes are piled neatly on the wooden floor; their owners sit with closed eyes and crossed legs on mats. Jasmine is leading a group of eight women and two men, between twenty and thirty-five years of age, in meditation. Tibetan paintings, which can be purchased in the shop, are hung on the walls. Jasmine's collection of singing bowls, purchased in Tibet and India, is distributed among the group. Following the meditation, the group splits into pairs. Jasmine demonstrates how to strike a bowl and move it in a slow, smooth motion around the body of each person's partner so as "to vibrate and resonate with their body and help them reach a calm and trancelike state" (plate 40). The metal bowls are heavy, making the movements quite strenuous for the therapist. After the session with the bowls, Jasmine encourages the group to share life experiences. The group's stories focus on the improvements they have experienced in respect to health, relationships, business, and happiness since they met a spiritual teacher and began their journey. During the session, a woman begins to feel unwell and lies down on a massage couch at the back of the room. Jasmine massages her with the bowls.

If places such as this one are not home in their own right, they can still be considered a refuge where the whole of one's life, including diet and physical well-being, is intimately relived and shared in ways that the compound might not fully allow. They offer a sense of escape, a space for integration, and the kind of emotional support provided in the past by extended families.

OF BOUNDS AND BOUNDARIES

If feeling at home in one's religious setting and practices is ultimately about the degree of intimacy one experiences, the emphasis on nurturing fellowship around food and meals becomes understandable. Halal shops and restaurants in Shanghai (which are often located close to one other) are striking examples of the discreet and yet pervasive forms of intimacy that can be found in public spaces (plate 30).[11]

Halal Ramen Restaurant (Qingzhen Lamian Guan) on Nanchang Road is no different from other Muslim-run noodle eateries found around the city.[12] The small space painted green is marked with a "Halal Food" sign in Chinese, English, and Arabic, which distinguishes the shop from other ramen restaurants run by Han or Japanese. It offers the Lanzhou specialty of beef ramen and is operated, as could be expected, by Hui migrants from Gansu. The Ma family migrated to Shanghai eight to ten years ago and only recently opened the restaurant. They normally attend the Pudong Mosque, where they feel more comfortable than in the neighboring Xiao Taoyuan Mosque. Their restaurant offers cheap, casual food to a young, white-collar clientele. In contrast with this modest family venture, Xin Mei Ju, on East Ninghai Road, is famous for its fresh mutton hotpot served in a traditional copper pot. "We were one of the first independent restaurants to open in Shanghai after the Reform and Opening policy began," the old woman at the counter says proudly, opening a magazine to a story on the restaurant and its owners. "We've run this mutton hotpot dining room for more than thirty years. Now we have four branches in Shanghai. The largest one on East Jinling Road is managed by my oldest grandson; another one is run by my second grandson," she continued. The restaurant is also halal, although it is famous enough that it does not need to advertise the fact. "Our clientele is made up mostly of old customers, and, especially during winter, we're full at dinner time. Our family originally lived in Henan, but we migrated to Shanghai eighty years ago, so now we're Shanghainese. I usually go to the Xiao Taoyuan Women's Mosque. Our family has donated more than several hundred thousand yuan to different mosques; we even donated a place to Yangpu Mosque. My eldest grandson has pursued Koranic studies in South Africa. He doesn't speak Arabic but does speak good English."

Another halal restaurant, GGJ (Guanguanji), on Middle Zhejiang Road, is an important address in the history of Islam in Shanghai (plate 31). In 1855, an Indian Muslim bought a plot of land, opened a cemetery for foreign Muslims in Shanghai, and built a little house as a provisional mosque nearby. In the 1870s, the house became a proper mosque, established and operated by Muslims from Henan and Shandong. Some famous Chinese imams, fluent in Arabic, English, and Chinese, trained there. During the Cultural Revolution, the mosque was made into a warehouse. In the 1980s, the house was returned to the Islamic Association of Shanghai. The former mosque now harbors two restaurants, three to four butcher shops, and three snack shops. The head manager of GGJ introduces his restaurant as a branch of the Shanghai

Islamic community, with most staff members coming from Gansu. They are mainly Hui, and other Islamic groups, notably the Dongxiang ethnic minority, are also represented. The restaurant also showcases an Islamic sense of social responsibility. It offers staff free accommodations and salaries ranging from ¥3,200 to ¥8,000 a month, excluding bonuses, for an average workday of twelve hours that includes the possibility of a night shift. All staff members are supposed to meet basic Islamic requirements, and a space inside the restaurant is set aside for daily prayers. During Ramadan, the restaurant offers the general public a free breakfast before sunrise.

These three restaurants display a variety of styles and histories, yet each constructs a home that closely associates food and faith. Different groups of customers relate in varying ways to the environment, but they all enter a space that bounds a single experience of intimacy and sacredness.

NEGOTIATING PERSONAL SPACE

Close spiritual bonding within a homelike congregation may become as oppressive as the bond within a family that assigns particular value to religious rules and a religious ethos. In both cases, individuals, while remaining strongly attached to their families or communities, often feel the need to negotiate boundaries that will allow them some personal space and freedom. A metropolis may provide an environment where they can reconcile the support drawn from spiritual intimacy with the distance that most urban dwellers treasure even when they complain of excessive isolation.

Emma, the twenty-three-year-old Kazakh Muslim who avoided the halal canteen at Fudan University, as the food was not to her taste (chap. 1), is now working for a communications company and has applied for a master's program in the United Kingdom. She is not able to pray during work time but says, "It's not really a problem. Most Muslims in China can't either. I know it's different in the UK though." Emma met her boyfriend, a twenty-seven-year-old Han from Hubei, at the university. He is not Muslim, but, she says, he loves to read the Koran.

> He says there can't be two gods, so Allah is the name I give to God, and Buddha is another. His parents don't share his Buddhist faith. He had an unhappy childhood as his father used to beat his mother. He was looking for something, and he began reading. He even looked at Daoism. He wanted to be a monk, but his mother stopped him. She wanted him to work in a company and get married. He doesn't go to the temple, as he is learning everything from books. My parents wouldn't allow me to marry him because he's not Muslim, but maybe he'll become one. He never goes to mosque or prayers because he doesn't know the language we use. But, for sure, you can pray in any language.

Emma is negotiating a situation in which two forms of intimacy are in conflict. She is also carving out a new spiritual space that accommodates the ethos of a metropolis, the demands of the Xinjiang environment she grew up in, and her boyfriend's worldview.

Religious groups generally favor marriage within the same congregation, although the strictness of the requirement varies widely, and customs or rules are subject to change. Catholic Shanghai of the nineteenth century and the first half of the twentieth century practiced systematic intermarriage, cementing religious and business connections.[13] Youth from boys' and girls' Catholic orphanages were presented to each other, and these marriages eventually formed the core of the modest, mainly working-class Catholic population in the district surrounding St. Ignatius Church until urban renewal drastically altered the neighborhood's sociological composition. Today, Catholic parishes in Shanghai organize regular parties for single young Catholics, where participants are encouraged to get to know one another through games and sharing. Moreover, marriage and particular friendships are favorite topics for parish talk and gossip (plate 32).

The situation of Xiao Man (pseud.) has led to many heated discussions at the Zhangjialou parish. Xiao Man, a successful businesswoman, owns her own company. Her boyfriend of six years, a lawyer and a Catholic, seemed ideal, all parishioners assumed that they would soon marry. However, after the 2015 New Year holiday, the lawyer brought a new girlfriend to mass, and Xiao Man attended with her new boyfriend who was sixteen years her junior. The young man puzzled the parishioners. He came from a traditional Catholic family in Hebei, he had been baptized as a child, and his devotional style was distinctly different from that of Shanghai Catholics. He could sing hymns in Latin, although he had never received any formal Latin education. He knew more about liturgical music than anyone else in the parish, but his level of formal education was rather low and he could not find a suitable job in Shanghai. So he moved in with Xiao Man and her family. The biggest surprise was that Xiao Man's parents approved of him and agreed to the marriage if the couple decided to proceed. The young boyfriend occasionally taught piano to children and spent a great deal of time serving the church.

In September of that year, the wedding of Xiao Man and her boyfriend was announced. The big excitement was the invitation of twenty priests and twenty nuns to the celebration. On the day of the wedding, more than one hundred parishioners were there to witness the event. Acolytes in white chasubles led the priests, fifteen in all (not as many as announced but an impressive number nevertheless), who would together raise their hands to bless the couple. When the main celebrant read aloud the words of blessing written on a certificate from Rome and held up the document, the assembly erupted in loud cheering. The public voice wholeheartedly blessed the private arrangements that had been the subject of communal worry and curiosity.

PRIVACY, INTIMACY, AND SACREDNESS

The cases discussed in this chapter encourage us to redefine the terms used to describe the way a personal and a communal ethos balance each other through devotional practices. We understand religious intimacies as a set of devotional practices rooted in a faith and the milieu that conveys it. Religious intimacies are what make a person "feel at home" inside a given creed and church. This sense of belonging can be expressed in one's home arrangement, body language at the temple or the church, or behavior in public spaces. In contrast, spiritual privacy is the capacity to foster an inner life that distances itself from the codes and requirements of one's community. Spiritual privacy is about the distance an individual creates from a religious community that is still recognized as that person's place of origin. Spiritual privacy is one dimension of the right to privacy, which generally is felt and manifested more freely and clearly in contemporary metropolises.

Ultimately, a sacred space results from a trade-off between three different dimensions: communal space and devotions provide the framework for experimenting with sacredness; the set of practices that we defined as religious intimacies allows one to creatively appropriate the sacredness dispensed by the community and assert it as one's own; spiritual privacy forms the inner space where one confronts and reworks the frontiers of the sacred and the prohibitions that go with them, thereby adjusting levels of commitment. Several people we interviewed testified to this triangular relationship between socially dispensed sacredness (the public), the way they appropriate it (the intimate), and the spiritual privacy they want to assert and maintain.

A self-employed Shanghainese woman in her early forties explains:

> What is sacred is what is inviolable. Sacredness is what we will unconditionally believe in and rely on. I believe in Buddhism. For me, all temples are sacred. Honestly speaking, I don't feel that Shanghai has places that feel particularly sacred. Shanghai is a foreign precinct that holds a wide variety of cultures, but not a place in which I can feel sacredness. I go to a temple in Wuxi for worshipping Buddha. When I'm there, I can truly empty my mind, and then I can experience a feeling of sacredness.[14]

Here, the interviewee asserts several things: a personal commitment to a socially sanctioned creed, Buddhism, and the sacredness of the places where this creed translates into liturgical practices; the personal distance that the subject feels vis-à-vis places that do not channel the truth and mystery inherent to this creed; and, finally, the possibility of appropriating (or reappropriating) the experience that nurtures her faith by operating displacement.

A male office worker, age twenty-eight, expands on the same topic:

> Sacred language should lead to the Good, and mystical language should not be constrained by social codes. But what gives you a sense of the sacred? My first answer is "Young Pioneers and the Communist Party"! Does it mean I've been brainwashed? Well, [the sacred] must have to do with a mission, be a lifetime investment, serving others rather than oneself. "Sacredness" is rather abstract, rather subjective. For example, if you go to the extreme, look at ISIS — they may feel that what they do is sacred. For me personally, nothing is sacred. You use the word "sacred" when you think about fighting for a thing with your life, but for me now, there's nothing I want to risk my life for yet. . . . Religion refers to places of pilgrimage, places where something special happened. Religions have [sacred] mountains, temples, but, for example, hippies may have felt that Woodstock was sacred. The love of music may be something abstract, but it becomes more concrete when associated with a place. You start to worship this place; this place leaves a trace, gives you inspiration. Yes, a place can give you inspiration.[15]

Even as he places himself at some distance from both religious faiths and civic religion, the interviewee does assert that sacredness has to do with a mission, a sense of transcending oneself to a point that he realizes is currently alien to him. Yet the focus on space and pilgrimage is striking: a sacred place is charged with the feelings and practices that the pilgrim ascribes to it.

Being in such places may require traveling, but for other interviewees, they are simply at hand. Such is the case for a thirty-five-year-old mother of one:

> I think family happiness is sacred. The happiest thing in the world is to live without quarrels or trouble. Harmony is sacred. . . . I'm a Buddhist, but I think my faith is not of the kind [you find in people who have] deep faith. Why am I a Buddhist? Because Buddha gives me a feeling of stability, so I'll put my Buddhist faith into my family life; the feeling of serenity that Buddha gives me makes my family feeling serene. . . . Home is sacred. Home is not just a place; it is rather the feeling of being with family members. It does not need to be a family of three; it can be a big family. In my view, being a family, living in harmony, this kind of feeling is sacred.[16]

After the interviewee has located her beliefs within the framework of Buddhism, she focuses on the private realm and brings spiritual privacy and religious intimacies together. Here, intimacy takes a rather absolute expression, as family life and values become the quintessence of a religious ethos and practices. Family intimacy *is* religious intimacy, making home the ultimate and possibly sole sacred space.

CHAPTER 5

Religious Waterways

THE CHANNELS STRUCTURING THE RELIGIOUS GEOGRAPHY WE HAVE described function like waterways, forming a communication grid that links the areas and communities now included within Shanghai's administrative limits. Waterways provide transportation, waste disposal, and sources of drinking water. Within the early walled city of Shanghai, roads and paths followed the course of the five main creeks and their tributaries (map 9), spanned by more than a hundred bridges.[1] Water's pervasiveness also determined the composition of the city's population. During the nineteenth century, small boats, both a means of transportation and housing, settled along the waterways leading into the city.[2]

Traditional communities weave their places of worship into a nexus, emerging groupings shape their own networks, and "religious waterways" occasionally substitute for fixed spaces, creeds, and affiliations. The geographic mobility that a section of the Catholic population of the city experienced in the past is now lived and expressed in a different fashion. Daoism, popular religions, and Confucianism are "relocating" along new paths and connections, as is Buddhism, with Animal Release rituals carried out around the city's waterways. The irruption of new actors and groupings into the religious field also happens along waterways developed on the margins of the traditional religious field. The dynamism channeled throughout such networks makes Shanghai a field of forces: waterways crossing over landmarks, compounds, and private spaces, displacing sacredness from its original realm and infusing it into a recomposed urban body.

MAP 9. Shanghai Main Waterways

Catholic churches were often built on piers, some of which were later transformed into roads as the network of waterways began to recede. In the suburbs, many church buildings are still located on riverbanks. Conversely, a majority of Shanghai's Protestant churches were built along roadsides or on street corners.[3] The Catholic preference for piers and riverbanks can be explained partly by earlier implantation (as in the case of the riverside Sacred Heart of Jesus Church in Jiading, built in 1616) and partly by the fact that evangelization had been comparatively more successful with the fishermen, whose testimonies remain alive and potent today.

A Fishermen's Village

Qingpu District is Shanghai's westernmost district, adjacent to Jiangsu and Zhejiang. This part of the lower Yangzi region has always been advantageous for lake and river fishing, and a population of fishermen developed accordingly. They lived in boats on the lake and waterways. Fishermen were converted to Catholicism beginning in the late Ming period.[4] Today, their descendants take pride in this early conversion to the faith.

Fishermen were poorer than farmers and considered social outcasts, not integrated into the ritual nexus centered on the gods of the land. They found some protection in the missionaries and the network of churches. Until the mid-twentieth century, the fishing boats of Catholic families were moored in groups near the churches at nightfall, ensuring mutual protection.[5] The Church also provided fishermen with educational opportunities, receiving some of their children into parish boarding schools. Even when a section of this population became richer (sometimes much richer) after shifting from fishing to transportation and trade, they remained staunchly Catholic and supported charitable works at their parishes.[6]

Qingpu was home to the most important fishermen's settlement in the region. A 1948 study based on parish statistics estimates that, in Qingpu District, there were 4,686 Christian fishermen against 1,400 who were not. Fishermen in the Qingpu parishes worked in an area that extended from the vicinity of present-day downtown Shanghai in the east to Jinze in the west, and from Songjiang in the south to the Shanghai-Nanjing railroad in the north. Some families had given up the trade to focus on transportation, while another two hundred families left their boats to work on fish or crab dams.[7] This floating population held on to a good part of its customs and ways of life during the first decades of the new regime. However, at the beginning of the 1970s, the local government decided to group fishermen together in "fishery villages." Seven villages were created in Qingpu District, one for each of the townships that the district counted at that time. Today, the biggest village is in Baihe Township.

One of these villages is under the jurisdiction of Huaxin Township. Nowadays, Huaxin Fishery Village counts around eighty families, but most of them do not make their living fishing. When we first visited the village on a Sunday in September 2015, one woman estimated that only ten or twelve people are still truly engaged in the trade. Regardless, people here continue to proudly define themselves as "fishermen." Boats can be seen in front of most houses, and there are fishing supplies inside the homes. Villagers preferentially wed members of other fishery village families, reinforcing the fisherman identity. The two younger sisters of a man we met for lunch married into families of the Baihe fishery village.

Huaxin Fishery Village has no church. In the 1970s and early 1980s, people sought out underground priests for mass and sacraments. One of these priests who was ninety-seven years old at the time of our visit and living in Anting, Jiading District, had baptized at least thirty people from the village and was highly revered in Huaxin Village. However, from the end of the 1980s onward, people began going to the official Qingpu Immaculate Conception Church, an impressive riverside church quite a distance from the village.

In 2002, with the population ageing, the multifunction meeting hall located in the village and managed by the township was approved as a worship place. It could be legally used for performing mass every second Sunday of each month and also for solemnities. It is officially defined as a "prayer place" (*qidaosuo*), and the prayer books used by the assembly are inscribed with the words "Huaxin prayer place." This spacious communal meeting hall also hosts weddings and celebrations of all kinds. There is a kitchen at the entrance, and, farther in, a large meeting room, with chairs and hooks for hanging banners on the wall. There is also a back room where liturgical paraphernalia is stored.

One Sunday in September 2015, colorful banners decorate the wall, chairs are set out for the assembly, a table has been converted into an altar, and the Stations of the Cross hang on the wall. A little cabinet on the wall behind the altar is open, revealing a statue of the Virgin adorned with plastic flowers. At the entrance to the room is a table on top of which lies what would appear to be a coffin covered with a funeral banner. (At the end of the ceremony, when the room is cleaned up and the banner removed, it will appear that the banner was simply covering a shorter table put on the top of the first one.) At one end of the table, families place photographs of deceased relatives. Above the funeral banner are photographs of two late bishops of the Shanghai diocese: Fan Zhongliang (d. 2014), the underground bishop, and Jin Luxian (d. 2013), the official bishop, who was recognized as an "auxiliary bishop" by the Vatican.

Around eighty people are assembled in the hall, mostly adults and older people accompanied by children. The only young attendees are female, but the adults are split evenly between men and women. Men here play an important role in liturgies and church management, although a group of three women manages financial contributions. A young seminarian from Taiyuan diocese, Shanxi (a rural place where the majority of seminarians registered in the Shanghai diocese originate), directs the singing rehearsal, and the priest, who is from Chongqing, sits on a chair to hear the confessions of penitents who kneel or sit on either side. During the mass, attendees sing songs known throughout the Chinese-speaking Catholic world, with short intervals of chanting in Qingpu dialect.

Immediately after the mass, the whole assembly gathers around the makeshift ancestors' altar. Two men replace three banners on two sides of the room with black banners. The priest recites the ritual prayers, starting with invocations for the two dead bishops. The altar and photographs are incensed and sprinkled with holy water. During the ceremony, relatives take turns depositing banknotes in the casket beneath the altar. After the priest has finished reading the prayers, participants line up for the sprinkling of holy water. They do so slowly, at their own pace, while a group of men proceeds outside, where the priest presides over a blessing of the cars. As the procession nears its end, the banners are taken down and folded, all decorations and liturgical objects are stored in the back room, and the cabinet with the statue of the Virgin and plastic flowers is carefully closed. The church is gone, and the room has become an ordinary village meeting hall again.

The liturgy for the dead takes place after each monthly mass. Participants insist that it is much simpler than in the past, when a liturgy was performed separately for each family, and the rite could go on for a very long time. Nowadays, families are grouped together. One attendee notes that this is still the practice in Wuxi, and the local priest there often complains to devotees that he cannot spend all his time saying prayers for the dead. However, when he complains too much, some of the faithful threaten to look for an underground priest if prayers are not said the way they have always been said.

In March 2016, a funerary meal is held in the same communal hall, just before the Easter Vigil. An old woman from the village passed away on Holy Thursday, and prayers have just been recited at her home. More than two hundred people come from the fishing villages of Qingpu to attend the dinner. On this occasion, an entire fishermen's network comes into view, with everyone wearing a white funeral garment over his clothes. A Mr. Pan, who has come from Baihe, recalls that the deceased was like a mother to him after the untimely death of his parents. His ancestors were Catholics, and like his whole family, he has kept the faith. None of them joined the Communist Party, although he was sent to fight in Vietnam in 1979, at the age of nineteen or twenty. What happened then still torments him. Mr. Pan stays for the Easter Vigil that follows, as do a good number of the attendees. Once the Easter fire is kindled, a procession unfolds in the narrow streets of the village. Those who did not join the preliminary gathering kneel in front of their houses and then follow the procession after it has passed their homes (plate 33). As soon as the entire communal territory has been blessed by the circumambulation, the hall, fully decorated, becomes a hallowed worship space.

The fishermen exemplify a "networked community" defined less by territorial affiliation than by lineage solidarity. This solidarity was expressed both horizontally, when fishermen grouped around churches and in charitable networks, and vertically, through Catholic rituals for the dead that replaced the land-based ancestors worship, from which fishermen were excluded.

Massaging the Disciples' Feet

On the first day of the new year, a Friday in 2015, St. Francis Xavier Church seems almost empty. The 11:00 a.m. New Year's English-language mass has attracted only a modest audience. Shanghai appears subdued, its mood dampened by the stampede the night before that left thirty-six people dead on the Bund, not far from the church. The neighborhood, a formerly vibrant part of old Shanghai, is now a maze of half-destroyed houses and enigmatic building projects.

It is now early afternoon. Since early morning, more than thirty people have gathered at the parish quarters in a room of around sixty square meters, which feels very warm on this cold winter day. Attendees are divided into two groups. The smaller group is composed of seven beginners to whom Teacher Fan explains the basic principles and techniques of foot massage. Teacher Fan has a textbook open on her lap, and she sometimes points to a diagram or presses the foot of an elderly woman sitting across from her as she illustrates the ways of acupressure. The second group, directed by Teacher Wang, comprises around twenty-five students, mostly women, divided into pairs who alternately receive and give massage. Teacher Wang is experienced in foot massage technique. She is a middle-school chemistry teacher who has come all the way from Handan City, in Hebei. At times, her instructions sound like the information provided by a typical health-related television program: "You can assess the health of someone by looking at the color of his foot. . . . The human body is an integrated whole. . . . Foot massage can solve many problems. There are five lines in a toe, each one like a cable connecting to a specific part of the body. For instance, the right big toe is associated with the left eye. Reflexology comes from the West, but the cartography of the body in Chinese medicine is different." At other times, her manner of speech reveals her Catholic background: "God has created humans as an organic whole, so when you don't know which organ has problems but just feel pain in your body, do a whole-set massage of the feet. Doing a whole-set massage is entrusting yourself and the body to God. . . . Each massage is directed toward someone in particular."

Today's training session gathers dedicated Catholics from five or six parishes. They have pledged to learn the trade in order to assist in the teaching of migrant workers, who, it is hoped, will be able to earn a living using the newly acquired skills. During January, the volunteers will undergo three days of instruction. They will then assist Teacher Wang in training thirty-five migrant workers in another three-day session. The project has been well thought out and planned. Teacher Wang's Hebei-based team is an officially recognized training center that awards certificates recognized by the Labor Affairs Office. Team members intend to help in setting up a branch in Shanghai. A local charity that focuses on migrant workers, founded in Shanghai by an Australian priest and a few expatriates, meant to seek out job opportunities for the newly trained migrants. Some local Catholics are even thinking of starting a company that will provide foot-massage service. But what is the goal of the project? And what does foot massage have to do with the Church?

Mr. Ren, a retired university professor and an active member of the Zhangjialou Sacred Heart Parish in Pudong offers an answer to the first question. His connection with Catholicism started with his interest in photography. "At first, I just wanted to take pictures of church buildings, and then through the buildings I met with priests. I talked with them, learning more and more about the faith. Finally, I became a Catholic. Now I come to the parish two or three times a week, for mass and activities. Even if I don't come to church, I spend a lot of time on photos and classical music, which for me are one with my faith."

Mr. Ren taught biology. He believes that people with health problems should request medical help rather than rely on prayer. However, he has met many believers who pray not only for psychological relief but also because they have been disappointed with medical help or cannot afford to be treated in the hospital. The matter has gradually shifted from an intellectual concern to a cause for action. So Mr. Ren has joined a group of five people overseeing the foot massage project. Its initiators are still debating the project's goals and methods. Evangelization through healing is key for some, job opportunities for migrants are the main motivation for other members, and self-help and the training offered to Catholics inspire the efforts of the others. Discussions on WeChat about organizing the program are sometimes heated but usually conclude with the recognition that everyone means well, because they are working together for God and the Church. Still, some problems prove difficult to resolve. Most organizers come from the Zhangjialou parish, but sessions do not take place there, as the parish priest seems to be suspicious of their motives. Not all members of the clergy harbor doubts, however. There are two priests in today's group, one a newcomer and the other already well trained in acupressure. The trained priest notes that he considers foot massage, a practice that helps believers relate to God's healing action through the whole of their souls and bodies, an antidote to an abstract spiritual outlook. As for Mr. Ren, he stresses that the Church's social concern is the best channel for evangelizing people who have never heard about the faith. He points to the large cross that stands on the wall behind the practicing pairs, an excellent reminder that this is indeed a faith-based initiative, he remarks.

The interest in foot massage started with Father Josef Eugster (Wu Ruoshi), a Swiss priest from the Bethlehem Missionary Society who has lived in Taiwan for several decades and became an apostle of reflexology.[8] The method he developed has spread Taiwanese-style reflexology throughout Asia. Teacher Fan holds one of the books published on the Chinese mainland by Father Eugster. Catholics in China were quick to notice the popularity of this foreign priest-turned-healer and appropriated reflexology for evangelization purposes. Some of them see it as spiritual healing with Catholic characteristics, in contrast to the Evangelicals' reliance on prayer. A training center was established in Hebei, which Father Eugster visited several times. This, in turn, caught the attention of Shanghai Catholics. International, national, and local Catholic networks now revolve around reflexology.

In August 2015, three sessions, each lasting four days, were held in different churches. The project had been affected by several changes. Parishioners who were willing to both learn and serve proved to be scarce. In contrast, the project reached out to a number of migrant families, who were willing to learn because foot massage alleviated various ailments afflicting their children. Very few envisioned foot massage as a possible trade but thought of it as an alternative health-care method. Mr. Ren decided to concentrate on this goal and eventually sacrificed his commitments in the parish in order to concentrate on foot-massage education. The project has been an effective way of dealing with the conflict between his scientific upbringing and the faith he has embraced.

The foot-massage project received new impetus in April 2016, when Father Eugster visited Shanghai with four Taiwanese assistants. Fifty-five local Catholics paid a registration fee of ¥200 each for a two-day training session in the spacious compound of the main church on Chongming Island, an alluvial island at the mouth of the Yangzi River, part of Shanghai Municipality. Most of the teaching is done by volunteers from Taidong, Taiwan, with Father Eugster ensuring benevolent and mostly silent supervision. The last afternoon focuses on "mission," with one of the Taiwanese volunteers introducing the ways foot massage can help families or elderly people, thus promoting Catholicism through service to others. The session concludes with a mass and a pledge to serve society and the Church through foot massage. Participants receive a certificate solemnizing their commitment. Teacher Wang even dreams of starting a lay "third order" centered on foot-massage service. A final day of training for the larger public takes place in the city, with fees taken in the morning, and a free session offered at St. Francis Xavier in the afternoon, which more than 150 people attend. However, some people go home disappointed after finding out that taking pictures with the founder of reflexology is prohibited, so as to avoid commercial appropriation.

In July 2017, Liang and Benoît meet again with the core leadership of the network, which has recently started to rent some space in a small Protestant church in northern Pudong, near the end of metro line 6. Courses and therapy will soon be offered there. The network retains an "itinerant" character, going to parishes and other places to offer treatment and instruction, but the process of institutionalization is under way. At the same time, it keeps its translocal character: leaders come from both official and underground communities; they interact with the Protestant congregation from which they rent office space, a fact unusual for a Catholic grouping; they share a number of stories about how unwelcoming local congregations can be and how much they wish to contribute to changing Shanghai's Catholic outlook. The network still tries to balance a desire to preserve its fluidity with the need it senses to anchor at some suitable place on Shanghai's religious waterways.

The Rainbow Warriors

One evening in February 2015, in an apartment on West Zhongshan Road, a Christian ecumenical Bible study group is meeting. The two women and five men are part of a gay and lesbian fellowship that regularly connects through an active WeChat group. Two participants come from Shaanxi and Jiangsu. One of the women is from Taiwan and arrived in Shanghai only a year ago. The apartment owner has returned to Singapore for the Chinese New Year holiday.

One man, around thirty-five years old, guides the group in reading sections of Psalm 35. He asks, "How should we react to someone who insults us?" A shy silence follows, and then the discussion begins. It is clear that the group is looking for guidance and support from the text for situations they experience in their daily lives. "We must release our pain to God and ask the Holy Spirit to come upon us," says the leader. Except for the woman from Taiwan, who converted in 1999, no one present has been a Christian for more than six years. After a break at around nine, the session continues with thirty minutes of open prayer, during which almost everyone speaks up.

The group and the other members of the network used to meet at St. Peter's Church, with the support of the parish priest. After a while, some parishioners petitioned against their presence. The priest was going to allow them to continue, but the leader of the group decided against it. There are conflicting versions of this story. Some of our interlocutors hinted that the nature of the network was not the only reason some parishioners felt uncomfortable; instead, the main reason may have been that although a Catholic was one of the main initiators of the network, a pastor had been invited to speak at a meeting held at the parish.

There are actually two, closely associated networks. The nationwide, ecumenical Rainbow Witness Fellowship (Caihong Jianzheng Tuanqi) started in 2009 and established its first branches in Beijing, Shanghai, and Hangzhou. It maintains contact with similar groups in Shenzhen, Chengdu, Chongqing, Fuzhou, and Wenzhou. In 2013, in close association with the fellowship, some of its members, along with a seminarian from Hebei, started a subsidiary network, China Catholic Rainbow Community (Tianzhu Caihong Tuanti). The main reason for initiating a new network was the fact that Catholic members of the Rainbow Witness Fellowship (including around twenty who had converted from Protestantism) were seeking more thriving liturgical activities, especially mass attended in common. The China Catholic Rainbow Community placed itself under the patronage of Our Lady of Seven Sorrows and J. H. Cardinal Newman. A brochure presents the group's aims as "providing counseling and spiritual companionship for LGBT Catholic believers, dedicated to promoting the full integration of individuals' body and soul; and engaging in peaceful and rational dialogue with the Church." Both networks offer support, education in the faith, and advocacy. In Shanghai, both networks jointly organize all activities. For instance, they held a retreat in Sheshan in 2014 and 2015. Most of the fifty or so people who attended were Protestant, but at the end of the gathering, all members went to the top of Sheshan for common prayer. In 2014, all participants undertook the Way of the Cross. In 2016, a national retreat took place in Hangzhou.

On January 24, 2016, the Shanghai Rainbow Witness Fellowship met, as it does every Sunday afternoon, in a large apartment close to the Guilin metro stop. The community subsidizes the apartment rent, and the five young men who live there often host other members of the community in times of need. It serves approximately eighty people and has a weekly attendance of around fifty. However, as this particular Sunday is abnormally cold and just a week before the Chinese New Year holiday, only sixteen men and three women attend. When all are comfortably seated, the gathering starts with singing accompanied by a keyboard and harp. Lyrics to Christian songs are projected on the wall against images of butterflies in flight, cats lit by sunlight, and raindrops on windows. After the opening songs, each attendee greets the others individually with a hug and the words "Jesus loves you." Every week, a selected member or visiting speaker delivers a two-hour lecture.

On this Sunday, Eros, the cofounder of both the Shanghai Rainbow Witness Fellowship and the China Catholic Rainbow Community, gives a talk on the basis of Christian meditation. His charismatic presentation is followed by a thirty-minute meditation, the start and end of which are announced by the striking of a Tibetan singing bowl. The assembly then breaks into two groups, sharing experiences, worries, and expectations. Eros is deeply involved in collecting and publishing the testimonies of Chinese gay Christians. In October 2015, he was the sole Chinese representative at the first Global Network of Rainbow Catholics' four-day conference in Rome, during the second Synod on the Family, and was also chosen to convene the steering group of the network's youth branch.

On Sunday afternoon, April 24, 2016, the Rainbow Witness Fellowship holds its first "worship concert" (plate 41), in a gay club in Shanghai Stadium.

Around 120 young men and a few women gather around the stage. Many are wearing T-shirts printed with "Rising to the light" (*zai guangzhong xingqi*); onstage, members of the worship band are wearing the same T-shirt in black. Photographers are reminded courteously not to record any faces. The event, scheduled from 2:00 to 6:00 p.m., combines prayers, teaching, and worship songs, with most attendees arriving before and staying well after the event. This first worship concert organized by the Rainbow Witness Fellowship in China had to take place in this city, notes Eros, because "Shanghai is special. The community is much more resourceful and stronger here."

◆ ◆ ◆

Despite obvious differences, there are several similarities among the fishermen, the informal foot-massage network, and the China Catholic Rainbow Community. All clearly share in the Church's heritage, but not primarily through parish anchorage. "Locality" is not what determines religious interaction. Rather, a form of marginality, more or less clearly perceived and recognized, fosters a sense of fellowship. This dimension is present, for example, in the foot-massage project. Mr. Ren, the project's leader, was converted late in life and is dissatisfied with the parish routine; many active participants are affected by illness, directly or through family members, and combine a desire for self-healing with an urge to help others; and the goal of benefiting marginalized migrant workers remains firmly anchored in the group's consciousness. This illustrates a latent dissatisfaction with the close-knit sociability that characterizes parish life.

These three cases do not illustrate the full range of Catholic networking styles. A group of Wenzhou entrepreneurs provides a different configuration. Father Tan (pseud.) has ministered to the group since 2006. These entrepreneurs often manage the Shanghai branches of their businesses, residing in the city for a few years while remaining strongly connected to their original community. Their solidarity network is reminiscent of the many local associations that were active in Shanghai from the mid-eighteenth century to the end of the 1930s. Historian Frederic Wakeman and others have labeled such people "sojourners."[9] Catholic Wenzhou businesspeople gather for Christmas, Easter, Mid-Autumn Festival, and a few other occasions. They organize two one-day retreats a year and regularly visit sick people from Wenzhou, as Shanghai hospitals attract well-to-do Wenzhou people. Three hundred to four hundred people usually attend the Christmas Party, which Wenzhou people call "Christmas Wine" (Shengdanjiu), as the food is meant to be exceptional on this day. In September 2015, the association's leadership was lunching at a restaurant close to Father Tan's parish, and we met there with a businessman whose younger brother is a priest, trained in France and

Germany. Now back in China, this priest manages a local Catholic charity founded with his shares in the family business. The charity is notably active in Guizhou and Yunnan. Such a circle can maintain features typical of a Chinese professional network. During the lunch, a member asked the association's chairman for the phone number of his wife, whose cousin is married to the daughter of one of Deng Xiaoping's nieces. The chairman eventually rejected the request with a joke.

Throughout Shanghai, other religious networks share many of the features found in the Catholic constellation. Charities often provide people of the same religion the channel through which to trespass local or parochial boundaries. In November 2014, Imam Jin Hongwei, leader of the Xiao Taoyuan Mosque and the Shanghai branch of the Islamic Association of China, describes the mosque's and the association's charitable endeavors. The key person happens to be Maryam, (pseud.), a Singaporean Muslim who supervises projects throughout China. Each year, sometime before Eid al-Adha, Maryam posts notices of suggested donations, for example, a sheep costs around ¥1,000; if a Shanghai-based Muslim does not intend to sacrifice, he can donate the monetary equivalent. After collecting all the donations, Maryam buys sheep from local farmers so that Muslims in Ningxia or Anhui may participate in the festival. With around a thousand sheep bought every year, it is a considerable operation. Maryam shares many pictures of the religious festivals held in rural areas online in order to establish trust and generate interest on all sides. Her brother leads similar endeavors, such as financing the digging of wells in northern China's Muslim villages.

RECLAIMING TERRITORIES:
POPULAR, DAOIST, AND CONFUCIAN NETWORKS

While Huaxin Fishery Village in Huaxin Township is home to the descendants of a population whose marginality probably encouraged the embrace of a new faith, neighboring settlements illustrate the situation prevalent in the region: wet rice-growing peasants were also making ample use of the waterways' system and developing a variety of handicraft skills, notably in cotton processing. On the westernmost tip of Qingpu District, Jinze Township has developed around the banks of Dianshan Lake and is bordered by both Jiangsu and Zhejiang. Along the waterways of this old town, sixty-six kilometers from the center of the metropolis, the visitor starts to feel the pulse of the Jiangnan Delta, a region traditionally known for its cottage industries and a dense communications network used by peasants, craftsmen, and merchants.[10] The intertwined economic and ritual networks that fostered the clusters of settlements were far more important than the particular village identities.

Jinze was situated just one kilometer away from the Grand Canal, on a section linking Suzhou and Hangzhou, and its fortunes or vicissitudes through history were heavily dependent on this major route. Bridges crisscrossed its channels, each bridge flanked by a temple. During some periods, there may have been up to forty-two bridges and forty-two temples, though only seven bridges are still in use.[11] By around 1930, there were twenty-three bridges and twenty-eight temples.[12] Today, Jinze's inhabitants number around sixty-two thousand, a large proportion of whom are elderly people. The place is becoming a tourist attraction, albeit on a modest scale compared to the neighboring Zhujiajiao water town.

According to official statistics, Jinze counts five places of worship: one Protestant church, one Catholic parish, and three Buddhist temples. The figure is misleading in many ways. First, two of the three temples are in fact not Buddhist; the devotional style and deities worshipped are fully inscribed into the popular religiosity typical of the region. Local officials and Buddhist monks openly acknowledge this fact, explaining that there were no Daoist priests to take care of the temples at the time they were reopened. The Buddhist Association was thus put in charge. The nine monks residing at Yihao Temple (Yihao Chansi), the only genuine Buddhist temple in the township, describe their role as mere caretakers of the two other places of worship. However, officials also recognize that taking these temples away from the Buddhist Association would create major difficulties, as the revenue these temples generate is far greater than that obtained from Yihao Temple.

Additionally, governmental records induce a skewed representation of Jinze's religious vitality because there may be no other place in Greater Shanghai where so many unofficial sites of worship operate openly. In the local parlance, these places are called "little temples" (*xiao miao*). These "little temples" are simultaneously invisible and visible for all to see. On festival days, as well as on the first and fifteenth days of the lunar month, people congregate near the bridges. In some places, families have built and manage makeshift structures; in other places, where temples were destroyed in the anti-Japanese war, a plaque or a few remains may be on display. But in most cases, worshippers light incense and pray, individually or in small groups, in the open, somewhere between the bridge and the adjacent public toilets. The presence of public facilities reveals a hidden side of the story. During the Cultural Revolution, temples aligned along the bridges were converted into hygienic facilities.[13] These structures have since been renovated, but their locations still mark the places where neighborhood temples used to stand. Dilapidated houses in the fields also shelter little altars where people burn incense (plate 36). Local officials estimate that there are more than twenty "little temples." Historian Atsutoshi Hamashima refers to the "temple sphere" (*miaojie*) in describing a congregation of households assembled around a worship place.[14] Although he restricts the term to the cult of local earth gods, it can be applied to the way temples defined (and are still defining in absentia) the sense of place and social networks in Jinze.

The ritual cycle of Jinze is organized around two festivals. The first coincides with the anniversary of Dongyue, the Supreme God of Mount Tai (Dongyue Dadi), on the twenty-eighth day of the third lunar month. The festival begins three days before the anniversary day itself. The second one, on the ninth day of the ninth lunar month, celebrates the Double Yang Festival, a time for showing filial respect to both the living and the dead. On both occasions, however, the focal point of worship is Yang Zhen, or, as he is usually called, Lord Yang (Yang Laoye), a deity who enjoys great popularity in Jiangnan. Yang Zhen was an incorruptible high official of the Eastern Han dynasty who committed suicide in 124 as a protest against the moral and political demise of the empire. Among other anecdotes, one concerns his reply to a solicitor who assured him nobody would know of the gold he was proposing to give him: "Heavens would know, Earth would know, I would, and you would. Then who wouldn't?" But are Jinze's inhabitants really worshipping the historical Yang Zhen? Even if there is no doubt that the temple is dedicated to this figure, there is a variety of Lord Yangs in Jiangnan. Many are praiseworthy officials. Another Lord Yang is a woman from Cangnan County, in Zhejiang, who saved sailors from an assault by pirates. Whoever Lord Yang may be, he inspires steadfast devotion. In Jinze, between 30 to 50 percent of people over sixty have been placed under the patronage (*ji ming*) of Lord Yang. The custom disappeared after 1960 but has been revived (especially among teenagers preparing for exams), though without adopting the Yang family name, as was often done in the past.[15]

Construction on Yang Zhen Temple in Jinze began in 1999, and it was recognized as an official worship place only in 2009. The temple was built on the site of the Posterior Hall of the former Dongyue Temple, which had been dedicated to worshipping the God of Mount Tai. In Jinze, therefore, this god's anniversary is celebrated in Yang Zhen Temple. Worship begins in front of the Dongyue statue; an adjacent shrine is composed of statues of Lord Yang's three wives. Somehow, the people's deity has been substituting for the one put forward by the authorities. Dongyue is a "state god" (a status confirmed by the conversion of many Dongyue temples into city god temples during the Ming period), in contrast to Lord Yang's local anchorage.

Besides Yang Zhen Temple, the other temple that was officially recognized in 2009 is the General Manager Temple (Zongguan Miao), placed under the patronage of Jin Yuanqi (also known as Jin Zongguan).[16] The term *zongguan* corresponds to a variety of higher administrative positions, but since the late Yuan dynasty, it has been associated in the Jiangnan region with the protection of tax grain transport by commanders of seaborne squadrons. Around

Jiangnan, Jin Zongguan appears in diverse incarnations, always as a fearless and selfless official who was sometimes said to have distributed state-owned grain to the people in a time of famine and subsequently committed suicide in atonement for his unlawful (as his gesture was not state-sanctioned) act of benevolence.[17] Some ritual texts present Jin Yuanqi as a Song dynasty official who lived near Dianshan Lake and, after his death, aided mariners on the sea.[18] In Jinze, he is familiarly presented as Yang Zhen's uncle. Yang Zhen's statue stands to the right of the General Manager's, and a collective deity, the incarnation of all Lord Yangs, stands to its left. Zongguan is a "people's god," as illustrated by the following anecdote: In 1846, Zongguan was one of four gods punished by the Prefect of Suzhou because oracles attributed to him had incited peasants to rebel. The deity's image was bound and exposed in the city god temple, a punishment akin to being exhibited wearing a cangue.[19]

On festival days, visitors to the Jinze temples arrive by bus from the neighboring cities of Jiangsu and Zhejiang. Places where the Yang Zhen Temple was reputed to possess a particular spiritual power (ling) are linked to Jinze by waterways and trade networks. Locals and visitors from the region follow the Jiangnan custom of burning incense in ten temples in one day, a feat made much easier by pilgrimages that have become organized bus tours.[20] Jinze's three operating temples (Yang Zhen Temple, General Manager Temple, and Yihao Temple) are at the center of a devotional sphere that encompasses the part of Jiangnan that covers the western area of Shanghai municipality and adjacent localities in Jiangsu and Zhejiang. Devotional associations in the surrounding townships and cities organize pilgrimages to these sites. As a ritual center, Jinze is also integrated into a larger worshipping territory that includes the celebrated temples of Lingyin in Hangzhou and Bao'en in Suzhou.[21]

Traditionally, pilgrims circumambulated both inside a given temple and within a nexus of temples. Inside the temple, the circuit along which deities were worshipped depended on their respective ranking in the celestial hierarchy, as well as their perceived capacity to answer specific petitions. Similar criteria were applied when determining the circuit the pilgrimage would follow. As temples are much less numerous than in the past, and as collective memories have been affected by political and cultural transformations, ritual circuits are more flexible than they used to be. Nevertheless, Jinze's older pilgrims offer clear indications of the ideal order to follow when visiting gods and temples.

May 5, 2016, corresponds to the twenty-eighth day of the third lunar month, the final day of the festival. Several devotional groups (xianghui) from the region have converged on Jinze.[22] In a back courtyard of Yang Zhen Temple, one group from Jiaxing City attracts special attention. Jiaxing, located in northern Zhejiang, lies on the Grand Canal. The city is an important center of the trade and transportation network that defined the region's culture and economy. The Jiaxing-based "Jiangnan Fishing Boats Association" (Jiangnan Wangchuanhui) introduces itself as a worshipping group descended from popular devotional communities dating back to the Song dynasty.[23] Members participate in temple festivals across the region, exhibiting their skill at suspending gongs or incense burners attached to fishing hooks inserted into their forearms (*zharou tixiang*). With gongs, drums, and flags, they solemnly turn around the compound of Yang Zhen Temple before starting a long procession around the township.

The custom of suspending weights from hooks attached to the flesh, as well as the large portions of meat deposited on the altars of Yang Zhen Temple, indicate the sacrificial nature of the rituals performed and the role of medium-spirits (*wushi*) in the process. And, indeed, present-day "devotional-group leaders" (*xiangtou*), mostly women over forty, are also spiritual intermediaries. In the Jiaxing community, the group leader is an old man who ensures through the incantations he delivers that the act of suspending weights from one's forearm will not result in blood spilling, a most inauspicious omen.

As noted by historian Li Tiangang, religious practices still observed in Jinze and other places in the Jiangnan Delta region shed light on the relationship between state and local cults during the Ming and Qing periods.[24] The "religious economy" at work can be described as follows: First, popular devotions were directed toward the gods entered in the "state register of sacrifices" (*sidian*), such as Dongyue and Guandi, on the one hand, and toward those deities who expressed the ethos and identity of a given territory (Yang Zhen and Zongguan in Jinze and the areas around Dianshan Lake), on the other. Second, even though many local gods were listed in the official register, their cults were still regarded with some suspicion by the authorities and were occasionally restricted. Third, worshippers were organizing the gods (and the temples in which they dwelled) into an imaginary geography and hierarchy, distributing specific roles to deities within the netherworld's administration. Some of these roles were changing according to economic and political transformations. (For instance, Zongguan was first tasked with the safety of maritime transport and then invoked as a grain supplier when the restoration of the Grand Canal made sea transportation irrelevant.) Officials presided over state sacrifices performed twice a year for the city god, and local communities took care of sacrifices to lower deities. Once the state sacrifice had been performed, the same communities also organized the processions of the gods worshipped throughout their territories. Both state-sanctioned and popular sacrificial systems were Confucian in that they extolled a common set of virtues — integrity, filial piety, and devotion to the common good—which, in the storied lives of the deities, often led them to sacrifice their earthly existence.

Jinze's current religious pattern presents some similarities to the one recorded in the Ming and Qing periods. The state recognizes and monitors temples, and it even participates in organizing large-scale festivals. It also unofficially condones worship at nonofficial sites, as long as these activities remain consistent with the values and practices observed at officially recognized places. This twofold worship system is the locus around which a microregion reformulates its memory, identity, and network of connections. Weakened by a restricted religious supply and historical traumas, Jinze's religious geography does not coincide with the community's mental mapping as it did in the past. Still, with its mix of popular Confucianism, Daoist rituals, and Buddhist devotions, Jinze's worship system continues to articulate a local, regional, and national sense of belonging in a remarkably resilient synthesis.

DAOISM AND THE LANGUAGES OF MODERNITY

Although Jinze is part of the administrative territory of Shanghai, its religiosity differs widely from religious expressions found downtown. Already weakened by the systematic state-led dismantling of its tradition from the 1950s to the early 1980s, Daoism (and the form of popular religiosity lived and expressed through its networks of temples and masters) had to deal with the cultural and communal transformations that later reshaped Shanghai (map 10). Analyzing the curriculum and teaching methods used at Shanghai Daoist College (Shanghai Daojiao Xueyuan), Der-Ruey Yang, a Taiwanese scholar, discusses the passage from "rituals skills" to "discursive knowledge," concluding that "this 'paradigm shift' . . . derives from an acute sense of a crisis of legitimacy, or even survival, of Daoism that is now widely shared among the Daoist clergy."[25]

When the state and the Daoist National Association collaborated in creating the college in 1985, Shanghai Daoism was in dire need of new, trained masters. A basic learning course was first organized and taught at White Clouds Monastery. The first class graduated in 1989, when thirty-three men received their degrees. Political turmoil affected the college, and it did not reopen until 1992. Since then, it has been training students and holding graduation ceremonies every three years. The college's educational system differs sharply from the apprenticeship tradition. Daoist lineages provided the young students, with preliminary family training centered on literacy and musical practice. The teenager was then sent to a master who did not belong to his family or lineage and learned ritual skills. Further family training combined with practical work followed, and esoteric skills kept in one's

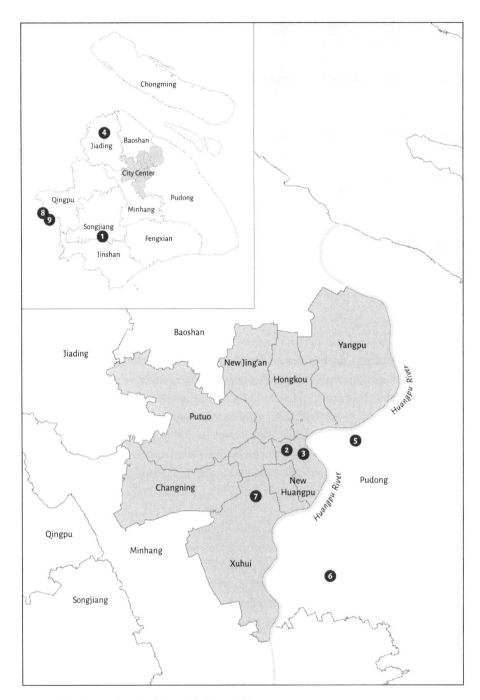

MAP 10. Daoist and Daoist-Related Fieldwork Sites

1 Dongyue Temple
2 White Clouds Monastery
3 City God Temple of Shanghai
4 City God Temple of Jiading
5 Qinciyang Hall Temple
6 Sanlin Chongfu Temple
7 Shanghai Qigong Institute
8 Zongguan Temple
9 Yangzhen Temple

family were taught at this stage. Students desiring to ascend as far as possible in the Daoist priestly tradition then entered an advanced apprenticeship under a senior master. A succession of exams and ordination documents confirmed the supernatural powers they had acquired through their mastery of a range of ritual skills that could be deepened by traveling to renowned temples.[26] The knowledge acquired centered initially on learning wind and percussion ritual instruments, writing and reciting scriptures, setting up and decorating altars, and making and drawing ritual artifacts and pictures. Once apprentices had mastered these basic skills, they could draw talismans, recite incantations, execute the right ritual gestures, and "dance out" magical charts. The efficacy of the rituals performed eventually depended both on the ability of the performer to communicate with divine powers through such skills and on his formal recognition by the heavenly bureaucracy, as confirmed by the certificates conferred on him. The cultivation of inner capacities and the quest for external confirmation were both necessary for the making of a full-fledged Daoist master.

In present-day Shanghai, Daoist schooling functions on an utterly different model. Lectures are at the core of the system; political and academic education (including theoretical and historical initiation to Daoism) is only partly balanced by instruction in some ritual skills (especially music and the reading of scriptures). The Daoist leadership encourages students to focus on academic knowledge so as to train a few scholars who may honorably represent Daoism in politics and lobbying. Daoist leaders are convinced that the capacity of a younger generation to expound doctrine through talks and media presence is a crucial factor in the survival of Daoism. Earning social respect and inserting themselves into larger social networks are goals shared by Daoist students and a number of their teachers: "The Daoist clergy in contemporary Shanghai has been caught up in the obsession with legitimizing itself through the others."[27]

The college is now located in the fully rebuilt Dongyue Temple (Dongyue Xinggong) in Songjiang District (plate 39). At the time of our visit in January 2014, fifty students between the ages of seventeen and twenty-seven resided there. History, English, Daoist doctrine, and music were key courses, and a daily meditation time had been added to the curriculum. The schooling is supposed to cultivate three basic capacities: knowledge of Daoism, managerial skills, and the ability to propagate the doctrine. In addition to the three years offered by any vocational training school (the original academic classification of the college), one more year is now prescribed, allowing students to obtain a BA degree in philosophy or religious studies from China East Normal University.

The "discursive nature" of contemporary Daoism is also manifested in the way the worship of Taisui is advertised. This deity is quite popular in today's Shanghai, as he reigns over individual (contrasted with communal) destinies. Especially at the time of Chinese New Year, all Daoist temples in Shanghai are filled with bright posters explaining how to assess one's destiny with regard to the sexagenary cycle and what ritual should be performed to rectify possible infelicities.[28] The "territory" reclaimed here is not primarily of a physical nature. Within the urban nexus, Daoism looks for legitimacy based on its body of knowledge regarding personal and cosmic equilibriums. The discourse through which this new position is justified borrows from both traditional culture and "scientific" justifications.

In this regard, Daoism should have benefited from the popularity that surrounds traditional practices such as tai chi and modern reinterpretations of martial arts therapy, exemplified by the various schools of *qigong*. All these practices are anchored to a common cosmological outlook but adapt well to modernity. In Shanghai, during the 1990s, Daoism certainly benefited from the interest in health and longevity techniques. In this period of transition, part of the Daoist tradition was reconstructed in the guise of martial arts. Some former foreign students of Fudan University remember their apprenticeship in the "art of spontaneous movements" (*zifa donggong*), a form of tai chi, under the direction of Master Shen Hongxun (1939–2011).[29] The classes were held on the lower level of a restaurant in Hongkou. At that time, different schools of *qigong* and tai chi were competing for the favor of urbanites in search of health-enhancing practices and inner balance. The repression that followed the fall of the Falun Gong movement in 1999 signaled the end of such semi-religious popular rebuilding.

Just before 1949, the year the new regime was founded, a small group of People's Liberation Army cadres had systematized ancient techniques of bodily cultivation under the label *qigong*, which they presented as a therapeutic method that harmonized traditional wisdom and the new scientific spirit.[30] The term *qigong* is indeed loaded with Daoist and medical overtones, thus taking on a new meaning as it sought to unify a corpus of techniques and beliefs anchored in a variety of local and sectarian traditions. The "invention" of *qigong* helped the Party and the state integrate practitioners of Chinese medicine with the ideological orthodoxy and the new health-care systems. However, during the Cultural Revolution, *qigong* was declared part of the corpus of old superstitions, and its practice was forbidden. Through the avowed support of important members of the state apparatus, *qigong* was rehabilitated in 1979. During the years that followed, "*qigong* fever" spread throughout China. At the same time, *qigong* practices were amalgamated into the craze for paranormal phenomena, especially the so-called extraordinary functions that *qigong* masters were often supposed to possess and display. *Qigong* fever was by no means limited to uneducated people. On the contrary, the most ardent supporters of the study and promotion of "extraordinary functions" were scientists who aimed to develop a new "somatic science" (*renti kexue*) integrating the best of China's body culture with the procedures of scientific inquiry. A plethora of masters taught disciples not only bodily, mental, and respiratory techniques but healing and "magical" methods as well. The lineages that composed the *qigong* world were federated through a channel of semi-official associations. Mass activities and conferences, television programs, press articles, colloquiums, and publications nurtured the myth of the *qigong* master, miracle man and promoter of the most advanced scientific theories.

Doubtful practices and sheer charlatanism slowly undermined the credibility of the *qigong* world. After 1989, the state reasserted its control of civil society. Though it failed for several years to effectively "rectify" the creeds and commercial activities of *qigong* associations and masters, it showed far more severity from 1995 onward, after a number of scientists and media people vigorously renewed their attacks on what they perceived to be sectarian movements gone out of control. The struggle proved to be uneasy, as *qigong* associations had grown more sophisticated, relying on commercial networks and cultural proselytism. Even bolder than its competitors, the Falun Gong movement was soon on a collision course with the authorities, as it seemed to directly challenge the Party's control of "spiritual civilization" (*jingshen wenming*). The demonstration it organized in April 1999, in front of Zhongnanhai — the central headquarters for the Party in China and the government in Beijing — went one step too far. Threatened at its core, the Party organized a systematic repression that not only crushed Falun Gong but also reduced other *qigong* organizations to silence.

In 2015 and 2016, visits to the Shanghai Qigong Institute (Shanghaishi Qigong Yanjiusuo), located in Xuhui District, testify to the break between Daoism per se and health-related practices. Established in 1984, the institute is attached to the Shanghai University of Traditional Chinese Medicine and flourished during the following decade. The small museum inside the institute recalls the roots of *qigong* theory and practice, including associations with Daoism, Buddhism, and popular traditions, and introduces visitors to medical perspectives on *qigong* techniques. Institutes such as this one are attached to the Ministry of Health, while the Ministry of Physical Education supervises other practitioners. If the institute offers free lessons to the public, it does so with caution, and keeps audiences modest in number. Its main networking activities take place with foreign institutions; interest in *qigong* seems to be more developed abroad and certainly does not encounter the political complications that continue to hamper its expression in China. While stressing the link between *qigong* and traditional culture, the institute's teachers and staff downplay its connections with religious Daoism, about which they seem to know very little. They also recognize that in Shanghai, *qigong* and tai chi have been largely supplanted by yoga.

However, numerous groups continue to practice one form or another of Daoist *qigong*-like traditions, even if they prefer to do so in a private or semi-private setting. On April 4, 2016, eight "muscle-bone strengthening" (*yijin-jing*) practitioners listen to the teacher's lecture on "peace of mind" at Zen One Clubhouse. Yan Weibing holds lectures throughout China, propounding a technique that relies on imitating the movements of animals, such as birds flying and landing. Practicing together is an important element of the program, as it fosters "a stronger energy field." Both teachers and students regard muscle-bone strengthening exercise as a form of "ascetic practice" (*xiuxing*) grounded in Daoism. One student comments that she felt the effect much more quickly than when she practiced yoga.

Daoist traditions still foster communal affiliations in peripheral parts of Shanghai, but worshippers at urban temples come on a personal or family basis, mainly for rituals linked to anxieties about one's own fortune (*ming-yun*). The small number of Daoist temples in central Shanghai contrasts with the relative abundance of Buddhist sanctuaries, to which the faithful will subsequently turn. On a visit to Baoshan Temple, we saw Daoist-like fortune-tellers lingering in the doorways of the Buddhist complex. In more ways than one, Daoism is indeed located at the periphery, even if a number of its traditional beliefs and practices have been absorbed by the social body as a whole. The promotion of "Daoist literacy" tries to create a new territory for this religious tradition, at the junction of traditional Chinese culture and the language of modernity. The parallel development of bodily techniques aimed at mental and physical well-being could legitimize and reinforce such a quest. However, political predicaments as well as the development of alternative offers have hindered this redeployment. In present-day Shanghai, Daoism's territory remains fragile and threatened. Still, the historical resilience of this tradition precludes a hasty conclusion.

CONFUCIANS AT WORK

Although Shanghai Daoism is currently suffering from a lack of discursive legitimacy, an excess of it may restrict the re-rooting of Confucianism in the city. The political and religious status of Confucianism in contemporary China is a lingering question. By the late nineteenth century, the spread of Western knowledge, categories (science, religion, politics), and social institutions (universities, churches, the press, and parties) challenged Confucianism's self-image as an epistemic, cosmological, and ritual system. Attempts

PLATE 33. Catholic fishermen's procession, Huaxin Fishery Village, Qingpu, 2016. A man prays in the courtyard of his house as the Easter procession of the Catholic fishermen's community passes his home. Huaxin Township is located in Shanghai's westernmost district of Qingpu.

PLATE 34.   Candlestick maker's workshop, St. Teresa's Catholic Church, Jing'an District, 2015. St. Teresa's Church stands in one of the largest *lilong* of Shanghai, comprising some seven hundred houses. In recent years, a major relocation project has left many of these structures empty. The remaining church complex contains a number of artists' workshops, including that of a nationally renowned stained-glass artist. Images and objects of piety are important cultural markers for Shanghai Catholics, and the community has developed its own tradition of craft.

PLATE 35. Procession, Jinze Town, 2016. Twice a year, people come to join the residents of Jinze Town, located on the outskirts of Shang-hai, to celebrate the birthdays of the town's local gods. Members of devotional groups from across the region display their skill at suspend-ing gongs or incense burners attached to fishing hooks inserted into their forearms.

PLATE 36. Shrine near a bridge, Jinze Township, 2014. Villagers established this small, unofficial shrine where a temple once stood. In Jinze, temples that were located near every bridge were destroyed or converted to other uses during the Cultural Revolution. Some residents still pray at these sites, and new, smaller constructions sometimes appear, on either a provisional or a more permanent basis.

PLATE 37. Animal Release gathering, Changning District, 2015. The traditional East Asian Buddhist practice of freeing captive animals in order to accrue good karma has flourished in recent years, along with the rise of social media networks and the ease of online money donation. Monks or devout laypeople organize weekly devotional gatherings throughout the city's public space.

PLATE 38.   Animal Release gathering, Shanghai ferry port, 2015. The traditional Animal Release ritual, which is allowed in public areas, is performed on the waterways that flow throughout Shanghai. Participants regularly change locations, as observant fishermen often lay out nets to recatch the "liberated" fish.

PLATE 39.   Shanghai Daoist College at Dongyue Temple, Songjiang District, 2014. The college is one of three official Daoist learning centers in China. The fifty students study academic subjects such as English and history, as well as Daoist doctrine and ritual practice. Daily meditation time in a state-of-the-art climate-controlled room has been added to the curriculum.

PLATE 40. Singing-bowl therapy session with Jasmine, Tibetan Buddhist center, Xingfu Road, 2014. Jasmine left her job as a Western medicine doctor in order to study traditional Tibetan Buddhist therapies. She offers Tibetan singing-bowl therapy to mostly Chinese clients at a members' club in Shanghai. A Shanghai businessman, who currently lives in Tibet, established the club "to share with other spiritual people."

PLATE 41. Rainbow Witness Fellowship gathering, 2016. The first musical worship event organized by this network of LGBT Christians was held at a gay club in Shanghai Stadium.

PLATE 42.   Fire ceremony gathering on Chongming Island, 2016. Yoga has flourished in Shanghai in recent years, generating interest in Indian spirituality and traditions. An Indian yogi hosts a monthly fire ceremony for Chinese devotees at a farm on Chongming Island.

PLATE 43. Sanskrit reading class, Shimao Riviera Garden, Pudong, 2015. Hindu families lead active spiritual lives, gathering for Sanskrit-reading classes and devotional singing groups in their homes.

PLATE 44. Ritual bridge, White Clouds Monastery, 2015. A model bridge used during funeral ceremonies to help the deceased proceed into the next life. Daoist ritual objects are said to possess spiritual efficacy.

PLATE 45. Fushouyuan pagoda room, Qingpu District, 2015. With an ever-growing population, Shanghai lacks space on the ground for the city's deceased. The commercial group that owns Fushouyuan Cemetery Park built a pagoda at the center of the cemetery. Inside are rooms of cabinets for keeping the ashes and memorabilia of loved ones.

PLATE 46. Weekly music practice at Chongfu Temple, southwest of Pudong, 2015. Music is central to Daoist ceremonies. An apprentice Daoist must learn to play various instruments in order to perform rituals beautifully and efficiently.

PLATE 47. Faithful at Jing'an Temple, 2015. The faithful put their hands over a nephrite stone invested with "spiritual efficacy."

PLATE 48. Shanghai Shabbat, 2016. An American-born Jewish woman celebrates the traditional Friday night Shabbat with her Chinese husband and their two children.

to save the encompassing character of the Confucian teaching (*jiao*) led to its reformulations, either as religion (conceived in relation to and contrasting with Christianity) or as philosophy. After the Maoist storm, Confucian reconstruction passed through different stages and strategies. Researchers have found evidence of the vitality of a "popular Confucianism" organized around lineage temples (*citang*) aimed at ensuring communal harmony. The rise of China and the Asian Tigers has stoked lively debates on Confucianism's socioeconomic effectiveness as an ever-growing body of reinterpretations of the Confucian canon targets different publics. Corollary questions arise as to Confucianism's religious nature, its social function, and its incorporation in state discourse.[31]

Western scholars have paid close attention to the political and religious reconstruction of Confucianism, focusing on the writings of scholars and publicists, on educational institutions launched mainly by entrepreneurs, and on local or national large-scale initiatives, such as those in Qufu and Guiyang.[32] In Shanghai, private discussions about such attempts are ordinarily met with skepticism, even when the interlocutors are avowed Confucian intellectuals. While these interlocutors stress the significance of continued ancestor worship on the occasions prescribed by tradition, they often see state-based or intellectual reconstructions as an altogether different matter. Even the so-called national studies (*guoxue*) fever, focused largely on the reading of the Confucian Classics, may be less significant than is sometimes asserted. In informal discussions with students from private and public companies enrolled in national-studies programs managed by a leading Shanghai university, we noted that teachers professing a religious-like fervor toward the Confucian inheritance were noticeably less popular than those offering a balanced, critical perspective. Students' motivations were about reconnecting with their cultural lineage while retaining the ability to refer to a variety of viewpoints.

Some Shanghai-based academics have engaged in Confucian activism. Professor Ke Xioagang, head of the philosophy department at Tongji University, for example, advocates widespread reading of the Classics while criticizing the trend toward reverential memorization of the texts and pleading for a focus on practices such as calligraphy, painting, and meditation. He gave a talk on the Reading the Classics Movement at the plenary meeting of the Shanghai Confucian Studies Society (Shanghai Ruxuehui) on May 7, 2016, a year after the society's creation.[33] The event took place in the Confucius Temple of Jiading. An article about the occasion emphasized that the meeting started with a "simple and solemn offering ceremony" that included the reciting of one of the Odes to Confucius penned by Confucian scholars in recent years.[34] This was as far as ritual and religious Confucian reconstruction could go at the time.

One of the major rituals performed by faithful Buddhists throughout China is the controversial practice of Animal Release, or Fang Sheng.[35] Many Buddhist groups gather donations for Animal Release in Shanghai and perform the ritual on the waterways that crisscross the city, mapping the city in a way other than drawn by the location of Buddhist temples (plate 37).

Tim is a member of a Shanghai group of lay Buddhists who organize themselves via WeChat and QQ. They volunteer at temples and donate money to the group online via Alipay.[36] With the donations, they buy fish and birds from markets, and then release the fish into the Huangpu River and the birds into the sky. They practice Animal Release every Saturday and expect around one hundred participants, who come from all over Shanghai to join them. Once a month, participants hold a large-scale performance presided over by a monk that draws around four hundred attendees. In the winter, they tend to start early in the morning, during the brightest, warmest time of day, and on longer summer days, they start in the afternoon. Most people discovered the group via Weibo or WeChat.

On January 3, 2015, the group gathers on the banks of Suzhou Creek, in Putuo District. Around nine thirty, two cars of volunteers arrive and begin to set up. At the bustling fish market, the group's founder heads straight to one seller and spends thirty minutes trying to make a deal on the price and quantity of fish. Shanghai-born and around forty years old, he used to be the CEO of his own company. After retiring five years ago, he founded the group and was joined by another retired businessman. According to the founder, the group currently has almost three thousand members, most of them contributing through Weibo or WeChat. Images are a key marketing tool. A young woman carefully notes the price and quantity of cartons of fish and then communicates this information to donors who are unable to attend the event. Larger fish and shellfish are too expensive, so few are bought and shellfish are privileged. On this occasion, the cost of fish purchased reaches ¥40,000, exceeding the average of ¥20,000.

The volunteers pull on custom-made yellow bibs with the group's name printed on the back. A loudspeaker is the first item to be brought down onto the large boardwalk next to the river. Music blasts out, defining the territory of the group's activity. A table is set up in front of a concrete wall covered with colored cloths. The leader of the group removes a thirty-centimeter-high Buddha statue from a box and, placing it on the table, proudly explains that it comes from Donglin Temple in Jiangxi, where several prominent members of the group go for retreats. Another table positioned at the entrance to the boardwalk displays free books from Donglin Temple, and a man seated at the table collects and registers donations.

Before the performance begins, Tim is eager to show the clothes he wears for such occasions, which he pulls out from his rucksack. He purchased the items at a temple but admits that most people buy them from the popular Taobao online shop, which offers lower prices and is more convenient. People arrive slowly, and by 10:30 the ceremony begins. Around 150 people attend. Women, who represent around 70 percent of attendees, stand on one side and men on the other. The leader directs the chanting in front of the altar with Tim and another assistant standing on either side. After forty minutes of chanting and prayer, everyone parades around the boardwalk four times. Then, the containers of fish are loaded onto a boat. The attendees form an orderly queue, waiting their turn to board the boat and throw the fish into the water. When all the containers are empty and everyone is back on dry land, the group continues its prayer. A few people leave at this point. Books are handed out to guide the last round of chanting. The ceremony finishes at 1:00 p.m. with a practical note of thanks from the founder.

The ceremony testifies to a ritual ethos that re-creates a public sacred space through the combination of vestments, gestures, music, and choreography. Attention is placed on decorum and details. The reason may lie in the underlying sense that Shanghai is somehow a "desecrated" space on which such rituals confer new meaning and a chance of redemption. At the very least, young Buddhist converts see strict ritual observance as a channel through which to reconstruct order in their lives. Photography and videotaping not only reflect but also contribute to the choreography of the event, and choreography is indeed what turns a ritual into a performance.[37]

At the close of the ceremony, the two leaders drive the core group of twelve people back to central Shanghai, where they share a lunch at the large restaurant in Xiahai Temple. While they are waiting for the dishes to be served, the founder opens large packets of "Buddhist kimchi" (kimchi without onion or garlic) that he has brought back from South Korea. The bill comes to ¥352, and after scrutinizing it, the founder's wife complains to the waitress that rice for twelve people came to ¥60. When the restaurant refuses to lower the bill, she retorts that they will bring their own rice next time.

On February 14, 2015, another Animal Release group meets on the prominent public walkway next to the Shanghai ferry port (plate 38). More than a hundred people gather on the boardwalk around plastic sacks and buckets containing large amounts of shellfish and river fish. High-rise buildings, partly obscured by a polluted haze, rise up behind them across the water. After an hour of chanting, participants split into two lines and begin moving the fish from the buckets into the water. Jessica discovered this group, started by a monk from Dongtai, Jiangsu, in 1997, via their WeChat group. Organized bus tours regularly transport people from Shanghai to events at the temples of Dongtai, around two hundred kilometers away. The young monk eventually settled in Shanghai in search of a larger number of believers. "It's not so important to have a designated temple; the most important thing is to be able to gather many people," Jessica emphasizes. Besides participating in Animal Release events (the most popular activity), the followers meet monthly for classes on Buddhist doctrine at the monk's large apartment in Puxi. None of the events follow a regular schedule, and members find out about upcoming activities and locations through their WeChat group.

Yet another group met in Minhang District on September 27, 2015, the night of the Mid-Autumn Festival in this year. Participants were Tibetan Buddhists who usually gather in the evening. The event began with a fire ceremony. Vehicles and three buses were in service to pick up devotees, filling the dead-end street. The chanting ceremony lasted around ninety minutes. The group was made up of about one hundred people, including many young singles and families with children. Following common practice, participants released a particularly tiny kind of fish; as Animal Release has become widespread in Shanghai, so has the fishermen's alertness, and groups routinely check the waterways for nets before releasing any fish. On this evening, after the chanting ended and the release of fish was about to begin, the group discovered nets, and all the attendees drove to another agreed-upon location along the waterway.

On all occasions we observed, chanting, ornaments, vestments, and ritual gestures are mobilized to create a public choreographed solemnity. When they gather along the waterways, city dwellers ritually re-enchant an urban landscape marred by pollution and unceasing reconstruction. The flux of lives and encounters is channeled into practices that confer a new depth and breadth to a public space that practitioners aspire to redeem and appropriate.

NEW PLAYERS ON THE SCENE: SPIRITUAL FLUIDITY

Although actively reinventing their presence through new forms of interactions, Catholic, Daoist, and Buddhist followers are already firmly inscribed onto the religious map of Shanghai. But religious and spiritual expressions new to the city are creating modes of connection, solidarity, and assembly that contribute to Shanghai's religious remapping (map 11). The inventiveness displayed by new players is apparent, as is their interconnection, regardless of the extent to which they belong or do not belong to an institutionalized religion.

Being Baha'i in Shanghai

Eros, cofounder of the Shanghai Rainbow Witness Fellowship, introduced us to a Chinese Baha'i group facilitator, who then connected us to Aidin

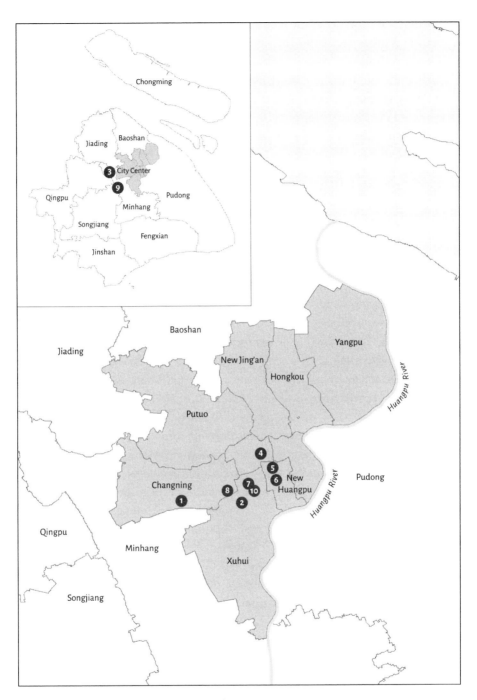

MAP 11. Alternative Spiritualities Fieldwork Sites

1 Floatessence
2 Just Yoga Xujiahui Studio
3 Just Yoga Minhang Studio
4 My Soul Yoga West Nanjing Road Studio
5 My Soul Yoga Fuxing Park Studio

6 Centre for Spiritual Living–Shanghai (CSL)
7 Shantih Shala Holistic Arts
8 Tibetan Tea Club
9 Kundalini Studio
10 Octave

(pseud.). Aidin was born to Iranian parents who are followers of the Baha'i faith and grew up in the United States. He earned a master's degree in chemistry from University College London and was an active member of the Baha'i community in the United Kingdom. Now he is working while studying for his PhD and also serves as the facilitator of Baha'i groups. He moved to Shanghai in 2000.

Upon request, the city's religious affairs bureau gave the foreign Baha'i community of Shanghai approval to meet once a month in a hotel in Xujiahui District. Five people are in charge of general affairs, but Chinese nationals must operate independently from foreigners. Aidin emphasizes the Baha'i adherence to the rules of the country of residence:

> The government gave us three restrictions; no groups over twenty people, limited mixing between Chinese and foreigners within groups, and not to gather in public spaces. All of these suit us well. . . . Our groups grow through word of mouth. We do not seek publicity but hope to be visible through the way we transform society for the greater good. The emphasis is on the significance and impact of the individual. In Shanghai generally it is people between twenty-four and thirty-five who become interested, although other places in China tend to recruit people over thirty-five.

In March 2016, two young Chinese women join a Baha'i family (father from the United States, mother from Taiwan, and two children) in their apartment for dinner during the period of fasting leading up to the Baha'i New Year. All are sharing their first meal of the day. Another couple arrives late, as the study session starts.[38] "The pillars of spiritual health are prayer, both together and alone. Sacred space is in our minds and in the shared minds of a group," stresses the American leader of the group. He later comments,

> China is a community of great importance, and the freedom we have is wonderful. There may now be around seven hundred foreign people leading study circles, but the Chinese community by far exceeds in number the foreign one.[39] Everyone is encouraged to begin their own study circle as soon as they feel ready; they don't have to complete the [Baha'i sacred] seven books before they begin. . . . WeChat is a great support to the community growth, and we don't hide what we do from being published there.

Weiwei (pseud.), from Anhui, discovered the Baha'i faith two years ago. She attends study circles three times a week, while she and her partner lead beginners' study sessions for Chinese friends. "I've started many circles, but people often leave partway through for practical reasons. No one in this city has time," she laments.

On March 20, 2016, Weiwei has been tasked with organizing the Baha'i New Year festivities. Around twenty Chinese, most of them between twenty and thirty-five years old, and four foreigners share the food they have brought. At the end of the meal, a group picture is quickly uploaded and printed out so that each person will have a memento of the day. Next, everyone settles around the ample sofa for prayer and sharing; the latter soon becomes deep and intimate. Participants joke that a Baha'i meeting is the right place to pick up a partner or a job, and indeed it appears that several people are or have been colleagues. The mother of nine-year-old twins then shared her educational concerns,

> My husband and I are from Shanghai. Two years ago we felt the
> need for a faith for our family. My grandmother is Buddhist, and my
> mother is Christian. I went with a friend to the church, but we didn't
> feel that it could really offer anything to our family. The strong element
> of children's education in the Baha'i faith attracted us, so we began
> studying together every Saturday. . . . We have learned so many things
> here, even cooking. My husband and I had never cooked before, as his
> mother cooks in our home, but he's very good! I've tried to introduce
> many other friends to the Baha'i faith, but it's very difficult in China,
> as people are worried about it being too sensitive or see it as a waste
> of time. We both believe that it's more important than English and
> math for our children. It offers a whole different structure of family
> life. Traditionally in China, a man gives money to his wife for the
> children's education, but in the Baha'i community, we all learn
> together.

Additional observation confirms that the Chinese Baha'i community emphasizes its willingness to cultivate good relationships with the government and academics, insisting that "civil law [trumps] religious law in the Baha'i faith"[40] and Baha'i leaders being careful not to put pressure on Chinese officials. The interaction between foreign and Chinese believers does not currently extend to monthly official worship but is nurtured through study circles and regular pilgrimages. Baha'is underline the rational character of their beliefs and the spirit of service they foster. More practically, the insistence on family life and values is extremely attractive for some middle-class Shanghainese families in search of an alternative educational model. In many respects, the Baha'i communal spirit is akin to the ethos and aspirations of many Shanghai urbanites.

Healing and Sharing

In a metropolis that is unanimously described as living life at a hectic tempo, accrued well-being, or mental and physical healing, is sought at any cost. Such a trend associates "spiritual consumerism," physical or mental practices, and religious quests. The fluid nature of the pursuit explains its networked character. Pilgrims try, adopt, or relinquish a variety of masters and methods; they exchange advice and information; they intertwine experiences and affiliations.

Octave (Yinyu Tingtang), an exclusive, holistic wellness center, opened in 2015.[41] It boasts a central downtown location as well as stunning architecture and interior design that fuse an old structure with modern materials. Light is an intrinsic design element. The client support team declares that 70 percent of the members are local and the rest foreigners. Nearly all the therapists are highly trained Chinese. Personal transformation and self-discovery are a particular focus. Octave activities include pilgrimage retreats in Suzhou and Sichuan.

The center is far from the only one of its kind in Shanghai. People attracted by Octave's approach may also try Floatessence, a floatation-tank therapy center.[42] Although flotation is a relaxation technique, many clients describe the experience lyrically as, "disembodying." It would be an exaggeration to label the carefully designed flotation rooms "sacred spaces," but they certainly operate as places of meditation that transcend daily routines.

Josephine is from Malaysia and was educated in Britain. She has been living in Shanghai for many years now and leads weekly Reiki sessions in her three-room apartment near the Shanghai Library.[43] Like many other "sacred home spaces" in Shanghai, the place is difficult to find, identified only by a small Hindu symbol stuck to the door. Most people learn about Josephine's activities through her WeChat account.

On February 21, 2016, eight people join the Reiki session. Some participants know others through the Centre for Spiritual Living–Shanghai (CSL-Shanghai), a place frequented mainly by expats that offers "classes, events and retreats for our bodies, minds and spirits."[44] The session room is just large enough for everyone to sit in a circle. Josephine invites participants to select a crystal from a collection laid out on a side table. Those who receive energy are instructed to place the crystal at a point on their bodies. There is little explanation given; participants are simply encouraged to work with their intuition when receiving and giving energy. The two first-timers are invited to experience the ten-minute healing session first, while those who are giving energy take positions around the ones who are lying down. The session runs more than two hours, after which they all share their experiences. There is a red box at the door to collect the modest ¥50 fee per session.

Josephine also offers sessions in yoga and Reiki at the center and eagerly describes her involvement there.

> For me, CSL-Shanghai is a sanctuary; it is also like an all-you-can-eat soul buffet. It's unique to this transitional city, as the classes are defined by the emotional character of the different kinds of people who come through the door. More and more people want this kind of support within the Shanghai chaos; the work itself is timeless. Seventy percent of those who come are foreign. The Chinese who come have to really open up beyond the confines of Chinese culture. Reiki is becoming very popular, and there are quite a few teachers in Shanghai, some Chinese. I run separate classes in Chinese for locals. . . .
>
> When I arrived in Shanghai, there were only four yoga centers. Now there seem to be hundreds. Shanghai is producing far too many yoga teachers now; it's like a conveyer belt in a factory. . . . I hardly use the word "spiritual" in describing what I do, but I use the word "sacred" all the time. I find that the connection born out of what I do is sacred, a sense of oneness with others. . . . One of my Chinese yoga clients asked me to lead a yoga class with sixty staff from her company as a farewell event for their company executive. They wanted to do something more soulful than the usual dinner.

Just as Eros led us to Aidin, Josephine introduced us to Rama (pseud.), a Chinese yoga teacher who was a member of the Hare Krishna community for a while. New players in Shanghai's sacred landscape nurture networks that are rarely mutually exclusive. These networks not only associate foreigners and Chinese with more ease than in other environments; multiple belongings or at least mutual connections are commonplace.

Rama has transformed a small centrally located apartment into a yoga studio with white walls and a wooden floor. The empty space is filled by a warm light filtering through the wooden shutters, blocking out the surrounding gray high-rises outside the large window. Rama is Shanghai-born and sees the city as "different, extreme in many ways, spiritually, intellectually, both extremely inhuman and human, at once extremely commercial and compassionate." He remembers the real growth of the yoga phenomenon beginning in 2004 as people began to recognize its commercial potential. At the time, Rama was a schoolteacher and discovered Hare Krishna through his practice of hatha yoga. He joined the community, which then numbered thirty people, for a few years but realized that it did not offer the support and meaning he was searching for.

> Around 2010, the city really opened up to alternative practices. The Chinese Sikh community orients itself around the practice of Kundalini yoga.[45] They offer a different brand of Kundalini yoga than the one you find in yoga studios. I helped translate the teacher's training material, which was half Sikh faith and half yoga practice. It's a sacred sandwich! [*He laughs.*] Their studio is also part shrine.
>
> The new generation in Shanghai sees no boundaries. They have no religion, and they want to explore. . . . I believe in the inner sanctuary. Hare Krishna was only about the outside — eating, chanting, dancing. Spirituality must be linked to everyday life. It's like eating a banana. When the banana is finished, the plate [the peel] becomes a sanctuary.

Although he has left the community, Rama introduces us to two Chinese Hare Krishna devotees, whom we meet in April 2016. Latha (pseud.) entered the movement at the age of twenty-nine, after having joined a yoga association. Sanjib (pseud.) discovered the movement in his home province of Guangzhou at the age of thirteen.

> The Chinese Hare Krishna movement started in the 1980s, moving from Hong Kong and then to Canton. The Bhagavad Gita was then translated into Chinese, but the movement met with problems after 1989, and then again around 2000, when Falun Gong was crushed. We continue to face many challenges, not only from the government, but also because of the Chinese social context. There are so many rules to follow for being a Hare Krishna! Many people join but then find it too much. The movement can attract Chinese because of its similarities to Buddhism, but we still have a long way to go. Other movements, like Baha'i, are spreading much faster. Our numbers in Shanghai are very limited, approximately one hundred now, but the community is much larger and organized in Beijing. Here we have no real place to meet.

The group rents a yoga studio hall for community events every month and meets in members' homes at other times. Latha is not as troubled as Sanjib by the peripatetic nature of the community.

> The most important thing is to maintain the life form that Krishna taught us. Unfortunately we have to conform to the life of the city and regular jobs — many of us are yoga teachers — but we maintain everyday rituals. We're encouraged to get up before sunrise and meditate before

making *prasad* (religious offering of food), which we distribute to others throughout the day. Cooking and sharing represent an important Hare Krishna ritual.

Then Latha offers cookies that she made this very morning. The symbol of Krishna is printed on the plastic packaging. "I give them to my coworkers and everyone I meet with!" she smiles.

As Rama noted, Kundalini yoga is well represented in Shanghai. Jocelyn's (pseud.) studio is difficult to find. A wealthy woman in Shanghai offered her space in an old factory compound on the outskirts of the city, free of rent. A platform in front of the wood-floored studio is surrounded by an army of large gongs, handmade in Hamburg and shipped to Shanghai. Jocelyn, originally from Taiwan, has spent many years in the United States. Her daughter and grandson live in Vancouver. She started practicing yoga in Shanghai and, after an injury, was introduced to the practice of Kundalini meditation by her teacher.

> A Sikh developed Kundalini yoga, and thus it includes Sikh philosophy and chanting. A yogi brought it to China, although many people reject the chanting element here. It is all about energy and strengthening the nervous system. Our nervous systems these days are very fragile, as we experience too much external stimulation. Just think of the chaos of Xujahui Ring Road for example! It is harder than any other yoga, it takes discipline, long hours of practice, holding positions for extended periods of time to break through the pain barrier and the blockages in our bodies. Eventually, on a yoga teacher training retreat in Thailand, I saw a white light, and I felt an overpowering, warm surge of energy.

Inspired to share the transformative experience with others, Jocelyn established and registered the first authorized Shanghai-based Gong Centre in 2014.

> I specialize in gong practice, which enhances the balance of harmony with the world. It helps us tune in to the rhythm of the planets. These gongs are tuned in to the frequency of the planet. I teach detailed rituals for everyday living, starting from the way one should shower in the morning. . . . As for my turban, it protects the thirty-six meridian points on the head. It creates a personal safe place. I didn't believe it at the start, but I once led a practice without a turban, and I had a terrible headache for days. There's an element of secrecy to every practice, I was recently on a yoga retreat, and the woman I was sharing a room with was lying on her bed chanting. When I inquired about her healing

practice, she said it was very simple, but she had signed a contract with her Daoist teacher that prohibited her sharing it with anyone. It was something only for the master and disciple. Likewise, to become a Kundalini yoga practitioner, there is a system of initiation.

Irina, a Chinese yoga teacher who also specializes in Kundalini, similarly practices in a white gown and turban. After several years of practicing other types of yoga, she and her husband discovered Kundalini. The path helped with their marriage, declares Irina. More generally, she speaks of Kundalini as guiding her through successive transformations — from a girl, to a woman, a wife, and a mother — and improving her ability to communicate with others. "Kundalini is not a religion, but rather a way of perception, a diamond that shines over different facets of your life."

India and Yoga in Shanghai

Yoga practices are thriving in Shanghai as in most metropolises. However, the local significance of the trend derives partly from the Indian presence in Shanghai. The experience of displacement and minority status induces a reassessment of one's spiritual roots and practices.

In March 2015, at a weekly Bhagavad Gita class, Seema, of Hindu birth, who has lived in Shanghai for twelve years with her Sikh husband and two children, spoke of how spiritual interaction developed among Hindus and Sikhs.

> We had nothing here, so we had to create a structure. In India, we're surrounded by religion, so we don't feel the need to get together for a weekly reading class, but now that we've begun, it has become important. As a family, we read two *shloka* every morning now, and I think we'll carry on doing this wherever we go. We've come to rely on these practices.

Seema is part of a group of eighteen Indian women who gather weekly to study the Bhagavad Gita for two hours. They take turns leading the class and hosting the event in their homes. An Indian expatriate who came to Shanghai for her husband's job established the group. A Bhagavad Gita textbook written by one of Seema's uncles was her initial inspiration. The founder currently lives in London but talks via Skype with the group every Sunday. The network of groups now extends to Bangalore, Canada, Delhi, Mumbai, Singapore, Switzerland, the United Kingdom, and the United States.

Other classes spread knowledge about the Indian and Hindu traditions (plate 43). Mansi, another participant in Seema's group, notes that many Chinese people know about Hinduism.

Once, Sri Sri Ravi Shankar was going to visit, and more than a thousand Chinese people signed up, so the government cancelled it.[46] I've been to Chinese Hare Krishna worshippers' houses; they do the practices and keep vegetarian. Once, Seema invited me to a weekly event in Zhongshan Park, where "Chinese Hindus" were dancing, chanting, doing yoga, and eating *prasad*. . . . Of course, they're Hindu. Anyone can be Hindu if one follows the guidelines. . . . Well, I see they replicate Hindu activities, but I'm not sure they understand it the same way.

The multifaceted activities of Atul and Charat may illustrate how spiritual connections develop. Atul offers members of the small Hindu community fire ceremonies in their homes, yoga/meditation practice, and discussions on Hindu philosophy. He is clearly an important spiritual presence for the community. Every Saturday between 7:30 and 9:30 a.m., Atul leads a class in yoga and meditation for about ten people in a rented room in the Pudong compound where many Indian expatriates live. Based in Shanghai since 2005, Atul began leading meditation for a small group of Chinese attendees. He takes multinational groups of around thirty people to India on a spiritual retreat twice a year and maintains his Chinese visa by teaching twenty-one lessons a week for a large yoga-training company.

Along with his teaching duties, Atul and a fellow Indian, Charat (both studied under the same yogi teacher), regularly hold fire ceremonies for a group of Chinese Hindu devotees. The ritual takes place on Chongming, the island where the foot-massage network held its training session. On January 19, 2016, in a car driving toward Chongming, Shanti one of the two core organizers of the Chinese Hindu community, relays news of an annual retreat at an ashram in India, from where she has just returned. Twenty Chinese from Shanghai and the surrounding area took part in the twenty-one-day event. The group's final destination is a cluster of old farm buildings next to a small lake. It is raining, so the event will be held indoors. The ceremony starts at 10:15 a.m. and lasts for an hour and a half. Around twenty people fill the small room, sitting crossed-legged around the fire. Charat reads and chants in English and Sanskrit from a book, Shanti translates the English into Chinese, and the group chants in response. The ritual continues with constant chanting and the throwing of ghee and rose petals mixed with nuts onto the fire (plate 42). A lengthy photo session follows, with pictures immediately uploaded to the WeChat group. While devotees share a vegetarian meal, Charat recounts his own journey.

I first came to Shanghai in 2005 to teach yoga. Three years later, I moved with my company, Pure Yoga, to Singapore. I returned to Shanghai in July 2013 and found a much more active yoga scene. A friend introduced me to this organic farm, and the owners let me hold a little retreat here and then showed me the old buildings, which were covered in bushes and almost derelict. I spent a long time clearing everything, fixing the doors and roof myself. You can do the fire ceremony anywhere. Wherever I go, I start a group to share with. In Shanghai, people are always traveling, so 50 percent are regular attendees and others come and go. People come for many reasons; some think it gives them fortune or good health. . . . I welcome anyone who feels the call to come.

The attendees, mainly middle-aged, middle-class women, have come to the event through their yoga practice. The group's outlook is far from unique, although the fire ceremony practice is a rarity. Even commercial yoga studios participate in the urbanites' quest for spiritual enlightenment and physical well-being. Ganesh, a Hindu, established two Just Yoga centers in Minhang and Xujiahui Districts. They offer yoga, meditation, and group retreats and sell organic health shakes. Both centers contain small Hindu shrines. Photographs of groups performing yoga poses in front of Buddhist temples are pasted to the notice board. Interviews conducted with Chinese practitioners in Shanghai yoga clubs reveal an array of motivations for joining. Jialin (pseud.), a woman of around thirty-five, explains,

> I was attracted to yoga because of its spiritual bases; however, after I started practicing in a "specialized" yoga club, I found I was truly doing bodily exercise. I didn't choose tai chi, because at my middle school, we were taught tai chi as a sport, cut off from its roots. I can understand why many people, especially women, prefer yoga; it's a "soft" and "mysterious" way to exercise. Tai chi now seems to be for old people, too slow for the young if they don't understand the meanings encompassed in every movement.

Cai Yan (pseud.), a woman of twenty-eight, elaborates on the difference between Chinese traditional breathing techniques and yoga:

> One should do *qigong* in an open place, so as to receive energy and let your body be part of nature. Is Shanghai the place for such practice? Yoga is just the opposite; it works both inside and outside. Also, *qigong* relates to traditional Chinese medicine, and its principles should be known before exercising correctly. Yoga is easier; you can emphasize the physical or meditation, whatever you feel like. Additionally, *qigong* has to do with a quest for longevity, while yoga helps one lose weight, which is much looked for in the city.

My Soul Yoga manages two studios, catering mainly to white-collar Chinese women who work around West Nanjing Road and Yandang Road.[47] Daily classes run from 7:00 a.m. to 9:00 p.m. and are led by foreign and Chinese instructors in either Chinese or English. Students usually follow the teacher's orders in a regimented and almost religious manner. During weekends and public holidays, the studios buzz with women in stylish Lycra, speaking softly, drinking tea, and playing on their smartphones between classes. Few men brave the feminine environment, and those who do are usually the women's partners.

The yoga craze is fostering networks of spiritual sociability that substitute for traditional religious fellowships. On the first morning of 2017, My Soul Yoga studios offered a session that featured an Indian yogi who led participants in sutra chanting and bindi painting. "Yoga is not a religion," he insisted firmly. But pressed with questions on yoga's ultimate purpose and its relationship to Buddhism, he specified, "Yoga is a huge tree; several religions, including Hinduism, Buddhism, and even Christianity are its branches and leaves, which form their own shapes and colors." Studios have somehow become sacred compounds.

◆ ◆ ◆

Religious waterways link compounds, homes, and landmarks on a map of sacred geographies, enshrining markers into urban history and buildings. Networks tend to materialize as fixed meeting places, and virtual connections prepare for actual gatherings. Thus, waterways are places where one lives, spends time, finds a dwelling, and navigates from one abode to another. Physical, personal, and virtual connections all play these roles, enlarging and reshaping believers' sense of sacred space.

Having explored the various dimensions of Shanghai's sacred territories, the concluding chapter will apprehend the religious fabric of the metropolis in the variety of its dimensions. How is sacredness personally delineated and celebrated in a global city that juxtaposes so many expressions of it? And, in return, how do these innumerable individual experiences coalescence into a spiritual cityscape? Finally, what does the exploration of Shanghai teach us about contemporary urban religious spaces, in the Chinese world and beyond?

The Sacred Tapestry

A town is from afar a town. But, as we draw near, there are houses, trees, tiles, leaves, grass, ants, limbs of ants, in infinity. All this is contained under the name of town.

— Blaise Pascal, *Pensées*

And as the same city, looked at from various sides, appears quite different and becomes as it were numerous in aspects; even so, as a result of the infinite number of monads, it is as if there were so many different universes, which, nevertheless are nothing but aspects of a single universe, according to the special point of view of each monad.

— Gottfried Leibniz, *Monadology*

"WHICH ONE LOOKS NICER? I JUDGE BY APPEARANCES."[1] IN A SMALL shop inside the Zhangjialou parish compound, Qian Yi (pseud.) shyly points to two images of Jesus hanging on the wall. She speaks quickly in an excited voice, "Every night I pray before going to sleep. What time of the day is best for prayer? When I soak my feet in hot water, am I allowed to pray? I want to hang crosses and images of Jesus in every room in my house!"

Such scenes occur daily at a church counter dedicated to the sale of objects of piety, but this day in July 2013 is very special for Qian Yi: she is making her purchases after the first Sunday mass since her baptism. As a new Catholic with no family Christian heritage, she is immersed in excitement, anxious to learn more about Catholic rites and equally anxious to conform to the model of a "good Catholic," a desire she will mention again several times.

The new identity that Qian Yi has adopted implies that a number of "holy things," such as crosses and images, are going to appear in her life. In addition to visible objects, deep and lasting changes will affect her life and schedule. For her, Sunday will be not just a day of rest but also a "holy day" hallowed by mass and prayer. Her questions about the best time to pray and what she is allowed to do while praying reveal some anxiety, as her faith will need to blend into her everyday practices. Religion is becoming a lived reality for Qian Yi, a reality that combines belief and practices, doctrines and their contextual expressions, the spiritual and the physical, the sacred and the profane.

Such questions are at the heart of how religion is being practiced, experienced, and expressed by ordinary people in Shanghai, and how such experiences and practices translate into lived sacred spaces. Five Chinese characters or lexical compounds will serve here to help us map the sacred geography we have wandered into and to enrich and modify the Durkheimian sacred/profane paradigm sketched in this book's introduction. To do so, we will consider the opposition between what is "right" (*zheng*) and "erroneous or perverse" (*xie*); the "spiritual quality or power" (*ling*) attached to certain objects and spaces; the contrast between what is "vacuous" (*xu*) and "real" (*shi*); the pair formed by "movement" (*dong*) and "quietness" (*jing*); and finally the ancient concept of "resonance" (*ganying*).

ZHENG: CONVERTS AND THE QUEST FOR ORTHOPRAXY

In the Zhangjialou parish, catechumenal courses extend over a period of around three to four months and contain about ten lessons. The course is arranged in a meeting room on the compound's second floor every Sunday morning after Mass, until the day of baptism. There are no strict rules for catechumens to follow except that they need to sign up each time they attend the class and can petition for baptism only after attending at least six classes.[2] Most catechumens, like Qian Yi, knew little about Catholicism before participating in the catechumenal process. These instruction classes serve as a necessary path for any adult wishing to convert to Catholicism and also as a process of transition by which people from different backgrounds come to know one another better. When joining a parish, Shanghai's new Catholic converts enter faith communities that have long been shaped by common memories and practices, as well as by a territorial model that in the past often associated parishes and lineages into sociohistorical units. At the same time, traditional parishes have been fractured by political vicissitudes and — maybe even more so — by urban renewal. This remolding makes it easier to integrate new converts and old Catholics into communities in which all participants need to find ways of living and expressing their faith within an unsupportive larger social and cultural environment.

Qian Yi, a young woman with a positive outlook, was one of the catechumens in the 2013 spring course. She came to Shanghai from northeastern

China after graduating from university and accepting a job in a bank. If she had not left her hometown, her current life would be better, she acknowledges, but she does not regret her decision. She recalls her connection with Catholicism:

> In my hometown, there's a beautiful church near my house. Whenever I passed by the church, I was attracted to it. I don't know how to interpret such a feeling, as no one in my family is Christian. But I never pushed open the door of that church. Here in Shanghai, one day I went for a walk with my boyfriend and came upon this church, which reminded me of my past feelings. This time, the door was open to me, and someone invited me to participate in the catechism class. That's how I came here.

Chen Ming (pseud.), who participated in the spring 2013 catechism class and was baptized afterward, attended the course again during the fall of the same year. Nicknamed "Miracle Hunter" in our field notes, he is a twenty-seven-year-old Shanghainese who looks younger than his age. He has long been unemployed but worries only about a chronic disease that he has had since childhood. One day, his mother, who is not Christian, brought him to a church close to their house, and going to the church eventually became part of his routine. He never missed a catechism class. He often appears absent-minded and slow, but when the word "miracle" is mentioned, his spirits rise.

When he met with Zhang Liang again in the fall of 2013, after the summer break, he began their exchange by asking, "Do you believe in miracles?"

"It depends on what you mean by 'miracle.' Could you give an example?"

He thought for a while and then said, "Apparitions of the Heavenly Mother."

"You've been baptized, but you still question this?"

"I believe that the Virgin Mary exists, but seeing her with my own eyes would be very important."

Chen once joined a fellowship organized by Protestants in which others claimed they had the experience of being filled by the Holy Spirit. He could not understand why he had neither seen the Virgin Mary nor felt the presence of the Holy Spirit, so he continues to attend various classes or lectures, whether organized by Catholics or Protestants and given by lay teachers or clerics.[3]

Wei Hongxuan acted as a catechist for both Chen Ming and Qian Yi. He is a confident, young engineer employed by an international company. He was raised in a traditional intellectual family; his father is a retired Party official, though he prefers to call him a "public servant." Before he failed his first qualifying exam for postgraduate studies, he had never met with a real setback, making him realize how self-satisfied he had become. After passing his qualifying exams the next year, he met a classmate who was a Protestant. Under her influence, he started to learn about Christian culture. As a science geek, he knew little about Western culture at the time. Before graduating, he had received several job offers, and after choosing one, he moved to Shanghai. Soon enough, his capabilities won him recognition in the workplace, but he felt that "[his] life was losing weight."

> I could live comfortably, but without economic pressure, it was like the meaning of life was becoming obscure. As I knew that others were also feeling like me, I began observing them and then observing myself again, and I realized that I needed to change myself — although I didn't know how to start. One night, I passed the Sacred Heart of Jesus Church. At that moment, I could not even tell whether this was a Catholic or Protestant church. The door was open, and when I stepped inside, I decided that this was the beginning of my change.[4]

The narratives of these converts may not provide clear reasons for approaching the Catholic Church in particular. They express a strong sense of contingency, but contingency is interpreted as leading to a result that was meant to be. Further interpretation of these stories also reveals a quest for the self with characteristics that vary from one catechumen to another. Wei Hongxuan describes with precision the inner travail that led him to enter the Church; Qian Yi speaks about a search for the beautiful and an attraction to Western aesthetics. Chen Ming implies that his illness had made him aimless, as it was difficult for him to participate in outdoor activities, and his inner quest substitutes for the endeavors he feels unable to undertake. Finally, the symbol of the church's wide-open door makes the element of chance in their religious encounters take on the sense of inevitability.

Praying and Doubting

After Qian Yi and Chen Ming were baptized, on July 21, 2013, Wei Hongxuan told the neophytes, "Baptism is just the beginning of your faith journey." As they travel along the same path as their new community, these new converts internalize a certain number of practices that they receive from the surrounding tradition. They also deal with challenges that may require them to take the initiative and display their inventiveness. In their conversations, the topic that arises most frequently has to do with the meaning and effectiveness of prayer. In asking themselves how they should pray, Catholics, especially recent converts, are trying to define an orthopraxy.

When looking at Chinese Catholics' understanding and practice of prayer, one should keep in mind the deep influence of traditional popular worship. Embedded in Chinese culture, popular worship is both a ritual expression of one's wishes and a set of practices that remains remarkably elastic, with specific words or postures left to the discretion of practitioners or passed down within families (although there are some socially prevalent customs regarding the way to kneel or the wording of petitions). Furthermore, ways of praying and petitioning are largely similar across Buddhism, Daoism, and folk religion.

Both communal and individual forms of prayer can be observed within the Sacred Heart Church congregation. Communal prayers are not limited to those enacted at mass, although some are grouped around the Eucharistic celebration. Before each Sunday mass, some of the Mysteries of the Rosary are chanted in local dialect by a group of longtime Catholics, using a regular rhythm and inflections reminiscent of the chanting performed at Buddhist temples.[5] After mass, the same group recites the Rosary again in thanksgiving. Although Catholics worldwide pray the Rosary, the chanting in Chuansha dialect makes it a specific tradition of this parish, practiced by old local parishioners. Most young Catholics, including Shanghainese from other districts, cannot understand the chanting and are unwilling to learn.

Another form of communal prayer cements closer links among young Catholic adults. Started by a young Shanghainese Catholic who had traveled to France, Taizé prayer meetings are regularly held in St. Michael's parish and sometimes in other locations as well, creating an inter-parish youth network. On the night of December 20, 2013, five prayer sessions, each lasting for around an hour and a half, with breaks for faith sharing, led some of the participants to stay until six in the morning. During a break, our contact explained that he was going to stay until six and then go to his parish church to put up Christmas decorations.

Personal prayer is a different matter. Aunt Lan (pseud.), a retiree who was baptized in spring 2015, is typically Shanghainese in looks and behavior; everything must be kept neat and tidy, including interpersonal relationships. Thus, she seldom talks with other parishioners, except when the conversation turns to the subject of prayer. Then she is willing to share her experience. "I pray every morning. After I get up, I pray for one hour with the Bible in my little room. It's very useful! I've been praying this way for three months already, and now I feel better."

Hua Xia (pseud.), a young ethnic Tujia woman who received a master's degree from a famous university, similarly stresses the role of prayer in her life. After she became accustomed to her workplace, she asked her mother to move from Guangxi and live with her in Shanghai. Three years ago, she went though a difficult time; feeling at a loss, and a random walk brought her to the church. After receiving instruction for three months, she and her mother were baptized together. Nowadays, when she prays "the right way," she strongly feels "the grace of God"—when she mentions this, tears fill her eyes. Conversely, if she prays "the wrong way," she experiences God's absence, a cause for worry. However, she believes that God is always protecting his children in a mysterious way.

> A few weeks ago, three other friends and I had planned to meet at Xujia-hui Cathedral at 1:00 p.m., and another friend would drive us to Jinze, where we would prepare to start an Emmaus meditation and retreat at 2:00 p.m. But many incidents delayed our driving to Jinze, which worried me again. However, on the way to Jinze, I calmed down, sitting peacefully and praying continuously that we wouldn't be late. Something really happened! We did arrive before 2:00 p.m., and the best part is that when we arrived, the organizer told us that the time for starting the activity had changed to 3:00 p.m. Amazing! God has his own arrangement for you, for me, and for everyone.[6]

The way God answers prayers is the subject of much questioning. For instance, Li Zhongrui (pseud.), a Catholic who was baptized more than five years ago, realizes that he still does not know how one can pray for other people. His friend, Long Bin (pseud.), similarly wonders how one knows that one's prayers have been heard and recognize that they have been answered? There are also questions about what can be prayed for. Teacher Ren, the leader of the foot-massage network, explains, "Recently, a parishioner came to the church to pray so as to find her lost pet dog. She was sure that her dog had a spirit and would return."

Praying and healing are the core areas in which the faithful wish to translate their faith, often a newfound faith, into concrete practices and ways of life. In the process, they repeatedly deal with a question that leads to perpetual readjustments, "Do I practice my faith according to what is expected from me?" As uncomfortable as it may sound, this question is the one that nurtures the personal and collective inventiveness of the faithful. Partly based on the Church's local and global devotional tradition, and partly triggered by the Chinese megacity's specific environment, painstakingly and hesitantly a new orthopraxy is being fashioned.[7]

The emphasis on doing what is "right" (*zheng*) is not restricted to Catholic converts. It remains true that Catholics are especially prone to detecting "erroneous" doctrines or practices. At the same time, Chinese Catholicism has to defend itself against accusations of heterodoxy from two different directions. First, Chinese Catholicism was labeled a "perverse cult" (*xiejiao*) from the mid-eighteenth to the mid-nineteenth century and today it is suspected of being "un-Chinese" because of its relationship with Rome. Second, Chinese Protestants are often strongly prejudiced against Catholicism, which is seen as not being truly Christian. Catholics likewise express similar prejudices, but in society at large, Protestantism generally is associated with Christianity.[8]

Tim is typical of a group of converts who could be called "Evangelical Buddhists." He is eager to talk about how Buddhism inspires his daily life. Every day after his studies, he attends language school for two hours. "I want to learn English so I can spread the word about Buddhism, and using my computer skills, I'll make a website about Buddhism. . . . I have a clear goal in life." He does not come from a practicing Buddhist family and grew up thinking that all religion was superstition. Eight years ago, while studying Internet communications at Shandong University, he discovered Buddhism by accident. A waitress inspired him with her "Buddhist happiness" to pick up one of the books available for free at the local temple. "Nobody encouraged me to do it. I was amazed by the wisdom and intelligence in the books. Not all Buddhism is good Buddhism. I should follow the books, not the teachings of men." He felt that before he came to Buddhism, he had a negative attitude toward life and lacked confidence. Now his lifestyle is shaped by his beliefs. He abstains from alcohol, smoking, oily food, and meat. He is not attached to any given temple. "I go to many, many temples. At every one I feel more comfortable than at home. I think in another life I was a monk. . . . Besides, every day I pray in my apartment in front of a Buddha statue for fifteen minutes to one hour. When I pray, I feel the Buddha around me. I often cry, and afterward I feel comforted. We should remind ourselves that the Buddha helps us and exists."

He also listens to monks' speeches online. "If I don't understand, it's ok." He also proudly describes his pilgrimage to a temple in Jiangxi, where he slept rough during four days on the road. He aims to make a pilgrimage every holiday time. Through prayer, pilgrimages, participation in reading, and Animal Release gatherings, Tim is crafting his own Buddhist orthopraxy.

LING: SPIRITUAL POWERS AT WORK

Catholics' local sacred geography revolves around the home, the parish, and some hallowed places such as Sheshan. The pilgrimages they undertake enable them to somehow re-enchant their environment, but still, Shanghai Catholics strictly differentiate between "sacred" and "secular" spaces. Adherents of other faiths may arrange the separations that structure their imagined religious geographies differently. Tan Dong (pseud.), a twenty-seven-year-old male tattooist, shares his experience of the world opening up in front of him.[9]

When I was in second year of university, I went to Jiuhuashan to do some sketches.[10] At the foot of Mount Jiuhua I bought a string of prayer beads. At the top of the mountain, an old monk asked me whether I wanted to do "the opening" (*kaiguang*).[11] I did not understand at that time, so I agreed, and the monk recited something over a bundle of incense and then gave the string of beads back to me. I think he was a very powerful old monk. Later, I felt there was some spiritual power (*ling*) in this little string of prayer beads, so I gradually came to believe in all this. For example, once there was an English exam, and before it, I was turning the string of beads. I wanted to arrive early in the morning to grab a good seat, but I would never have thought that all good seats would be already taken when I arrived. I would have imagined even less that, once we were all seated, the examiner would tell us to change seats according to matriculation numbers, and that I would sit down where I originally wanted to be! So I think that Heaven was helping. Later on, I wanted to find a chance to make the acquaintance of a girl I often encountered. A semester had passed, and I still had not met with this person. Graduation was coming soon, and there would be no chance in the future. I came up with the prayer beads, asking to be given a chance. I went to school the next day, sitting on bus 946, to the stadium. On the way, I realized that the string of beads was loosening, and that it would certainly break very soon. I remembered that a classmate had said that there was a place for repairing prayer beads nearby, in Xujiahui. I stopped and bought a Chinese knot at the repair shop, then I sat at McDonald's for a moment, and then I again took bus 946, in which, all of a sudden, I met the girl I had been looking for all that time, . . . and I was able to make her acquaintance. Before that, I had never seen her on the 946.

Afterward, I reflected that, in fact, our lives are arranged in advance: the ones we call the deities (*shenming*) operate in our [human] space in ways we cannot foresee. What this world calls "miracles" may be the result of some kind of telepathy or resonance (*ganying*), some arrangements. Since then, I rather believe in those things. My string of prayer beads is broken now, and I keep it at home. Sometimes when I go to a temple, I bring this string of beads with me, and I communicate with the deities. I think we can communicate with them. For them, we are like a game (*youxi*), just like the ones we play in virtual reality ourselves, with set rules and procedures.

Tan Dong's narrative sketches an "enchanted geography" that gives urban trajectories mysterious depths. It speaks of plays and rituals, in which human agents are more objects than subjects; it gives a contemporary resonance to the Chinese notion of "spiritual power (efficacy)" (*ling*) that seizes objects and spaces (plate 44). In Tan Dong's discourse, a traditional notion is associated with an outlook that considers the urban space-time as a kind of divine chessboard in which artifacts and locations are invested with specific values.

We often met with other expressions of the importance given to "spiritual efficacy," though generally not in a narrative as elaborate as Tan's. In Jing'an Temple, people gathered around a magnetic jade (*hetianyu*) often come up with miraculous stories that justify their belief in the power of specific places and objects (plate 47). For instance, a certain Mr. Cai was traveling with his wife to Mount Putuo (Putuo Shan), a favorite pilgrimage destination for Buddhists from the greater Shanghai area. Although it was raining heavily that day, he took a picture in front of a stone on Mount Putuo. To his surprise, the picture showed sunlight above him and his wife. Since that time, he believes deeply in Buddhism, and he keeps the photo with him as testimony.

Especially for Buddhist and Daoist believers, the efficacy conferred on some objects and places is one with the sacredness of these objects and places, and it determines the way they will be used and treated. Although more discreet, and sometimes even outwardly denied, similar beliefs and practices can be detected among Christian believers. For Catholics, places of pilgrimage, rosaries, and images are easily invested with unspoken powers (plate 34). With the Protestants we met in Shanghai, their relationship to the material object that is the Holy Book may unconsciously compensate for the disenchantment of the material world; the well-worn volume opens up wherever and whenever they need its insights. In many ways, the material environment of urban dwellers is invested with powers and meaning, as is the case in villages where trees, stones, or fountains become channels of religiosity. However, in traditional settings, the community determines the hierarchy and geography of spiritually loaded places and objects, while in the metropolis, individuals insert the shining pearls created by religious imagination into their own thread.

XU: VIRTUAL SPACES

Xuni is the Chinese compound used for translating the word "virtual," with the first character (*xu*) playing a defining function. It is often translated as "vacuous," in contrast to its opposite, *shi*, which means "real," "full," "material." The term has been used in a variety of religious contexts. If its Buddhist usage makes it analogous to "vacuity," Daoist philosophy preserves the original idea of "nebulosity," of a void already filled with potentialities, which legitimizes its use for rendering the contemporary concept of virtual.[12] In the Daoist classic *Zhuangzi*, *xu* is the space where the "fasting of the heart" (*xinzhai*) liberates the mind from all affects, so as to grasp the continuous flow of all things. The semantic history of the word is loaded with connotations that are more spiritual or religious than is the case for its English-language equivalent (even if the latter is anchored in the history of scholastic philosophy).

Tan Dong's testimony shows the importance in spiritual parlance of metaphors anchored in games and virtual reality. Interviews of younger subjects, such as this fifteen-year-old female International School student, offer confirmation.

"What comes to mind when one speaks of sacred?"

"Sacred? The Temples of the Gods (*Shenmiao*) . . ."

"Where is the sacred?"

"Above, in the open, the wilderness, where there are no people. The Temples of the Gods are sacred."

"Do you have some personal experience of it?"

"No, I've only been to Jing'an Temple in my neighborhood, but it's full of people. There is no feeling. I need to go back to what I've read before, such as 'Notre Dame de Paris,' and to things more recent, like 'Temple Spring,' 'Pillars of the Earth,' and then there's such a feeling."

"In Shanghai, there are many churches. When you pass them, do you have that kind of feeling?"

"I did not go there, nor did I feel anything."[13]

In fact, the virtual nature of religious activities has long been recognized. "When Confucius offered sacrifice to his ancestors, he felt *as if* (*ru*) ancestral spirits were present. When he offered sacrifice to other spiritual beings, he felt *as if* they were present. He said, 'If I do not participate in the sacrifice, it is *as if* I did not sacrifice at all'" (*Analects*, 3.12). Confucius insisted that attentive and respectful participation in a ritual would gradually transform one's thoughts and ways of proceeding in such a way that the worshipper would be united with what he was celebrating.[14] The rituals we witnessed were all characterized by this sense of attentiveness and respect (*jing*). The spiritual pathways that people experience and narrate are both the *result* and the *trigger* of the practices and rituals in which they engage.

Spiritual pathways are the *result* when practicing religion is not a matter-of-fact state of affairs. In such an environment, the faithful engage in forms of practice based on what they have already felt, intuited, or even, at the extreme, simply out of a desire for conformity that still reflects the strength of a group encounter. In all cases, some kind of experience precedes and directs the ritual action that takes place, be it personal or collective.

Spiritual pathways are the *trigger* when the performance of a ritual produces effects that deepen, challenge, or modify the nature of the experience on first engaging in ritual practice.

People gather in spaces that are inscribed into the sacred geography, the "second nature," so to speak, shaped by the megalopolis. Such spaces may or may not be officially sanctioned. They may be citywide or part of a small neighborhood; they may offer large, public facilities or be limited to a room, a private altar. In any case, spaces are made functionally sacred — even temporarily — by the way they are marked for specific practices. Within these spaces, further spatial arrangements facilitate the performance of rituals (plate 45). At a lower level of this inverted spatial pyramid, the minds and bodies of practitioners are converted into inner spaces reshaped by ritual performance.

So far, we have identified three ways through which the religious territory of the city can be described as virtual: believers evoke the spiritual powers they refer to as being potentially present in their daily spaces and activities and model their behaviors accordingly; approached as plays or art forms, rituals reorganize spaces and conduct so as to further actualize the spiritual presence that guides and gathers believers; and traces of ritual activities (such as photographs that document the religious fabric of Shanghai) create icons that memorize the effects of such rituals and potentially trigger new effects.

A fourth way of engineering virtual religious territories is linked to the role played by social networks, such as the omnipresent WeChat, in cementing religious sociability. WeChat triggers donations for Animal Release and other causes; it gathers groups that receive daily Bible quotes, schedules of fire worship, or information on healing techniques. Communities gather around official WeChat accounts.

Among other unofficial Evangelical groups in the city, Shanghai Little Lamb Church (Shanghai Xiaoyang Jiaohui) was founded in 2008 as an extension of the Hangzhou-based mother congregation. Its leaders were all trained at the School of Theology of City Harvest Church (Chengshi Fengshou Jiaohui), a megachurch in Singapore known both for its discerning use of new media and for recurring financial scandals.[15] One of the church leaders, Dongfang Yue, is an experienced journalist and program host, with stints at CCTV and local cable stations. Calling herself a "Gospel preaching volunteer" or, more recently, a "watcher" (*shouwangzhe*), she is an avid microblogger. She started Radio Spirituality (Lingxiu Diantai) and moved her program from Lychee FM to the Ximalaya FM platform in 2015. Both stations are mobile application platforms that allow users to set their own radio station, record their programs on their phones, and make them available in podcast form. Lychee FM is "the country's first mobile phone blog application," according to its official website. Within two years, 200 million people downloaded the phone application, with 80 million users, 1.5 million podcasts, and 20 million minutes of original audio programming.[16] In 2016, Dongfang

Yue was broadcasting one ten-minute program per week, with an audience of 3,800–28,000 listeners, the mean averaging 10,000. The broadcasts are carefully conceived and edited. Prose and poetry introduce Bible stories and topics such as the best way of overcoming procrastination.[17] Supported by close-knit religious communities, initiatives such as Radio Spirituality aim to reach out to a larger public, inscribing themselves into the cultural codes of young urbanites and contributing to the shaping of mobile cities. Virtual channels are the waterways of today, linking spiritual compounds with scattered, mobile customers who may or may not wish to eventually join a more stable community.

DONG: NOMADS AND DWELLERS

The networks explored in chapter 5 are characterized by the sense of mobility they offer their members. Throughout our narrative, we met a number of "homeless" believers, in search of a place of their own, and others, like the taxi driver in chapter 4, who seemed to enjoy their wanderings. Mobility is experienced physically; the streets of Shanghai are a space of religious recruiting.

On a Friday afternoon, near People's Square, Liang meets with two young women, Jin Wei (pseud.) and Guo Hani (pseud.), who suggest that they read the Bible together in the nearby Starbucks. (Such encounters are far from uncommon.) Subsequent meetings indicate that they belong to a fringe group, probably of Korean origin. The biblical reading they champion unveils the existence of a Heavenly Mother alongside the Heavenly Father; it also includes interpreting figures found in the Books of Revelation and Daniel. One of the truths unearthed there is that the pope's demonic power began to wane in 1789. As a rule, the two women will not enter a church. "We find the atmosphere in churches gloomy. For worship, it suffices to have a few sisters gathered to celebrate the day, in one house or another. Sisters of our congregation are like family to us. We clean the room, we keep feast day observances, and we feel happy together."

Pilgrimages are another way of entering a mobile religious space. This devotional practice is very popular, especially among Buddhist faithful. Peter Zhang, a volunteer receptionist at Zhangjialou parish, is an enthusiastic Catholic pilgrim. He usually dresses in a green T-shirt with an Emmaus logo printed on it alongside a rose and a fish and, below, in English, the word "Shanghai." He is the proud owner of seven of these T-shirts, one for each day of the week. Peter likes to speak of his pilgrimages. They all led to Sheshan, within the limits of Shanghai. He was quite apprehensive the first and second times he underwent the experience, as the road alongside the urban landscape is neither easy nor agreeable. And both times he got wet. But afterward, he became more confident. He never misses a chance to repeat the journey. It is both physical and spiritual exercise and has become part of his life.

Tim (from Shandong), Peter (from Hebei), and Jin Wei and Guo Hani (from Yunnan and Hebei) are all outsiders. Most probably, their "household registration" (*hukou*) remains listed as their place of birth, as is the case for around 40 percent of Shanghai's population.[18] The believer's inner journey is often rooted in actual experiences of displacement. Physical or virtual displacements are always about the discovery of potential, a new reality, something filled with promise. Religious displacements, whatever their paths, express and sublimate the risks and opportunities linked to the experience of entering a metropolis such as Shanghai.

The sociologist Nancy Ammerman has suggested accounting for "family resemblances" among people who do not necessarily belong to the same creed by distinguishing among various "spiritual tribes."[19] The adjectives "nomadic" and "sedentary" are associated with the term "tribes," which can be either one or the other. In a contemporary urban context, the term "religious sedentism" may apply to people who group together in communities that provide them not only with stable locations but, more importantly, with a spiritual style and a set of devotional practices that solidly frame their religious space and calendar (whatever the intensity of belief and the level of religious attendance). These people can also be described as "dwellers." In fact, in Shanghai and China, people who belong to underground communities, though often led to change their location, nevertheless dwell in a stable religious environment. Religious nomadism or peripateticism may refer to people crossing a variety of religious paths with a fluid sense of affiliation, as is the case for a number of the "new spiritualities" practitioners we met. However, nomadism and sedentarization are at opposite ends of a continuum. People may belong primarily to a stable community while adding up practices such as pilgrimage or networking. This may compensate for what the religious home or compound does not offer. In exploring additional religious spaces, they find a way of expressing a sense of displacement that comes from both personal exploration and social insecurity. In another configuration, people may wander around a restricted spiritual territory, mirroring the one covered by a countryman whose mobility is enhanced by the use of a boat and/or seasonal work opportunities, as was the case for people inserted into the networks of Jiangnan's popular religiosity.

The lexical contrast between "quietness" (*jing*) and "movement" (*dong*) may further illuminate the attitudes at issue. The character *jing* originally referred to the action of pacifying a territory. *Jing* gradually came to mean tranquility, absence of desire, and immobility (an attitude allowing the capacity to examine and discern, according to the specific sense found in the ancient *Shuowen* dictionary).[20] *Dong*, its antonym, refers to movement as a property of living beings; hence it is related to forces stirred by desire or emotion.[21] At the same time, chapter 40 of the *Daodejing* teaches "Returning is the movement of the Way" (*fanzhe dao zhi dong*). This may be read merely as a cosmological statement, which the return of the seasons exemplifies. However, the fact that this statement is immediately followed by "Weakness is the functioning of the Way" (*ruozhe dao zhi yong*) leads one to think that "returning" connotes the course of a force that knows how to "weaken," to revert to its origin once it has accomplished its effect. In no way does the *Daodejing* separate the cosmological, ethical, political, and ontological realms. In every order of reality, quietness and movement alternate and equilibrate.

This contrast is reminiscent of the one developed by the sociologist Thomas Tweed, between "the kinetics of homemaking" and "the kinetics of itinerancy," which he describes as the two poles of religious experience.[22] We fully acknowledge the rapprochement; however, our analysis does not aim at drawing a general theory of religion, as does Tweed's. Tweed takes "dwelling" and "crossing" as two constitutive dynamics of religion proper, "religion as dwelling [situating] devotees in time and space—including in the body, the home, and the cosmos—and religion as crossing [imagining] an ultimate horizon of human life and [prescribing] ways of crossing it."[23] Our study focuses on agents, insisting that, if both dynamics can be found in all subjects and communities, there remains a kind of opposition between "homemakers" and "nomads."

GANYING: RESONANCE

The lexical compound *ganying* is often translated as "correlative resonance," "stimulus and response," "induction," or, in common parlance, "response," "interaction," or even "telepathy."[24] *Ganying*, a notion that emerged in ancient Chinese thought and was conceptualized in early imperial times, refers to a process of "dynamic influences exchanged through the energetic medium of qi."[25] The idea of responses occurring between active agents takes the place of the concept of linear causation in Western philosophy. Attention given to the acoustic phenomenon of sympathetic vibration coalesces in a theory of cosmological resonances.[26] In the political approach developed by the philosopher Xunzi (3rd century BCE), sounds and harmonies affect the body, eliciting different emotions and subsequent moral responses, which eventually shape or threaten the social order.[27] *The Huainanzi* (an encyclopedic treatise of the second century BCE) rather insists on the spontaneous ordering of cosmic and social phenomena when human agents enter into a state of mutual resonance with all things.[28] Later, in Buddhism and in Daoist religion, the term refers to the way the faithful can trigger the deity's empathy, especially through good deeds, so that they may see their prayers answered. The expression is commonly used today. It amalgamates cosmological and moral meanings into an integrative approach to spiritual realities. We refer to it, first, to give an account of our subjects' apprehension of sacred spaces and moments and, second, to attempt a final sketch of Shanghai's religious fabric.

Although in contemporary, urban contexts the sacred and the secular are located on a mental and geographic continuum, which (as noted) makes it sometimes difficult to strictly separate between the two, there still exists a process through which sacred space-times are somehow crystallizing. A number of such crystallizations come to mind: home celebrations before Chinese New Year and visits to temples on the first morning of the year, sweeping ancestors' graves or visiting a columbarium at appropriate times, caring for hungry souls wandering through the neighborhood during the ghost month, celebrating Christmas in one of the city's churches, re-enchanting the urban landscape through a short-length pilgrimage or Animal Release rituals, circumambulating one's territory according to a temple festivals calendar, communing as a close-knit brotherhood in a makeshift place of worship, exchanging and reinforcing energies in a healing session. Each of these fragile sacred space-times may be compared to an echo chamber. Within it, correlative resonances link the worshippers and link worshippers with ancestors and/or other spiritual powers. The design and intensity of these acoustic configurations depend on the time, place, and creed that gather the community. Sacred music itself speaks not only of a creed and a religious sensitivity but also of the ethos of the worshipping community, of the universe it creates for itself (plate 46). When community support is lacking, it becomes much harder for urban dwellers to imagine the city as a conduct of sacredness. At the same time, interviews conducted by Chen Jia-ren in January 2016 testify to the fact that, even for spiritual loners, the idea of the sacred — seen as the "other" of the profane world of the metropolis — remains operative.

A twenty-seven-year-old male freelancer observed, "Buddhist places of worship, Christian churches — these places are more sacred than others. I think it has to do with the mind emptying itself, as if starting from zero. When entering that kind of place, it feels like the soul is being washed — a new beginning, cleanliness. It seems that one does not have this kind of experience in Shanghai."

Several other interviewees had similar opinions of Shanghai's sacred places. A small-business owner, a woman of about forty, commented, "I believe in Buddhism. For me, all temples are sacred. Honestly speaking, I don't feel that Shanghai has places that feel particularly sacred. Shanghai is a foreign precinct that holds a wide variety of cultures, but it's not a place in which I can feel sacredness."

A male freelancer, thirty-five years old, responded, "Shanghai is not sacred. Sacredness has little contact with daily life. It's found only in some exceptional environments, that is, when you go to some scenic spots, cultural remains, or in African villages."

To these three interviewees, the density of Shanghai's urban environment and the hectic lives of its inhabitants disturb the process by which privileged places foster communication and response between divine, cosmic, and human energies. In such a context, the heart (*xin*) becomes the ultimate echo chamber, as another interviewee, a female retiree, fifty-six years old, explained: "Sacredness lies in my own heart. One shouldn't too easily tell other people about it. I put this at the bottom of my heart and tell myself about it.... Deep down, there is this thing: I'm conversing with myself. This is the feeling."

People who question the megalopolis's capacity to generate sacredness are prone to imagine sacredness as cross-fertilized by nature and mysticism. (Tibet is regularly mentioned as the ultimate sacred place.) Such people are often spiritual loners. For worshippers attached to a community, however small it may be, the experience of sacredness is generated primarily by the group performance of rituals at specific times and places. A space becomes sacred when the ritual that awakens its capacity to reverberate has been put into motion.

How do the sacred resonances awakened by one space-time or another blend or discord with the ones created by the other religious enclosures of the city? Sacred space-times respond to (rather than dialogue with) each other. Representations of religious interactions within a given urban or national space often insist on their dialogical and/or hostile nature.[29] We have seen relatively little of either in Shanghai, although Chinese Internet forums sometimes feature growing feelings of uneasiness among religions, notably between Buddhism and Christianity. Curiously, the clearest allusion to religious hostility we found appears in an official report. A study commissioned by the Jinze Township government sees the vitality of popular religion in the area as an effective containment against Christianity and contrasts it with the situation prevalent in Greater Shanghai. According to the report, there are only five hundred to six hundred followers of Protestant Christianity in Jinze, most of whom come from outside the town. Even in the adjacent water town of Zhujiiajiao, it notes, Christians, ten times more numerous, are mostly locals. Zhujiajiao's pastor explains that the struggle against superstitions in the 1950s to 1970s was much more rigorous in Zhujiajiao than in Jinze. This created a religious vacuum that was filled by Christianity from the 1980s onward. In today's Jinze, notes the report, the few elderly people who converted to Christianity are ostracized by their relatives. If illness strikes a family that counts a Christian among its members, the misfortune is automatically attributed to the lack of filial piety exhibited by the foreign creed. Adverse reactions to the Christian way of celebrating funerals are so strong that most Buddhist worshippers and followers of popular religion (*bai Pusa de ren*)[30] do not want to eat with Christians. And when the church's glass windows were broken, the local shop refused to sell new ones.[31]

We found and heard very few comments and stories similar to those quoted here. Shanghai's religious scene is better illustrated by the performance described in the introduction to this book—groups gathered on a stage by state authorities, playing tug-of-war before returning to relative isolation. Direct dialogue is a rare occurrence, even among friends and colleagues. Still, religious communities respond to each other. They are watchful of the competition and observe the proselytizing of others. They locate religious buildings on the map, pleased with their own landmarks, or, for unofficial groups, lament the invisibility imposed on them by governmental policies while taking paradoxical pride in it. They respond to the state's attempt to control them and build alternative sacredness through tactics that they endlessly devise and adapt for preserving and developing spaces of their own. From an outsider's viewpoint, spaces and groups respond to one another by contributing to the city's varied religious landscape (plate 48). As with Leibniz's monads, described at the beginning of this chapter, religious spaces and groups are viewpoints from which to appreciate Shanghai's religious universe. Though each of them gives rise to a different world, these monads taken as a whole are like the innumerable facets of one and the same universe.

FASHIONING A SACRED SPACE-TIME

Durkheim was already fashioning an approach to sacredness based on space-time when he combined polarities in spatial location with seasonal alternations. In his account, some places were set apart from normal use, so as to foster the full efficiency of rituals without contaminating social relations in their entirety, and the season of sacred effervescence contrasted with the season dedicated to the quest for subsistence. Accrued social complexity, especially in an urban context, comes with the multiplication of coordinates that must be taken into account, to the point of considering sacred space-times as continuums rather than as combinations of discrete entities organized according to a rigid system.

Our exploration of Shanghai enables us to integrate Chinese resources into a global approach to contemporary religious life, drawing on practical observation as well as the Chinese lexical and conceptual toolbox. They do not apply only to Chinese realities; rather, they frame the social and religious field the same way the Latin vocabulary around the word "sacredness" helped us approach it initially. Our discussion includes five essential features.

First, those who enter into a specific religious setting transition from a nebulous to a legible religious universe, which a community makes welcoming enough that a new practitioner can dwell in it. This goes along with the development of an orthopraxy, which gives accrued meaning to spatial and temporal divisions. Orthopraxy contributes to give differentiated values to moments and spaces, and it determines the way both are used. The effort to discriminate between what is "correct" and "incorrect" remains a basic feature of any consciously organized religious universe.

Second, particular qualities are attributed to some objects, moments, and spaces that magnetize and orient the spiritual universe in which the religious seeker dwells. At certain times and locations, particular epiphanies, which may be mediated by objects and people with specific spiritual efficacy (*ling*), confirm, alter, or reveal the structure and meaning of the universe the believer inhabits. Ideally, the sum of all events that create texture in a religious community composes its space-time.

Third, religious events are time spans dedicated to personal prayer, collective celebrations, meals, and other symbolic actions and decisions. These events are also lived as if they are occurring in virtual reality, that is, as if revealing the potentialities hidden within everyday existence. As lived by those who are immersed in it, a religious space-time is a virtualized version of social existence. This virtualized space-time in turn affects the features of the collective reality from which it originates.

Fourth, another polarity opposes a secure dwelling within the limits of one's community to the enlarging of the existing universe or the crossing of its frontiers. There is a perpetual trade-off between the sense of belonging and the thrill of exploration. Individuals eventually achieve their own balance. Scenarios of accommodation may include firm commitment or a weak level of religious affiliation, passage from one community to another, or regular poaching in another religious universe with a return to one's original dwelling.

Finally, the resources offered by the notion of correlative resonances helps structure the preceding perspectives into a whole. First, worshippers live sacred space-times as echo chambers; second, like-minded "spiritual monads" tend to aggregate into spiritual tribes that can be disbanded and reshaped; and third, different religious space-times function within the same territory as multiple viewpoints on a shared sacred universe.

These perspectives cannot fully represent the depth and multiplicity of a spiritual seeker's experiences. Rather, they try to reconcile the focus on religious inventiveness as an interweaving of personal journeys with its study as a patterned social phenomenon. The quote from Pascal that opens this chapter insists on the limitless divisibility of observed realities, while the quote from Leibniz points toward their harmonization as a theoretical horizon.[32] Neither stance should be ignored. Both quotes make use of the metaphor of the city as the exemplar of a universe that is whole and yet endlessly fragmented. This concept resonates with our experiences throughout Shanghai. Disconcertingly diverse and contradictory in its expressions, the metropolis fosters an ethos that suffuses spaces, groups, and personal quests, which all appear as fragments of the same collective adventure. Embedded in the culture and destiny of the nation to which it belongs, while sharing some defining features with other world metropolises, Shanghai has developed its own spiritual being, protean and yet recognizable, multifarious and continuously unfolding. All the religious expressions we have studied, and many others, texture the sacred tapestry that weaves patterns from the wandering lines scribbled throughout the city by residents and sojourners.

APPENDIX

Fieldwork Sites

The following is further location information for the fieldwork sites labeled on the maps in this book.

SYMBOLIC SHANGHAI (MAP 2)

1. Shanghai Government 上海市人民政府
   200 Renmin Avenue 新黄浦区人民大道200号

2. Shanghai Museum 上海博物馆
   201 Renmin Avenue 新黄浦区人民大道201号

3. The Bund 外滩

4. Xintiandi 新天地
   Lane 191 Taicang Road 新黄浦区太仓路191弄

5. China Art Museum (Chinese Pavilion of Expo Shanghai 2010)
   中华艺术宫 （中国2010年上海世博会中国国家馆）
   205 Shangnan Road 浦东新区上南路205号

6. Yu Garden 豫园

7. Shanghai Tower 上海中心大厦
   51 West Lujiazui Road 浦东新区陆家嘴西路51号

8. Jin Mao Tower 金茂大厦
   88 Century Avenue 浦东新区世纪大道88号

9. Shanghai World Financial Center 环球金融中心
   100 Shiji Avenue 浦东新区世纪大道100号

10. Oriental Pearl Radio and TV Tower 东方明珠广播电视塔
    1 Century Avenue 浦东新区世纪大道1号

11. Pudong International Airport 上海浦东国际机场
    300 Qihang Road 浦东新区启航路300号

12. Hongqiao International Airport 上海虹桥国际机场
    2550 Hongqiao Road 长宁区虹桥路2550号

13. Xu Guangqi Memorial Park and Hall 光启公园
    17 Nandan Road 徐汇区南丹路17号

14. Shanghai Jewish Refugees Museum (former Ohel Moishe Synagogue)
    上海犹太难民纪念馆（摩西会堂旧址）
    62 Changyang Road 虹口区长阳路62号

15. Shanghai Exhibition Centre 上海展览中心
    1000 Middle Yan'an Road 新静安区延安中路1000号

16. Former residence of Sun Yat-sen 上海孙中山故居纪念馆
    7 Xiangshan Road 新静安区香山路7号

17. CWI Children's Palace 中国福利会少年宫
    64 West Yan'an Road 新静安区延安西路64号

18. Shanghai Disney Resort 上海迪士尼乐园
    Shanghai Disney Resort, Chuansha Town, Pudong New District
    浦东新区川沙新镇上海迪士尼度假区

LANDMARKS OF CIVIC SACREDNESS (MAP 3)

1. People's Square 人民广场
   Renmin Avenue 新黄浦区人民大道

2. Memorial Hall of the First National Congress of the Chinese
   Communist Party 中国共产党第一次全国代表大会会址
   374 South Huangpi Road 新黄浦区黄陂南路374号

3. Shanghai Municipal History Museum 上海城市历史发展陈列馆
   Oriental Pearl Radio and TV Tower, 1 Century Avenue
   浦东新区世纪大道1号东方明珠广播电视塔

4. Shanghai Monument to the People's Heroes 上海市人民英雄纪念塔
   500 Zhongshan Dongyi Road 新黄浦区中山东一路500号黄浦公园

5. Longhua Revolutionary Martyrs' Cemetery 上海市龙华烈士陵园
   180 West Longhua Road 徐汇区龙华西路180号

6. China Art Museum (Chinese Pavilion of Expo Shanghai 2010)
   中华艺术宫（中国2010年上海世博会中国国家馆）
   205 Shangnan Road 浦东新区上南路205号

7. Shanghai Exhibition Centre 上海展览中心
   1000 Middle Yan'an Road 新静安区延安中路1000号

8. City God Temple of Shanghai 上海城隍庙
   249 Middle Fangbang Road 新黄浦区方浜中路249号

9. Shanghai Confucian Temple 文庙
   215 Wenmiao Road 新黄浦区文庙路215号

10. Jiading Confucius Temple and Examinations Museum 嘉定孔庙
    183 Zhennan Street 嘉定区镇南大街183

11. Songjiang Guangfulin Relics Park 广富林遗址公园
    Guangfulin Relics Park, Sheshan Hill 松江区佘山广富林

12. Fushouyuan Cemetery Park 上海福寿园
    600, Lane 7270 Waisong Gong Road 青浦区外青松公路7270弄600号

13. Longhua Crematorium and Funerary Museum 上海市龙华殡仪馆
    210 Caoxi Road 徐汇区漕溪路210号

14. Xu Guangqi Memorial Park and Hall 光启公园
    17 Nandan Road 徐汇区南丹路17号

15. Shanghai Songhu Anti-Japanese Campaign Memorial Hall
    上海淞沪抗战纪念馆
    1 Youyi Road 宝山区友谊路1号

RELIGIOUS LANDMARKS (MAP 4)

1. St. Ignatius Cathedral (Xujiahui Church) 圣伊纳爵主教座堂
   （徐家汇天主堂）
   158 Puxi Road 徐汇区蒲西路158号

2. Sheshan Basilica of Our Lady Help of Christians 佘山進教之佑圣母大殿
   Western Peak of Sheshan Hill 松江区佘山山顶

3. St. Francis Xavier Church (Dongjiadu Church) 圣方济各沙勿略堂
   （董家渡天主堂）
   185 Dongjiadu Road 新黄浦区董家渡路185号

4. St. Nicholas Church 圣尼古拉（尼克莱）教堂旧址
   16 Gaolan Road 新黄浦区皋兰路16号

5. Former Ohel Rachel Synagogue 拉结会堂/西摩路会堂
   500 West Shanxi Road 新静安区陕西北路500号

6. Moore Memorial Church 沐恩堂
   316 Middle Xizang Road 新黄浦区西藏中路316号

7. Hengshan Community Church 上海国际礼拜堂
   53 Hengshan Road 徐汇区衡山路53号

8. East Shanghai Church 基督教沪东堂
   350 Guohe Road 杨浦区国和路350号

9. Grace Church 怀恩堂
   375 North Shanxi Road 新静安区陕西北路375号

10. City God Temple of Shanghai 上海城隍庙
    249 Middle Fangbang Road 新黄浦区方浜中路249号

11. White Clouds Monastery 上海白云观
    239 Dajing Road 新黄浦区大境路239号

12. Qinciyang Hall Daoist Temple 钦赐仰殿
    476 Yuansheng Road 浦东新区源深路476号

13. Xiao Taoyuan Mosque 小桃园清真寺
    52 Xiaotaoyuan Street 新黄浦区小桃园街52号

14. Fuyou Road Mosque 福佑路清真寺
    378 Fuyou Road 新黄浦区福佑路378号

15. Songjiang Mosque 松江清真寺
    75 Gangbeng Xiang 松江区缸甏巷75号

16. Jing'an Temple 上海静安寺
    1686 West Nanjing Road 新静安区南京西路1686号

17. Jade Buddha Temple 上海玉佛禅寺
    170 Anyuan Road 普陀区安远路170号

18. Longhua Temple 龙华寺
    2853 Longhua Road 徐汇区龙华路2853号

19. Shanghai Dongling Temple 上海东林寺
    150 Donglin Street, Zhujiang Town 金山区朱泾镇东林街150号

20. Eaglewood Pavilion 沉香阁
    29 Chenxiangge Road 黄浦区沉香阁路29号

21. Dongyue Temple 上海松江东岳庙
    9, Lane 196 Middle Zhongshan Road 松江区中山中路196弄9号

1. Fuyou Road Mosque 福佑路清真寺 (又名"穿心街回教堂", 俗称"北寺")
   378 Fuyou Road 新黄浦区福佑路378号

2. Songjiang Mosque 松江清真寺 (俗称"云间白鹤寺")
   75 Gangbeng Xiang 松江区缸甓巷75号

3. Xiao Taoyuan Mosque 小桃园清真寺 (俗称"清真西寺")
   52 Xiaotaoyuan Street 新黄浦区小桃园街52号

4. Xiao Taoyuan Women's Mosque 清真女寺
   24 Xiaotaoyuan Street 新黄浦区小桃园街24号

5. Pudong Mosque 浦东清真寺
   375 Yuanshen Road 浦东新区源深路375号

6. Huxi Mosque 沪西清真寺 (俗称"老寺")
   3, Lane 1328 Changde Road 普陀区常德路1328弄3号

7. Jiangwan Mosque 江湾清真寺
   86 Zhengfu Road 杨浦区政府路86号

8. Jinshan Mosque 上海金山清真寺
   136 Lipu Road 金山区荔浦路136号

Note: Private or unofficial places of meeting and worship are not listed.

CATHOLIC FIELDWORK SITES (MAP 6)

1. Sheshan Basilica of Our Lady Help of Christians 佘山圣母大堂
   Western Peak of Sheshan Hill 松江区佘山山顶

2. St. Francis Xavier Church (Dongjiadu Church) 圣方济各沙勿略堂
   (董家渡天主堂)
   185 Dongjiadu Road 新黄浦区董家渡路185号

3. St. Ignatius Cathedral (Xujiahui Church) 圣伊纳爵主教座堂
   (徐家汇天主堂)
   158 Puxi Road 徐汇区蒲西路158号

4. St. Michael's Church 曹家渡天主堂
   1066 Wanhangdu Road 长宁区万航渡路1066号

5. Christ the King Church 君王堂 (巨鹿路君王堂、巨鹿路天主堂、帝王堂)
   361 Julu Road 新黄浦区巨鹿路361号

6. Sacred Heart of Jesus Church (Zhangjialou) 张家楼天主堂
   （耶稣圣心堂）
   151 Hongfeng Road 浦东新区红枫路151号

7. Sacred Heart of Jesus Church 川沙天主堂（川沙耶稣圣心堂）
   15, Lane 42 Zhongshi Street, Chuansha New Town
   浦东新区川沙新镇中市街42弄15号

8. Our Lady of Lourdes Basilica 唐镇天主堂(唐墓桥露德圣母堂)
   50 Tangzhen Old Street 浦东新区唐镇老街50号

9. St. Peter's Catholic Church of Nanqiao New Town 圣伯多禄堂
   Nanqiao New Town, Fengxian District 奉贤区南桥新城

10. Sacred Heart of Our Lady Church 怒江路天主堂(圣母圣心堂)
    638 Nujiang Road 普陀区怒江路638号

11. Saint Joseph's Church 四川南路天主堂(洋泾浜圣若瑟堂)
    36 South Sichuan Road 新黄浦区四川南路36号

12. St. Teresa's Church 大田路天主堂(小德肋撒堂天主堂)
    370 Datian Road 新静安区大田路370号

13. St. Peter's Church 圣伯多禄堂
    270 Chongqing Road 新黄浦区重庆南路270号

14. Catholic Prayer Hall of Huaxin 华新镇祈祷所
    Fishery Village, Huaxin Town, Qingpu District 青浦区华新镇水产村

15. Sacred Heart of Jesus Church 虹口天主堂(虹口圣心堂)
    246 Nanxun Road 虹口区南浔路246号

16. Our Lady of Peace Church 惠民路天主堂（和平之后圣母堂）
    692 Huimin Road 杨浦区惠民路692号

17. Sacred Heart Church of Chongming Island 崇明大公所天主堂
    （耶稣圣心堂）
    Gangyan Town, Junma Village 崇明县港沿镇骏马村

Note: Private or unofficial places of meeting and worship are not listed.

PROTESTANT FIELDWORK SITES (MAP 7)

1. Hengshan Community Church 上海国际礼拜堂
   53 Hengshan Road 徐汇区衡山路53号

2. Hongde Church 鸿德堂
   59 Duolun Street 虹口区多伦路59号

3. Moore Memorial Church 沐恩堂
   316 Middle Xizang Road 新黄浦区西藏中路316号

4. Young John Allen Memorial Church 景灵堂
   135 Kunshan Road 虹口区昆山路135号

5. Grace Church 怀恩堂
   375 North Shanxi Road 新静安区陕西北路375号

6. All Saints Church 诸圣堂
   425 Middle Fuxing Road 新黄浦区复兴中路425号

7. Jiangwan Church 江湾基督堂
   1717 Shuidian Road 虹口区水电路1717号

8. Abundant Grace Church 鸿恩堂
   455 Hongfeng Road 浦东新区红枫路455号

9. Protestant Church of Nanqiao New Town 耶稣堂
   Nanqiao New Town 奉贤区南桥新城

10. East Shanghai Church 基督教沪东堂
    350 Guohe Road 杨浦区国和路350号

Note: Private or unofficial places of meeting and worship are not listed.

BUDDHIST FIELDWORK SITES (MAP 8)

1. Xilin Temple 西林禅寺
   666 Middle Zhongshan Road 松江区中山中路666号

2. Changren Temple 长仁禅寺
   2 Wangqiao Street, Chuansha New Town 浦东新区川沙新镇王桥街2号

3. Zhiye Temple 知也禅寺
   Songjiang Guangfulin Relics Park 松江区广富林遗址公园

4. Sanguan Temple 三观堂
   359 Wan'an Road 虹口区万安路359号

5. Baoshan Temple 宝山寺
   518 Luoxi Road 宝山区罗溪路518号

6. Yongfu An 永福庵
   2, Lane 351, Nanchen Road 宝山区南陈路351弄2号

7. Jinhuang Temple 金皇讲寺
   Feng Village, Dachang Town 宝山区大场镇葑村

8. Guangfu Temple 广福寺
   Guangfu Village, Gu Town, Baoshan District 宝山区顾村镇广福村

9. Chan Yi Club House 禅一静观堂
   1, Lane 91 Changshou Road, Jing'an District 新静安区长寿路91弄1号

10. Eaglewood Pavilion 沉香阁
    29 Chenxiangge Road 新黄浦区沉香阁路29号

11. Jade Buddha Temple 玉佛寺
    170 Anyuan Road 普陀区安远路170号

12. Longhua Temple 龙华寺
    2853 Longhua Road 徐汇区龙华路2853号

13. Jing'an Temple 静安寺
    1686 West Nanjing Road 新静安区南京西路1686号

14. Qingjing Temple 清净庵
    Deyun Cun, Chenjia Town, Chongming District 崇明县陈家镇德云村

15. Baohua Temple 宝华寺
    1000 Gaoping Road, Pengpu Town 新静安区彭浦镇高平路1000号

16. Zhenru Temple 真如寺
    399 Lanxi Road, Zhenru Town 普陀区真如镇兰溪路399号

17. Jinshan Wanshou Temple 万寿寺
    1148 Jinwei Town, Weizhen 金山区卫镇金卫村1148号

18. Yihao Temple 颐浩禅寺
    12 Yingxiang Street, Jinze Town 青浦区金泽镇迎祥街12号

19. Xiahai Temple 下海庙
    73 Kunming Road 虹口区昆明路73号

DAOIST AND DAOIST-RELATED FIELDWORK SITES (MAP 10)

1. Dongyue Temple 东岳庙
   9, Lane 196 Middle Zhongshan Road 松江区中山中路196弄9号

2. White Clouds Monastery 白云观
   239 Dajing Road 新黄浦区大境路239号

3. City God Temple of Shanghai 上海城隍庙
   249 Middle Fangbang Road 新黄浦区方浜中路249号

4. City God Temple of Jiading 嘉定城隍庙
   314 Dongda Street 嘉定区东大街314号

5. Qinciyang Hall Temple 钦赐仰殿
   476 Yuanshen Road 浦东新区源深路476号

6. Sanlin Chongfu Temple 崇福道院
   555 Yangnan Road, Sanlin Town 浦东新区三林镇杨南路555号

7. Shanghai Qigong Institute 上海市气功研究所
   650 South Wanping Road 徐汇区宛平南路650号

8. Zongguan Temple 总管庙
   8 Shangtang Street, Jinze Town 青浦区金泽镇上塘街8号

9. Yangzhen Temple 杨震庙
   61 Peiyu Road, Jinze Town 青浦区金泽镇培育路61号

ALTERNATIVE SPIRITUALITIES FIELDWORK SITES (MAP 11)

1. Floatessence 原宿漂浮
   96-1, East Ronghua Road 长宁区荣华东路96号-1

2. Just Yoga Xujiahui Studio 上海Just Yoga 瑜伽工作室徐家汇馆
   Tianping Hotel, 185 Tianping Road 徐汇区天平路185号

3. Just Yoga Minhang Studio 上海Just Yoga瑜伽工作室闵行馆
   360 Xingle Road 闵行区幸乐路360号

4. My Soul Yoga West Nanjing Road Studio, My Soul Yoga 南京西路会所
   3-4F, 218 Fengxian Road 新静安区南京西路奉贤路218号3-4楼

5. My Soul Yoga Fuxing Park Studio, My Soul Yoga复兴公园会所
   2F, 99 Yandang Road 新黄浦区雁荡路99号2楼

6. Centre for Spiritual Living–Shanghai (CSL)
   R. 311, Building 3, Lane 200 Taikang Road 新黄浦区田子坊泰康路200
      弄3号楼311室

7. Shantih Shala Holistic Arts
   Near Shanghai Library 上海图书馆附近

8. Tibetan Tea Club 安驿·茶中藏茶会所
   42-2 Xingfu Road 长宁区幸福路42-2号

9. Kundalini Studio 昆达里尼工作坊
   68, Lane 7611 Zhongchun Road, Minhang District
      闵行区中春路7611弄68号

10. Octave 音昱
    357 Jianguo Xi Lu, Xuhui District 徐汇区建国西路357号

NOTES

PREFACE

1 An initial presentation of our conceptual apparatus was published as Liz Hingley, Benoît Vermander, and Liang Zhang, "(Re)locating Sacredness in Shanghai." The theses first introduced in this article have been thoroughly reworked and expanded for the present publication.

2 Daoist buildings are also sometimes unaccounted for. For example, chapter 5 mentions visits to two Daoist temples that are officially registered as Buddhist, although observation immediately confirmed that worship at these places is purely Daoist or popular-religious in nature and the two temples were simply recorded under the district's Buddhist association at a time when the authorities looked on Daoism with suspicion.

3 Field reports on this topic by Ge Zhuang partly supplemented this gap. See Ge Zhuang, "Hushang wailai liudong Musilin qunti de jingshen shenghuo"; Ge, "Shanghai de qingzhen yinshi wenhua."

4 Schneider and Wright, *Between Art and Anthropology*, 12.

5 See Grimshaw, *The Ethnographer's Eye*.

6 Bell, *Ritual*, 82.

7 Chopra, "Robert Gardner's 'Forest of Bliss,'" 3.

8 Henri Franses has suggested seeing Byzantine icons as both conductor and partial insulator of the sacred, structuring the experience in a way "sensory but not visceral, engaging but not terrifying" ("Partial Transmission," 187). This may well characterize the "effects" created here by the photographs.

9 As it is beyond the scope of this study, we do not offer an extended analysis of the global city concept, understood here simply as an urban center that plays the role of an especially important node in the global system, not only in its economic and financial dimensions but also in its manifold cultural manifestations. For an approach to the concept and its applicability to Asian metropolises, see, notably, Roy and Ong, *Worlding Cities*. For studies of Shanghai as a global city, see, among others, Wasserstrom, *Global Shanghai*; Greenspan, *Shanghai Future*.

10 See Long Finance, "GFCI 20 The Overall Ranking," accessed January 7, 2017, www.longfinance.net/global-financial-centres-index-20/1034-gfci-20-the-overall-rankings.html.

11   Among recent publications, see Veer, *Handbook of Religion*, which focuses on the interaction between religious aspirations and the Asian urbanization process; and Garbin and Strhan, *Religion and the Global City*, which gives special attention to identity and migration issues. For a historical perspective on religion and globalization in the Chinese context, see Jansen, Klein, and Meyer, *Globalization*.

12   On the application of the notion of montage to visual ethnography, see Suhr and Willerslev, "Can Film Show the Invisible?"

INTRODUCTION

1   The United Front Work Department (Tongzhanbu) is an agency that manages relations with influential non–Communist Party individuals and organizations. Among other duties, it supervises relations with religious groups and ethnic minorities. It has branches at all administrative levels.

2   In 2015, Shanghai's permanent residential population was 24.15 million, with 40.6 percent of the total not recorded under local household registration. Zhang Ningning, "Shanghai's Non-local Population Drops for First Time in 15 Years," *Shanghai Daily*, March 1, 2016.

3   Shanghai Commission for Ethnic and Religious Affairs, "Short Presentation of Religions in Shanghai" (Shanghai zongjiao jianjie), December 25, 2014, accessed January 15, 2016, www.shmzw.gov.cn/gb/mzw/shzj/index.html. The same page lists 1,235,300 believers, but it is hard to assess the significance of this figure, as there is no explanation of how the number of Buddhist and Daoist faithful was estimated, participants in Protestant home churches and Catholic underground communities are not counted, and estimates of practitioners without resident permits raise additional difficulties. We were able to compile a list of 416 sites by consulting all sections of this website and the websites it forwards to. The gap between the two figures (430 and 416) is not significant, and the listing we compiled from Internet sources did not include at least one "prayer place" (*qidaosuo*) that we had visited and know to be officially recognized. The figure of 430 for official places of worship is thus reasonably accurate, though it gives the outsider only a pale idea of Shanghai's religious vitality. There is no estimate of the number of unofficial places and communities.

4   Shanghai Commission for Ethnic and Religious Affairs, "The Situation of Buddhism in Shanghai" (Shanghai shi Fojiao gaikuang), October 14, 2015, accessed January 16, 2016, www.shmzw.gov.cn/gb/mzw/shzj/fj/index.html.

5   Zhou, *Shanghai jiaotang jianzhu ditu*, 11.

6   For the establishment in Shanghai of Ciji (romanized as Tzu Chi in Taiwan) a Buddhist organization that originated in Taiwan, see Huang, "The Bodhisattva Comes Out."

7   Working with a group of sixty overseas Chinese, Christian executives living in Shanghai, Joy Tong has found that forty-seven were members of a church before arriving in China, while thirteen became Christians after their arrival (Tong, "Christian Ethics").

8   Aelius Gallus, quoted by Festus, *Lexicon* 424. Cf. Schilling, "Sacrum et profanum," 954.

9   Festus, *Lexicon* 298. Cf. Schilling, "Sacrum et profanum," 954.

10 Trebatius, quoted by Macrobius, *Saturnalia* III, 3, 4. Cf. Schilling, "Sacrum et profanum," 954.

11 See, e.g., Jin, "Ruhe lijie zongjiao de 'shenshengxing,'" which is based on Eliade's premises.

12 Here we do not deal with the question of the specific historical sequence in which societies similar to the ones described by Durkheim may have appeared. Mary Douglas postulates the coexistence of strongly ritualized tribal societies with others that are very secular in outlook. However, as noted by Robert Bellah, Douglas remains quite Durkheimian in her approach, as she links degrees of religiosity to intensity of social organization. See Douglas, *Natural Symbols*, 99; Bellah, *Religion in Human Evolution*, 137.

13 Durkheim, *Elementary Forms*, 34.

14 Ibid., 35.

15 Durkheim, *Professional Ethics*, 143.

16 Durkheim, *Elementary Forms*, 215.

17 Ibid., 221.

18 Ibid., 322.

19 Ibid., 415, 416.

20 Rumor among locals is that business at Super Brand Mall, a major shopping center in Pudong, was bad, so the owners installed the shrine in front of the mall, and things improved. Many passersby stop and pray at the shrine in the heart of the business district.

21 Pickering, *Durkheim's Sociology of Religion*, 143–49; Lukes, *Emile Durkheim*, 25.

22 Scheid, *Les dieux, l'État*, 27–28.

23 Granet, *La religion des Chinois*, 103.

24 Ibid., 106–7.

25 Goossaert and Palmer, *The Religious Question*, 28.

26 See Veer, *Modern Spirit of Asia*.

27 *Grand Dictionnaire Ricci*, character 2452.

28 When a reference to semantic history makes it necessary, we provide the simplified and traditional forms of the character.

29 Shun, "Ren and Li," 54.

30 Harley, "An Existential Reading."

31 Ing, *The Dysfunction of Ritual*, 304.

32 Fingarette, *Confucius*.

33 Goossaert, *Dans les Temples de Chine*.

34 De Bary, *Self and Society*, ix.

35 Works anchored in structural analysis have often shown special sensitivity to the way in which social practices were balancing continuities and discontinuities in the representation of life processes. See Macherel, "Le pain."

36 For an overall presentation of Chinese communal religion toward the late Qing period, see Goossaert and Palmer, *The Religious Question*, 20–27.

37 The dictionary *Xiandai hanyu cidian* defines *shensheng* as "something inviolable" (*buke qinfan*), as is the national territory.

38 Vermander and Xie, "Avec leurs voix propres."

39 However, Chinese scholars studying contemporary Buddhism usually refer to this lexicon. See, for instance, Lin Xiangping, "Renjian Fojiao de shenshengxing."

40 Certeau, *Practice of Everyday Life*.

41 Ibid., xix.

42 Ibid., xviii.

43 Elias, *The Society of Individuals*, 32.

44 Ibid., 19–20.

45 Elias, *The Court Society*, 144.

46 Elias, *What Is Sociology?*, 130. These three analogies were brought together by Chartier, *On the Edge*, 111–12.

47 See Lenoir and Standaert, *Les danses rituelles chinoises*.

48 Wendling, *Ethnologie des joueurs d'échecs*.

49 Hamayon, *Why We Play*. In French, the word *jeu* refers to both games and play. Published in a series dedicated to Maussian studies, Hamayon's book focuses on *le jeu* in the way Mauss was studying *le don*.

50 Wei-cheng Lin, *Building a Sacred Mountain*, 5.

51 Ibid.

CHAPTER 1. MAPPING SHANGHAI

1 Lee, *Shanghai Modern*; Fogel, "The Recent Boom."

2 Xiong, "20 shiji Shanghai shi yanjiu"; Zuo Yuhe, "Zhongguo jindaishi yanjiu de fanshi zhizheng yu chaoyue zhilu"; Liu and Jiang, "Panluan yu xiandaixing."

3 For a detailed official narrative, see Ruan and Gao, *Shanghai zongjiao shi*. See also Li, *Renwen Shanghai*. General histories of Shanghai in Western languages (notably, Bergère, *Shanghai*) often include rich analyses of religious developments.

4 Brook, "Xu Guangqi," 92.

5 On the aggiornamento, see Ge, "A Survey"; on urban Daoist culture, see Liu, *Daoist Modern*.

6 Goossaert, "The Heavenly Master," 243.

7 Hamashima, "Communal Religion," 129.

8 Johnson, "Shanghai," 154.

9 Elvin, "Market Towns and Waterways."

10 Li, "Jiangnan zhenxiang jisi tixi zhong de difang yu guojia," 78. There was already a temple to Tianhou (Mazu), deity of seafarers, in the Yuan dynasty (1279–1368); however, temples in other maritime provinces were attracting more attention.

11 Brook, "Xu Guangqi," 73–75.

12 Ibid., 77–84.

13 Wakeman, *Policing Shanghai*, 25–26. See also Lu, "Huidaomen."

14 The common-trade associations may also be thought of as "guilds" and "corporations."

15 Johnson, "Shanghai," 168–69.

16 Goodman, *Native Place*, 25.

17 Henriot, *Scythe and the City*, 48.

18 Goodman, *Native Place*, 92–103.

19 Bai, "Yisilanjiao zai Shanghai."

20 Ma, "Cong Haifurun anjian kan Qianlong dui Huizu de tongzhi zhengce"; Luo, "Haifurun shijian," 206.

21 Bergère, *Shanghai*, 17.

22 See Yang Rongbin, *Minguo shiqi Shanghai Huizu shangren qunti yanjiu.*

23 Ruan and Gao, *Shanghai zongjiao shi*, 566–98.

24 See Shanghai Census, accessed June 7, 2016, www.stats-sh.gov.cn/sjfb/201203/239823 .html. The Chinese census does not ask about religious affiliations. The estimated number of Muslims was derived by adding up the population of ten ethnic groups that traditionally are Muslim.

25 See Shi, "Christian Scholar Xu Guangqi," 203.

26 La Servière, *Jusqu'à l'établissement d'un vicaire*, 111–14.

27 Wiest, "Les jésuites français."

28 Des Forges, *Mediasphere Shanghai*; Liang, *Mapping Modernity in Shanghai.*

29 Meng, *Shanghai,* xxv.

30 Quoted in La Servière, *Jusqu'à l'établissement d'un vicaire*, 24.

31 This paragraph is based on Vermander, "Jesuits and China."

32 Anonymous, *La Compagnie de Jésus*, 28.

33 On Lu Baihong and, more generally, the ethos of Catholic Shanghai before 1949, see Mariani, *Church Militant*, 14–26.

34 Ristaino, *The Jacquinot Safe Zone.*

35 Denison and Ren, *Building Shanghai*, 52–54. For a general history of the Protestant mission in China, see Latourette, *History of Christian Missions.*

36 Hibbard, *The Bund Shanghai*, 338.

37 Garrett, "The Chambers of Commerce," 236.

38 Ibid., 230–31.

39 Lee and Chow, "Christian Revival from Within," 47–48; see also Lee and Chow, "Publishing Prophecy."

40 Honig, *Sisters and Strangers*, 217–24.

41 On Wenzhou, see Cao, *Constructing China's Jerusalem.*

42 See Xi, *Redeemed by Fire*, 26–41.

43 Mungello, "Reinterpreting the History of Christianity," 547.

44 Elvin, "The Administration of Shanghai," 259.

45 Ibid., 248–49.

46 Zhang, "Shanghai Fojiao xuexi Jidujiao," 32.

47 Ge, "Survey of Modern Buddhist Culture," 84–85. See also Tang, "Minguo Shanghai jushi Fojiao cishan de yunzuo moshi, tedian yu yiyi"; Tarroco, "City and the Pagoda."

48 Liu, *Daoist Modern*, 8.

49 Ibid., 204–5.

50 Ibid., 73.

51 Ibid., 275.

52 See Ge, "Jindai Shanghai shehui zongjiao de jiaorong jiaohui"; and Ge, "Shanghai de chengshi fazhan yu zongjiao wenhua yingxiang."

53   See Aveline-Dubach, "Revival of the Funeral Industry."

54   Welch, *Buddhism under Mao.*

55   Liu, *Daoist Modern*, 9.

56   Goossaert and Palmer, *The Religious Question*, 146–65.

57   Mariani, *Church Militant.* See also Lefeuvre, *Shanghai.*

58   Jin, *Learning and Relearning*, 288.

59   The Three-Self Patriotic Movement (Sanzi Aiguo Yundong), a Protestant umbrella organization, was founded in 1954. Its name refers to the three principles of self-governance, self-support, and self-propagation.

60   Keating, *A Protestant Church*, 89–104; Wickeri, *Seeking the Common Ground.*

61   Lee and Chow, "Christian Revival from Within," 49–50.

62   Perry and Li, *Proletarian Power*, 11–12.

63   "Gang of Four" is the name the Chinese Communist Party gave a posteriori to four people who played a central role in the events occurring during the Cultural Revolution, although the leadership group was wider. Their downfall happened in October 1976.

64   Perry and Li, *Proletarian Power*, 191.

65   Smith, "Talking Toads," 411–12.

66   *Wanbei Ribao*, April 10, 1950, quoted in Pang, "Dialectics of Mao's Images," 408.

67   Pang, "Dialectics of Mao's Images"; Zuo, "Political Religion."

68   Jin, *Learning and Relearning*, 288.

69   "Dongjiadu Cathedral" is the familiar name for St. Francis Xavier Church.

70   Knyazeva and Sinykim, *Shanghai Old Town*, 95.

71   Jin, *Learning and Relearning*, 283–87.

72   Fenggang Yang, "Religion in China," 28. See also Fenggang Yang, "Lost in the Market."

73   Shanghai Commission for Ethnic and Religious Affairs, "Short Presentation of Religions in Shanghai" (Shanghai zongjiao jianjie), December 25, 2014, accessed January 15, 2016, www.shmzw.gov.cn/gb/mzw/shzj/index.html.

74   Hong, *Price of China's Economic Development*, 168–69.

75   Pan Mingquan, "Shanghai zongjiao huodong changsuo de shehui dingwei he shehui guanli zouyi."

76   Cary Y. Liu, "Encountering the Dilemma of Change," 120.

77   Li et al., "Residential Clustering," 122.

78   Zhang Ningning, "Metro Pays a Price for Its Success, Says Report," *Shanghai Daily*, February 11, 2017.

79   Shiqiao Li, *Understanding the Chinese City*, 106.

80   See Shanghai Government, Shanghai Yearbook 2016, accessed July 3, 2017, www .shanghai.gov.cn/nw2/nw2314/nw24651/nw42131/nw42174/u21aw1232708.html.

81   Liang, "Where the Courtyard Meets the Street," 501.

82   For a phenomenological attempt at capturing the urban experience from the viewpoint of Chinese philosophy, see Shen, "Dao in the City."

83   Cristi and Dawson, "Civil Religion in America," 269.

84   Pierard and Linder, *Civil Religion*, 22–23. Our summary is based on Okuyama, "'Civil Religion' in Japan?"

85 Parsons, *Perspectives on Civil Religion*, 42.

86 Scheid, *Les dieux, l'État*, 166.

87 Denton, "Museums, Memorial Sites," 571.

88 Though less frequently used, the alternative translation "China Art Palace" is closer to the Chinese (Zhonghua Yishu Gong).

89 See "Shanghai Names 20 Red Tourism Sites," April 11, 2005, China.org, accessed June 16, 2016, www.china.org.cn/english/culture/125400.htm.

90 See Névot, "Le Rouge de Chine."

91 Feuchtwang, "School-Temple and City God."

92 Zhou, *Shanghai jiaotang jianzhu ditu*, 96.

93 See Fushouyuan Group, accessed June 20, 2016, http://sh.fsygroup.com. On the origins of Fushouyuan and the history of Shanghai's funerary industry, see Aveline-Dubach, "Revival of the Funeral Industry."

94 Yang Meiping, "Jewish Memorial Park Opens in Local Cemetery," *Shanghai Daily*, September 6, 2015.

95 Design Milk, accessed June 20, 2016, http://design-milk.com/shanghais-rainbow-chapel-coordination-asia/.

96 "Classic Duet Performance, May 21, 2016," Shanghai Museum of Glass, accessed June 20, 2016, www.shmog.org/classic-duet-performance/, 20 June 2016.

97 Stephanie Thomas, "Beastly Tales: Unearthing Shanghai's Nine Dragon Pillar," April 22, 2010, CNN, accessed June 20, 2016, http://travel.cnn.com/shanghai/play/unearthing-shanghais-nine-dragon-pillar-509418; interviews with informants, March–June 2015.

98 Favraud, "Les 'Voies rapides surélevées,'" 41–46.

CHAPTER 2. CALENDARS AND LANDMARKS

1 Between November 2015 and February 2016, Chen Jiaren interviewed a dozen older residents of the former Zhabei District (merged with Jing'an in November 2015) in order to compare their descriptions and practice of calendrical observances with those recorded in literature or gathered during our earlier fieldwork. Our assessment of the degree of importance of traditional feast days and customs is based partly on this inquiry.

2 See Fan, *Shanghai minjian xinyang yanjiu*, 225.

3 The day for welcoming back the Kitchen God changed from New Year's Eve to the last day of the Spring Festival toward the end of the Qing dynasty. See ibid., 226.

4 The festivities calendar proper for Shanghai's City God Temple follows closely the one sketched out in this section, though it includes a few other celebrations. Cf. Zheng and Liu, *Hucheng xingshi*, 118–20.

5 See the case of Jinze Township in chapter 5.

6 Testimony collected by Chen Jiaren, January 2016.

7 "Fireworks Ban Cuts Workload of Street Cleaners by 80 Percent but No Improvement in Air Quality," *Shanghai Daily*, February 8, 2016. The ban was also strictly applied in 2017, at least in downtown Shanghai.

8   See Fan, *Shanghai minjian xinyang yanjiu*, 257–60.

9   Literally, "Precious Hall of the Great Hero." The great hero is Sakyamuni, the Buddha of the Present.

10   For examples of the Water and Land Dharma Service as celebrated across Shanghai, see chapter 3.

11   Additionally, the thirteenth day of the ninth month marks the apotheosis of Guandi. Although his cult was not endogenous to Jiangnan, Guandi was the object of large processions in the countryside surrounding Shanghai. This rather complex figure was associated with both professional ability and exorcisms. If rain was falling on one of Guandi's feast days, it was considered an auspicious occurrence. See Fan, *Shanghai minjian xinyang yanjiu*, 262–65.

12   The first term, "Zhongyuanjie," is anchored in the Daoist tradition, while the second, "Yulanpen," refers to a Buddhist sutra narrating the story of Mulian saving his mother from hell. The festival is a synthesis of Buddhist and Daoist traditions.

13   Goodman, *Native Place*, 94–96.

14   Hu Min, "Huge Jams as Locals Head to Cemeteries for Dongzhi," *Shanghai Daily*, December 23, 2015; Chinese-language news compilation on Knews.com, accessed February 2, 2016, www.kankanews.com/a/2015-12-22/0037296558.shtml.

15   Hu Min, "Shuttles to Link Metro, Cemeteries," *Shanghai Daily*, December 17, 2015.

16   See the Chinese-language news compilation at Shanghai Xinhuanet, accessed February 2, 2016, http://sh.xinhuanet.com/zhuanti2015/2015qmj/index.htm; and Hu Min, "Qingming Numbers Down, but Still Gridlock," *Shanghai Daily*, April 6, 2015.

17   Lu, *Beyond the Neon Lights*, 301.

18   For a discussion of Catholic fishermen's villages, see the first section of chapter 5.

19   Bell, *Ritual*, 102–3.

20   See the section on Shanghai mosques in chapter 3.

21   Gillian Wong, "Alibaba Tops Singles' Day Sales Record Despite Slowing China Economy," *Wall Street Journal*, November 11, 2015.

22   Yu, *Shenming yu shimin*, 138–40.

23   See Fan, *Shanghai minjian xinyang yanjiu*, 214.

24   Ibid.

25   See "Religious Culture," Official Shanghai China Travel Website, accessed June 30, 2017, http://meet-in-shanghai.net/highlights/tourist-attraction/religious-culture.

26   The former Luwan District, in the heart of the French Concession, is now part of Huangpu District.

27   Orthodoxy in China, accessed March 1, 2014, www.orthodox.cn.

28   The former Orthodox Cathedral is located on Xinle Road, in Xuhui District. On May 15, 2013, Patriarch Kiril celebrated the first service there after a fifty-year hiatus. It is now being restored, but its final destination is not yet known.

29   Herzfeld, "Practical Piety."

30   Cary Y. Liu, "Encountering the Dilemma of Change," 123.

31   Some churches, modest in size, were built inside the walled city, as the foreign settlements were slow to develop and the missionary endeavor extended to the whole city.

32 Feuchtwang, "School-Temple and City God," 589.

33 Henriot, *Scythe and the City*, 286–87.

34 Processions from the City God Temple took place each year on Tomb Sweeping Festival, on the fifteenth day of the seventh month, and on the first day of the tenth month. The birthdays of the city god (the twentieth day of the second month) and his wife (the twenty-eighth day of the third month) were also occasions for large-scale gatherings. Fan, *Shanghai minjian xinyang yanjiu*, 219–20.

35 Goossaert, "Managing Chinese Religious Pluralism," 21.

36 Yu, *Shenming yu shimin*, 107–21.

37 Ibid., 149–74.

38 Ibid., 147.

39 Gui, *Shanghai Chenghuang Miao daguan*, 69–75.

40 Also called "Temple of the Compassionate Clouds" (Ciyun Chansi). The name Chenxiang Ge (lit., "Eaglewood Pavilion") applies to the pavilion where a replica of the original Guanyin statue is installed.

41 Fan, *Shanghai minjian xinyang yanjiu*, 259.

42 Promotional leaflets available at the temple; Cochini, *Guide to Buddhist Temples*, 105.

43 When referring to a Daoist establishment, the term *guan*, as in the Chinese name of White Clouds Monastery, can be translated as "temple," "monastery," or "complex." It normally indicates the presence of a monastic community, but historical hazards often make the character that marks the specific nature of a religious establishment (*guan*, *gong*, *tang*, *si*, *chansi*, *miao*, etc.) irrelevant. Buddhist and Daoist religious establishments are to be considered as being "temples," that is, places where people come to worship. A good number of Buddhist temples house a monastic community, the size of which varies greatly. The Daoist Quanzhen School also used to keep monasteries, but nowadays, at least in the cities, trained married priests, who return home every night, are tasked with all rituals performed in Daoist temples. (In Chinese history, married priests living in the midst of the community, especially those belonging to the Zhengyi School, have always performed the vast majority of Daoist rituals.) In addition, temples often house various facilities, such as restaurants, shops selling objects of piety, printing presses, or spaces for meetings.

44 Liu, *Daoist Modern*, 49–51.

45 On the official discourse at the time of the move, see Herrou, "La sagesse chinoise," 303–4. On the temple's personnel, see ibid., 284–85.

46 Taisui is both one and many. He is the god of the planet Jupiter and consequently the god of the calendrical cycle, but he is also divided into sixty figures, one for each year of the Chinese calendar. Taisui is under the authority of Doumu, the mother of the stars of the Dipper. For a description of a ritual to Taisui at White Clouds Monastery, see Herrou, "La sagesse chinoise."

47 Goossaert and Ling, "Temples and Daoists," 40.

48 Interviews with informants, April 2016. Shanghai's Commission for Ethnic and Religious Affairs indicates that a total of 150 *daoshi* were active in the thirty-three Daoist worship places registered in the city in October 2015. See Shanghai

Commission for Ethnic and Religious Affairs, accessed April 8, 2016, http://www
.shmzw.gov.cn/gb/mzw/shzj/dj/index.html.

49 Keating, *A Protestant Church*, 26–33.

50 Zhou, *Shanghai jiaotang jianzhu ditu*, 83.

51 Keating, *A Protestant Church*, 120.

52 This migrants' church is described in chapter 4.

53 Keating, *A Protestant Church*, 232.

54 Ibid., 104.

55 Hengshan Community Church is renowned for its musical energy and creativity.
See Feng, *Cong Guoji Libaitang kan Jidujiao yinyue zai Shanghai*.

56 Alpha is an evangelistic course offered worldwide by all major Christian denominations that seeks to introduce the basics of the Christian faith.

57 Keating, *A Protestant Church*, 212.

58 *Guide to Catholic Shanghai*, 41.

59 Ibid., 14.

60 See Zhou, *Shanghai jiaotang jianzhu ditu*, 69.

61 La Servière, *Jusqu'à l'établissement d'un vicaire*, 232–33.

62 Ruan and Gao, *Shanghai zongjiao shi*, 645–48.

63 Yang Jian, "Historic Building of Former Catholic Monastery in Xuhui to Reopen
after Revamp Restores Its Original Look," *Shanghai Daily*, January 11, 2015.

64 Clarke, *The Virgin Mary,* 192–93.

65 In December 2014, the Shanghai Commission for Ethnic and Religious Affairs
estimated the number of Chinese Catholics in the city at around 135,000; Shanghai Commission for Ethnic and Religious Affairs, accessed August 29, 2015, www
.shmzw.gov.cn/gb/mzw/shzj/tzj/index.html. This figure does not include Catholics worshipping outside officially recognized church communities. Around forty
priests serve underground Catholics in Shanghai, versus eighty for those worshipping in the official Church. The two communities overlap.

66 Madsen and Fan, "Catholic Pilgrimage to Sheshan."

67 Ma Daqin announced his resignation from the Patriotic Catholic Association the
day he was ordained a bishop and has been under house arrest in Sheshan Seminary ever since. The limits on his freedom have gradually decreased, although he
still cannot govern his diocese. He expressed public regret about his resignation
in June 2016 and was reinstalled in the local Patriotic Catholic Association as a
priest in January 2017.

68 Madsen and Fan, "Catholic Pilgrimage to Sheshan," 94.

69 WeChat is a mobile text and voice messaging service with multiple applications
that has become omnipresent in China.

70 Denton, "Museums, Memorial Sites."

71 See "Longhua Revolutionary Martyrs' Cemetery," Shanghai Xuhui, accessed January 9, 2016, www.qjtrip.com/info/ShowDetailEn.aspx?Id=330.

72 Denton, "Museums, Memorial Sites," 573–74.

73 There was a Longhua Township, but it was merged with another administrative
unit.

74 Tarroco, "City and the Pagoda," 45.

75   On the social and political influence of the temple, see Gao Zhengnong, "Lueshu Shanghai Yufochansi zai jiangou shehuizhuyi hexie shehui zhong suo qi de jiji zuoyong." See also Jue, "Dushi siyuan yu renjian Fojiao."

76   For examples of fears and rumors associated with the immediate surroundings of Jade Buddha Temple, see Tarrocco, "City and the Pagoda," 44–45.

CHAPTER 3. THE WALL AND THE DOOR

1   Zhou, *Shanghai jiaotang jianzhu ditu*, 25.

2   Information on this parish is from participant observation of around fifty catechumens and seven lay preachers conducted by Zhang Liang (spring 2013–spring 2014) during religious instruction (*mudaoban*) organized by the parish.

3   Zhou, *Shanghai jiaotang jianzhu ditu*, 111.

4   Ibid., 71.

5   Jessup, *The Householder Elite*, 20–21.

6   Ruan and Gao, *Shanghai zongjiao shi*, 156.

7   Kang, "Rural Women, Old Age," 49.

8   Prazniak, "Weavers and Sorceresses," 216.

9   Honig, *Sisters and Strangers*, 210–14.

10   Ge, "Hushang wailai liudong Musilin qunti de jingshen shenghuo," 152.

11   Jaschok and Shui, *History of Women's Mosques*, 198.

12   Shanghai Municipal Bureau of Statistics, accessed June 19, 2015, http://www.stats -sh.gov.cn/fxbg/201111/235919.html; Ge, "Hushang wailai liudong Musilin qunti de jingshen shenghuo," 148; and interview with informant, June 2015.

13   There are eight official places of worship — seven mosques and one "fixed establishment" (*guding chusuo*) — with eighteen imams attached to them. See the Shanghai city government's introduction to Islam in Shanghai, Shanghai Commission for Ethnic and Religious Affairs, accessed June 26, 2015, www.shmzw.gov.cn/gb /mzw/shzj/yslj/index.html.

14   Ge, "Hushang wailai liudong Musilin qunti de jingshen shenghuo," 150.

15   Interviews with informants, December 2012.

16   See, for instance, Chu, "China and the Vatican."

17   Harrison, *The Missionary's Curse*, 199.

18   The literal translation of "Zhangjialou" is "the storied building of the Zhang family."

19   Zhu Hongbo, *Chuansha xian zhi*, 189.

20   The Chinese expression for "True Cross" (Xunhuo Shizijia), or "The Cross That Was Found," refers directly to the alleged discovery of the relics of the cross by the Empress Helena, mother of Constantine.

21   Interview, September 2015.

22   This section was published in slightly different form as "From Ethnography to Theology: Religious Communities in Contemporary Shanghai and the Tasks of East Asian Theology," in *Korean Journal of Systematic Theology* 39 (2014): 7–35.

23   The Three-Self Patriotic Movement and the China Christian Council (Zhongguo

Jidujiao Xiehui) form the state-sanctioned Protestant Church in China, often called the Three-Self Church (Sanzi Jiaohui).

24 Deng, *Shimin shehui lilun de yanjiu*.

25 Yu, Jiang, and Zhou, *Zai canyu zhong chengzhang de Zhongguo gongmin shehui*.

26 See Gao Hong, "Dangdai Shanghai 'laoban Fojiaotu.'"

27 On interactions between entrepreneurs and the Buddhist world in Shanghai, see ibid.

28 The material from this section comes mostly from Sun Weiqiao, who generously allowed us to refer to his unpublished research. See also Sun, "Wu guishu de Fojiao yigong?"

29 Meyer, "The Sephardi Jewish Community"; Betta, "Myth and Memory."

30 Eber, *Voices from Shanghai*.

31 Moishe House, accessed March 31, 2014, www.moishehouse.org/houselist.asp.

32 "At a Party Like This, All Cultures Come Together," *Shanghai Daily*, December 17, 2008, available at Chabad Jewish Center of Pudong, accessed March 31, 2014, http://jewishpudong.com/media/pdf/251/MMJt2517855.pdf.

33 "Jewish Home Away from Home," *Shanghai Daily*, May 31, 2011, available at Chabad Jewish Center of Pudong, accessed March 31, 2014, http://jewishpudong .com/media/pdf/537/gqJW5379469.pdf.

34 "Former Jewish Refugees Return for 'Thank You, Shanghai' Trip," *Shanghai Daily*, March 27, 2014.

35 Jackson, "Raj on Nanjing Road," 1677.

36 Ibid., 1695.

CHAPTER 4. A SHRINE OF ONE'S OWN

1 Herzfeld, "Practical Piety," 26. See also Herzfeld, *Cultural Intimacy*, and Herzfeld, "The Performance of Secrecy."

2 See Herzfeld, "Practical Piety."

3 Li, *Shanghai Homes*, 6–7.

4 Ibid., 190.

5 Figures vary slightly among sources. Nevertheless, Amity Press is now the largest printer of Bibles in the world, publishing in a multiplicity of languages.

6 "Grandfather of the Soil" refers to Tudi Gonggong, and "Mistress of the Soil" refers to Dizhu Taitai, his wife.

7 Interview by Chen Jiaren, December 2015. Between November 2015 and February 2016, in addition to the interviews on calendrical observance recorded in chapter 2, Chen Jiaren conducted fifteen non-directive interviews on sacred spaces in Shanghai with people from different areas of the city. This series of interviews is used in this chapter and chapter 6.

8 La Servière, *Jusqu'à l'établissement d'un vicaire*, 230.

9 Yu, "Desensitising the Christian House Churches"; Gao and He, "The Central Problem." Both articles emphasize the differences between clandestine rural house churches; larger and more open structures that appeared later but are still typical of

rural sociability; and city churches. However, all are characterized by spontaneity, solidarity among members, and a family-like hierarchical structure.

10   On the development of Ciji in Shanghai, see Huang, "The Bodhisattva Comes Out."

11   See Ge, "Shanghai de qingzhen yinshi wenhua."

12   Ramen (*lamian* in Chinese) is wheat noodles served in broth.

13   Mariani, *Church Militant*, 17–20.

14   Interview by Chen Jiaren, January 2016.

15   Ibid.

16   Ibid.

CHAPTER 5. RELIGIOUS WATERWAYS

1   Denison and Guang, *Building Shanghai*, 22.

2   Henriot, "Slums, Squats, or Hutments?," 505.

3   Zhou, *Shanghai jiaotang jianzhu ditu*, 24.

4   Fang, *Zhongguo Tianzhu jiaoshi renwuzhuan*, 567.

5   Tsu, "La vie des pêcheurs," 139–40, 150–52.

6   La Servière, *Jusqu'à l'établissement d'un vicaire*, 336–37.

7   Tsu, "La vie des pêcheurs," 107–8.

8   Kathryn Treece, "Soul Work: How a Swiss Priest Popularized Reflexology throughout Asia . . . and Beyond," Father Josef's Method of Reflexology, accessed January 4, 2015, www.fjmreflexology.com/news.htm.

9   Wakeman and Yeh, *Shanghai Sojourners*.

10   An exact delimitation of the area covered by the term "Jiangnan" is still being debated. See Hamashima, "Communal Religion," 129.

11   Li Tiangang, "Jiangnan zhenxiang jisi tixi zhong de difang yu guojia," 77.

12   Jinze Township Government, "Chuangxin dui minjian xinyang de renshi he guanli," Qingpu District United Front, accessed May 9, 2016, http://tz.shqp.gov .cn/gb/content/2014-04/15/content_663298.htm. The report is based on collaboration between the local government and a team of teachers and students from Fudan University, though the final authorship remains unclear.

13   See Jinze Township Government, "Chuangxin dui minjian xinyang de renshi he guanli," Qingpu District United Front, accessed May 9, 2016, http://tz.shqp.gov .cn/gb/content/2014-04/15/content_663298.htm.

14   Hamashima, "Communal Religion," 153.

15   Jinze Township Government, "Chuangxin dui minjian xinyang de renshi he guanli," Qingpu District United Front, accessed May 9, 2016, http://tz.shqp.gov .cn/gb/content/2014-04/15/content_663298.htm.

16   As in many other popular temples, a plaque at the entrance of the General Manager Temple certifies that this is a site where religious activities are allowed.

17   On the various Zongguan deities, see Hamashima, "Communal Religion," 132, 159.

18 See Berezkin, "Connection between the Cults," 84.

19 Hamashima, "Communal Religion," 131.

20 Li, "Jiangnan zhenxiang jisi tixi zhong de difang yu guojia," 72.

21 Ibid., 73.

22 The word *xianghui* applies first to a pilgrimage to a sacred mountain or a temple. By extension, it also designates the (generally loose) groups or networks that organize such excursions.

23 See the association's introduction at Zhejiang Online, accessed May 6, 2016, http://jx.zjol.com.cn/system/2016/04/07/021100247.shtml, and Zhejiang Online, accessed May 6, 2016, http://jx.zjol.com.cn/system/2016/04/07/021100247.shtml.

24 Li, "Jiangnan zhenxiang jisi tixi zhong de difang yu guojia." See also Li, "Jiangnan zongjiao de xingshi."

25 Der-Ruey Yang, "From Ritual Skills," 81.

26 Ibid., 84–86.

27 Ibid.,102.

28 The sexagenary cycle is the traditional Chinese method for recording days and years. It is based on a combination of two terms, the first from a cycle of ten and the second from a cycle of twelve.

29 Arrault and Lippello, "In Memoriam."

30 This historical summary of the *qigong* movement is based on Palmer, *Qigong Fever*. The rise and fall of Falun Gong has been extensively covered elsewhere and is not discussed here. See Vermander, "Law and the Wheel."

31 Billioud and Thoraval, *Sage and the People*; Vermander, "Religious Revival."

32 For regular updates on Confucian scholars' positions and initiatives, see Rujiawang, www.rujiazg.com.

33 See Ke Xiaogang's May 7, 2016, talk, available at *Ruxue*, accessed May 21, 2016, http://rufodao.qq.com/a/20160508/030997.htm.

34 Yao Yuan, "2016: Opening of the First Shanghai Confucian Congress," *Rujiawang*, accessed May 23, 2016, www.rujiazg.com/article/id/8089/.

35 Shiu and Stokes, "Buddhist Animal Release Practices."

36 Alipay is the leading Chinese online payment platform.

37 Bell, *Ritual*, 159–64.

38 On the role of study circles in Baha'i propagation, see Palmer, "From 'Congregations.'"

39 Palmer estimates the number of adherents in mainland China to be well over twenty thousand. See ibid., 91.

40 Ibid.

41 Shanghai by Octave, accessed May 17, 2016, www.livingoctave.com.

42 Floatessence, accessed May 17, 2016, www.floatessence.com.cn.

43 Reiki is a form of alternative medicine with roots in Daoist meditation techniques. It was developed by Japanese Buddhist Mikao Usui.

44 Centre for Spiritual Living–Shanghai, accessed May 17, 2016, www.cslshanghai .com.

45 Kundalini yoga is a school of yoga influenced by Shaktism and Tantrism. The term "kundalini" refers to a primal energy, or Shakti, located at the base of the spine.

46 Sri Sri Ravi Shankar is the founder of the Art of Living Foundation. That the Chinese government cancelled his visit is unverified.

47 My Soul Yoga, accessed May 20, 2016, www.mysoulyoga.com.cn.

CONCLUSION

1 Literally, "I'm a member of the Good-Looking Society." A self-deprecating expression, recognizing that the criteria used to judge one's appearance are extended here to one's choice of objects of piety.

2 Courses may last a longer time in parishes with stricter attendance requirements for receiving baptism.

3 Interview by Zhang Liang, September 22, 2013.

4 Interview by Zhang Liang, September 8, 2013.

5 The Chuansha vernacular is a branch of the Pudong dialect, which is itself different from the Shanghainese spoken in Puxi west of the Huangpu River.

6 Interview by Zhang Liang, June 14, 2014.

7 Presently, this quest for orthopraxy often leads to the revival of traditions and obligations, such as Latin chanting or the Tridentine Mass, that are understood as being more authentically Catholic. Such revivals operate according to the local ethos.

8 In contemporary Chinese, the term *Jidujiao* applies equally to "Christianity" and "Protestantism."

9 Interview by Chen Jiaren, December 2015.

10 Mount Jiuhua, in Anhui, is one of the four sacred mountains of Chinese Buddhism. The Greater and Lesser Tiantai peaks are among its notable features.

11 The term *kaiguang* means to grant "light" (spirit, animation) to a sacred object through an ad hoc ritual. Said especially of statues, which can be opened by painting the pupils of the eyes.

12 See *Grand Dictionnaire Ricci*, character 4661.

13 Interview by Chen Jiaren, January 2016.

14 Cf. Wing-Tsit Chan, *A Source Book*, 23–25.

15 Yang Wenyi, "Xinxing ling'en chengshi jiaohui tezheng yanjiu," 16.; Danson Cheong, "City Harvest Attendance Declines Again," *Straits Times*, May 10, 2016, accessed July 3, 2016, www.straitstimes.com/singapore/city-harvest-attendance-declines-again.

16 Lychee FM, accessed July 8, 2016, www.lizhi.fm/about/aboutUs.html.

17 Cf. Ximalaya FM, accessed July 8, 2016, www.ximalaya.com/zhubo/29821709/.

18 Zhang Ningning, "Shanghai's Non-local Population Drops for First Time in 15 Years," *Shanghai Daily*, March 1, 2016.

19 Ammerman, *Sacred Stories, Spiritual Tribes*, 303–4.

20 See *Grand Dictionnaire Ricci*, character 2100.

21 See ibid., character 11830.

22 Tweed, *Crossing and Dwelling*, esp. 80 and 123.

23 Tweed, "Crabs, Crustaceans, Crabiness," 445–46.

24 The two characters composing *ganying* mean "moving" and "responding."

25 *The Huainanzi*, 875.

26 *The Xunxi* (chap. 20), *Zhuangzi* (chap. 23), *Lüshi chunqiu* (chaps. 2, 13), and the whole of *The Huainanzi* develop and comment at length on the analogy, although the compound *ganying* itself rarely occurs. Instead, the texts make use of expressions such as *gan er ying*, as they aim to describe a process rather than establish a concept.

27 Brindley, *Music, Cosmology*, 106–8.

28 Le Blanc, *Huai-nan Tzu*.

29 See Ammerman, *Sacred Stories*, 288–304.

30 This expression, used in the report, applies first to Buddhist devotees but more generally to practitioners of all forms of traditional Chinese religions.

31 Jinze Township Government, "Chuangxin dui minjian xinyang de renshi he guanli," accessed May 9, 2016, http://tz.shqp.gov.cn/gb/content/2014-04/15/content _663298.htm.

32 When discussing the union of the collective spiritual element and the physical individuation of the body in the emergence of the idea of the person, Durkheim (*Forms*, 273) uses the monad analogy: "All [monads] are consciousnesses that express one and the same object, the world. . . . However, each expresses it from its own point of view and in its own manner. We know how this difference of perspectives arises from the fact that the monads are differently placed with respect to one another and with respect to the whole system they comprise."

GLOSSARY

Chinese characters are simplified unless marked as traditional ("trad."). When a reference to semantic history makes it necessary, we provide the simplified and traditional forms of the character.

an 庵 nunnery; small temple

bai Pusa de ren 拜菩萨的人 Buddhist worshippers; followers of popular religion
Baihe Zhen 白鹤镇 Baihe Township
Baiyun Guan 白云观 White Clouds Monastery
Bao'en Si 报恩寺 Bao'en Temple
Baohua Si 宝华寺 Baohua Temple
Baoshan 宝山 Baoshan (District)
buke qinfan 不可侵犯 inviolable

Caihong Jianzheng Tuanqi 彩虹见证团契 Rainbow Witness Fellowship
Caihong Litang 彩虹礼堂 Rainbow Chapel
Caishen 财神 God of Fortune
Changren Chansi 长仁禅寺 Changren Temple
chansi 禅寺 Buddhist temple/monastery
chanxiu 禅修 Zen meditation
Chan'yi Jingguan Tang 禅一静观堂 Zen One Clubhouse
Chen Huacheng 陈化成 (1776–1842) Qing dynasty general responsible for the defense of Shanghai during the First Opium War; made one of the city gods of Shanghai by popular acclaim, from the time of the anti-Japanese war to the Cultural Revolution
Chen Jiaren 陈嘉仁
Chen Yingning 陈撄宁 (1880–1969) Daoist lay leader
cheng dao 成道 to reach perfection (Buddhism or Daoism); ascent to the rank of bodhisattva (*sambodhi*)
chenghuang miao 城隍庙 city god temple (lit., "temple of the walls and the moat," referring to the boundaries of a walled city). From the

beginning of the Ming dynasty onward, there was a city god temple in each district or prefecture. The City God Temple of Shanghai is probably the most notable one in China today.

Chengshi Fengshou Jiaohui 城市丰收教会 City Harvest Church (a megachurch in Singapore)

chengshi jiaohui 城市教会 city church (home church active in a large city)

Chenxiang Ge 沉香阁 Eaglewood Pavilion; located in the Temple of the Compassionate Clouds. The name Chenxiang Ge is often used to designate the temple in its entirety. *See also* Ciyun Chansi

Chi Song 持松 (1894–1972) abbot of the Buddhist Jing'an Temple from 1947 to 1966

Chongfu Daoyuan 崇福道院 Chongfu Temple

Chongming 崇明 Shanghai island and district

Chongyangjie 重阳节 Double Yang Festival

Chuansha Xinzheng 川沙新镇 Chuansha New Town

Chunjie 春节 Spring Festival

Chunwan 春晚 CCTV New Year's Eve Gala

Ciji 慈济 Buddhist Compassion Relief Tzu Chi Foundation

citang 祠堂 ancestral hall or temple

Ciyun Chansi 慈云禅寺 Temple of the Compassionate Clouds, generally known as Chenxiang Ge (Eaglewood Pavilion). *See also* Chenxiang Ge

Dabei 大悲 (1891–1971) Buddhist master, active in Shanghai principally during the Republican period

Dai Lizhen 戴丽贞 (b. 1918) Protestant pastor

danwei 单位 work unit

dao 道 the Way; in imperial times, prefecture, subdivision of a province

daochang 道场 ritual field (Daoism); space where the Law is taught, the place where the Buddha reached enlightenment (Buddhism); any area prepared for the performance of an ad hoc ritual

daoshi 道士 Daoist priest, Daoist master

Daxiong Baodian 大雄宝殿 the Great Hall of a Buddhist temple/monastery (lit., Precious Hall of the Great Hero, i.e., Sakyamuni, the Buddha of the Present)

denggao 登高 climbing a height

Dianshan Hu 淀山湖 Dianshan Lake

Dizang (Wang) Pusa 地藏（王）菩萨 Ksitigarbha (the bodhisattva of hells)

Dizhu Taitai 地主太太 wife of the God of the Soil. *See also* Tudi Gong(gong)

dong 动 movement (opposite of *jing* 静 "quietness")

Dong Qichang 董其昌 (1555–1636) artist and scholar

dongfang hong 东方红 oriental red; "The East Is Red" (revolutionary song)

Dongfang Yue 东方月 radio host

Dongfang Zhiguan 东方之冠 Oriental Crown (China Pavilion at Expo Shanghai 2010), now China Art Museum. *See also* Zhonghua Yishu Gong

Dongjiadu 董家渡 Shanghai street and neighborhood

Dongxiang (zu) 东乡（族） Dongxiang ethnic group

Dongyue Dadi 东岳大帝 Supreme God of Mount Tai

Dongyue Xinggong 东岳行宫 Dongyue Temple (in Songjiang District)

dongzhi 冬至 winter solstice

Doumu 斗母 Mother of the Stars of the Dipper

Duanwujie 端午节 Dragon-Boat Festival

Fagushan 法鼓山 Dharma Drum Mountain (Buddhist center in northern Taiwan)

Falungong 法轮功 Falun Gong

Fan Zhongliang 范忠良 (1918–2014) Joseph Fan Zhongliang (underground bishop of Shanghai)

Fang Sheng 放生 Animal Release (lit., Releasing Lives); Buddhist ritual of freeing captive animals

fanzhe dao zhi dong 反者道之动 "Returning is the movement of the Way" (*Daodejing*, 40)

Fei Qihong 费启鸿 (1845–1923) George Field Fitch (American Presbyterian missionary)

fen xiang er zuo 焚香而坐 burning incense and meditating

fu 府 prefecture (during imperial times)

Fu Xiliang 富锡亮 Orthodox Christian deacon

Fushouyuan 福寿园 Fushouyuan Cemetery Park

gan er ying 感而应 resonating (to an affect)

Gan'en Jie 感恩节 Thanksgiving Day

ganying 感应 resonance

Ge Zhuang 葛壮

gong 宫 palace; large temple

Gong Pinmei 龚品梅 (1901–2000) Ignatius Gong Pinmei (Kung Pin-Mei) (Catholic bishop of Shanghai, named cardinal *in pectore* [secretly] in 1979)

gongsuo 公所 common-trade association, corporation

guan 观 to contemplate; Daoist temple/monastery/complex

Guan Yu 关羽 (d. 220) military hero, revered under the names Guandi and Guangong

Guandi 关帝 "Emperor" Di, often worshipped as the God of War. *See also* Guan Yu

Guandi Miao 关帝庙 Guandi Temple

Guangfulin 广富林 site of a cultural park in Songjiang District

Guangong 关公 *See* Guan Yu and Guandi

Guanguanji Musilin Canting 贯贯及穆斯林餐厅 GGJ (halal restaurant in Shanghai)

Guanyin 观音 bodhisattva, the Goddess of Mercy (Sanskrit, Avalokitesvara)

guding chusuo 固定处所 fixed (religious) establishment

Gu'erbangjie 古尔邦节 Eid al-Adha (Festival of Sacrifice)

guiyue 鬼月 ghost month (name often given to the seventh month of the lunar calendar)

guoxue 国学 national studies (studies of Chinese culture and tradition)

haiqing 海清 inner piece of Buddhist monastic clothing

Hama Jing 蛤蟆精 Toad Spirit

hetianyu 和田玉 nephrite; Hotan jade

Hongde Tang 鸿德堂 Hongde Church

Hongmiao 红庙 / 虹庙 Red Temple

Huadong Shenxueyuan 华东神学院 East China Theology College

Huainanzi 淮南子 Daoist encyclopedia, 2nd century BCE

Huang Daopo 黄道婆 Woman Huang

Huating Xian 华亭县 Huating County

Huaxin Zhen 华新镇 Huaxin Town

Hui (zu) 回（族） Hui (Muslim) ethnic group

huidaomen 会道门 sects and secret societies

Huigen 慧根 (d. 1900) founder of the Jade Buddha Temple

huiguan 会馆 native-place association; guild

hukou 户口 household registration

Huo Guang 霍光 (d. 68 BCE) Han dynasty chancellor; one of the city gods of Shanghai

ji 祭 sacrifice

ji 纪 (trad. 紀) figurative knots

ji ming 寄名 placing oneself under the patronage of

Ji Yiwen 季怡雯

jia 家 home; family

Jiading 嘉定 district in Shanghai

Jiading Kongmiao 嘉定孔庙 Confucius Temple of Jiading

Jiang Kongkong 蒋空空

Jiang Xili 姜茜莉 present-day pastor at Moore Memorial Church

Jiangnan 江南 geographic region immediately south of the lower reaches of the Yangzi River, including the area of present-day Shanghai municipality

Jiangnan Wangchuanhui 江南网船会 Jiangnan Fishing Boats Association

jiao 教 teaching

jiaohui 教会 church, congregation (usually Christian)

jiaohui mudi 教会墓地 church graveyard

jiaotang 教堂 Christian church (building)

jiatang 家堂 place in the home for tablets of family ancestors or gods (sometimes referring to the ancestors or gods proper)

jiating jiaohui 家庭教会 house church (lit., "family church")

Jiaxing 嘉兴 city in Zhejiang

Jidujiao 基督教 Christianity; Protestantism

Jidutu Juhuichu 基督徒聚会处 Christian Assembly (Chinese Pentecostal Church), also known as "Little Flock," founded by Watchman Nee. *See also* Ni Tuosheng

jiemeihui 姐妹会 sisterhood

Jin Hongwei 金宏伟 imam (present-day chairman of the Shanghai branch of the Islamic Association of China)

Jin Luxian 金鲁贤 (1916–2013) Aloysius Jin Luxian (Catholic bishop of Shanghai)

Jin Yuanqi 金元七 a local god of the Jiangnan region often associated with an official of the Song dynasty. *See also* Jin Zongguan

Jin Zongguan 金总管 General Manager Jin. *See also* Jin Yuanqi

jing 静 quietness (opposite of dong 动 "movement")

jing 敬 respect, reverence

Jing Jianmei 景健美 pastor at Jingling Church and associated parishes

Jing'an Si 静安寺 Jing'an Temple

Jinghuang Jiangsi 金皇讲寺 Jinhuang Temple

Jingling Tang 景灵堂 Young John Allen Memorial Church

jingshen wenming 精神文明 spiritual civilization

Jingtu 净土 Pure Land (Buddhist School)

Jingyi Tang 敬一堂 Jingyi Church

Jinshan 金山 district in Shanghai

Jinze 金泽 township in Shanghai municipality

jishen 祭神 deity worship

Jiuhuashan 九华山 Jiuhua Mountain

Jixiang Cao 吉祥草 Lucky Veg (restaurant)

jizu 祭祖 ancestor worship

jūshi 居士 householder (a layperson who has vowed to follow Buddhist precepts)

juweihui 居委会 neighborhood committee

kaiguang 开光 imparting "light" (spirit, animation) to an object (especially a statue) through a ritual; consecrating an object

Kaizhaijie 开斋节 Eid al-Fitr (Breaking-the-Fast Feast), at the end of Ramadan

Ke Xiaogang 柯小刚 (b. 1972) professor at Tongji University and advocate of traditional Confucian education

kou 口 mouth

Kuaile Chan 快乐禅 Happy Zen

labazhou 腊八粥 porridge made during the twelfth lunar month

laji 腊祭 winter sacrifice

li 礼 (trad. 禮) rites; ritual. Especially in ancient China, the term also applies to all rules that govern behavior and contribute to ensuring social and political stability.

Li Tiangang 李天纲

Liang Zhun 梁准

Liji 礼记 (trad. 禮記) *The Book of Rites*

lilong 里弄 form of residential development centered on lanes or groups of lanes (alleyways)

ling 灵 (trad. 靈) spiritual power or efficacy

Lingxiu Diantai 灵修电台 Radio Spirituality

Lingyin Si 灵隐寺 Lingyin Temple

lixia 立夏 start of summer in the Chinese lunar calendar

Lixu Xueshe 利徐学社 Xu-Ricci Dialogue Institute

"Liyun" 礼运 (trad. 禮運) "The Conveyance of Rites," a chapter in *The Book of Rites* (Liji)

Lizhi FM 荔枝 FM Lychee (FM radio station)

long 龙 dragon

longhua (shu) 龙华（树） *nâga-puspa* (dragon flower) tree, under which Maitreya, the Buddha of the Future, teaches the law to all sentient beings after his Awakening

Longhua Lieshi Lingyuan 龙华烈士陵园 Longhua Revolutionary Martyrs' Cemetery

Longhua Si 龙华寺 Longhua Temple

longtang 弄堂 *See* lilong

Lu Baihong 陆伯鸿 (1875–1937) Joseph Lo Pahong (Catholic entrepreneur and philanthropist)

Lunyu 论语 *The Analects of Confucius*

luohan 罗汉 arhat

luohan song 罗汉松 *luohan* tree (*Podocarpus macrophyllus*)

Lüshi chunqiu 吕氏春秋 *Master Lü's Spring and Autumn Annals*

Ma Jinliang 马进良 imam (Jinshan District mosque)

manyi 缦衣 outer piece of Buddhist monastic clothing

Mazu 妈祖 goddess of the seafarers

menshen 门神 gods of the door

miao 庙 ancestral temple (initially); any kind of temple (today)

Miaofa lianhua jing 妙法莲花经 Lotus Sutra

miaohui 庙会 temple fair

miaojie 庙界 area upon which a temple extends its influence

ming 命 fate

mingyun 命运 destiny, fortune

mitan 密坛 Buddhist place of worship in the Zhenyan (Shingon)
    tradition

Mizong 密宗 Tantric Buddhism

Mose Yiluo 摩瑟伊萝

mudaoban 慕道班 catechism class; religious instruction

Mu'en Tang 沐恩堂 Moore Memorial Church

Mu'er Tang 慕尔堂 original Chinese name for Moore Memorial Church,
    "Mu'er" being the Chinese approximation of "Moore"

Nanshi 南市 district in Shanghai, merged with Huangpu District in
    2000

Nanzhili 南直隶 province (territory of Jiangsu and Anhui, directly
    governed by the central government during the Ming dynasty
    [1368–1644])

nei 内 interior

Ni Tuosheng 倪柝声 (1903–1972) Watchman Nee (Christian leader)

nianyefan 年夜饭 Chinese New Year's Eve dinner

nie 聂 family name; whispering in the ear

Pan Yunduan 潘允端 (1526–1601) official, founder of Yu Garden

ping'an guo 平安果 fruit of peace (name now sometimes given to the
    apple at Christmastime)

pingguo 苹果 apple

Pudong 浦东 district in Shanghai

Pusa 菩萨 Bodhisattva; (familiarly) the gods

Putuo Qu 普陀区 Putuo District, in Shanghai municipality

Putuo Shan 普陀山 Mount Putuo; one of the four sacred Buddhist
    mountains in China, located on an island in Zhejiang

qidaosuo 祈祷所 prayer place

qigong 气功

Qin Yubo 秦裕伯 (1295–1373) Ming dynasty official; one of the city gods of Shanghai

Qingbang 青帮 Green Gang

Qingjing An 清净庵 Qingjing Temple

Qingmingjie 清明节 Tomb Sweeping Festival

Qingpu 青浦 district in Shanghai

qingtuan 青团 dumplings of glutinous rice mixed with wormwood and filled with red bean paste

qingzhensi 清真寺 mosque

Qiujiawan Yesu Shengxin Tang 邱家湾耶稣圣心堂 Qiujiawan Sacred Heart of Jesus Church

Quanzhen 全真 Daoist School founded during the Jin dynasty (1115–1234)

Qufu 曲阜 city in Shandong known as the hometown of Confucius

ren 仁 benevolence

renjian Fojiao 人间佛教 humanistic Buddhism

Renshan 仁山 (1887–1951) Buddhist master and religious reformer

renti kexue 人体科学 somatic science

ru 如 as if

ruozhe dao zhi yong 弱者道之用 "Weakness is the functioning of the Way" (*Daodejing*, 40)

Sanguan Tang 三观堂 Sanguan Temple

Sanzi Aiguo Yundong 三自爱国运动 Three-Self Patriotic Movement (Protestant patriotic association)

Sanzi Jiaohui 三自教会 (informal) Three-Self Church (the state-sanctioned Protestant Church in China, as structured by the Three-Self Patriotic Movement and the Chinese Christian Council)

Shanghai Daojiao Xueyuan 上海道教学院 Shanghai Daoist College

Shanghai Guoji Libaitang 上海国际礼拜堂 Shanghai International Church, usually referred to as "Hengshan Community Church"

Shanghai Lingxuehui 上海灵学会 Shanghai Psychical Research Society

Shanghai Qingzhen Dongshehui 上海清真董事会 Shanghai Muslims' Board

Shanghai Ruxuehui 上海儒学会 Shanghai Confucian Studies Society

Shanghai Wenmiao 上海文庙 Confucian Temple of Shanghai. *See also* wenmiao

Shanghai Xiaoyang Jiaohui 上海小羊教会 Shanghai Little Lamb Church

Shanghaishi Qigong Yanjiusuo 上海市气功研究所 Shanghai Qigong Institute

shejiao huitang 社交会堂 social club

shen 神 spirit, holy

Shen Hongxun 沈洪训 (1939–2011) tai chi master

shendao 神道 sacred alley

sheng 圣 (trad. 聖) sage, saint

Shengdanjiu 圣诞酒 Christmas wine ("Christmas party" in Wenzhou parlance)

shengdi 圣地 sacred place

shengjie 圣洁 purity, inner holiness

Shengjijie 圣纪节 Mawlid (birthday of the Prophet Muhammad)

Shengyan 圣严 (1930–2009) Master Sheng Yen (founder of the Dharma Drum Mountain foundation in Taiwan)

shenmi 神秘 mysterious, occult

shenming 神明 deities

Shenmiao 神庙 Temple of the Spirits

shensheng 神圣 sacred

shenshenggan 神圣感 sense of the sacred

shenshengxing 神圣性 sacredness

Sheshan 佘山 She Mountain ("Zose" in Shanghai dialect)

shetuan 社团 altar community; association

shi 实 real, concrete (opposite of *xu* 虚)

Shi Hantao 施瀚涛

shifang conglin 十方丛林 universal (i.e., large public) monastery (Daoist or Buddhist)

Shijie Fojiao Jushilin 世界佛教居士林 World Buddhist Householder Grove

shisu 世俗 profane

shisu shang de ren 世俗上的人 people living mundane lives (in contrast to people dedicating their lives to a religious or spiritual ideal)

Shizhao yuebao 时兆月报 *The Signs of the Times*

shouwangzhe 守望者 watchman

shuichancun 水产村 fisheries village

Shuilu Pudu Dazhai Shenghui 水陸普度大齋勝會 Water and Land Dharma Service (Buddhist liturgy for the liberation of all sentient beings)

Shuowen jiezi 说文解字 Chinese dictionary, early 2nd century

si 寺 Buddhist temple

sidian 祀典 sacrificial ritual; register of state-sanctioned sacrifices

Songjiang 松江 district in Shanghai

Songjiang Fu 松江府 historical prefecture, now a district in Shanghai

su 俗 secular; vulgar

Sun Weiqiao 孙尉乔

taijiquan 太极拳 tai chi

Taisui 太岁 calendrical god

Taixu 太虚 (1890–1947) famous reformist Buddhist master, promoter of "humanistic Buddhism"

tang 堂 place of meeting or worship; temple. The term normally applies to Daoist temples but may be found for some Buddhist establishments when state authorities have engineered the devolution of the temple from Daoism to Buddhism at some point in history; the character is also used in the name of a Christian church building, Catholic or Protestant (e.g., Jingyi Tang, Mu'en Tang). *See also* jiaotang

Tianhou 天后 Heavenly Empress; title given to the goddess Mazu

Tianzhu Caihong Tuanti 天主彩虹团体 (China) Catholic Rainbow Community

Tianzhujiao 天主教 Catholicism

Tongzhanbu 统战部 United Front Work Department

touxiang 头香 the first incense offered, especially on New Year's Eve

Tudi Gong(gong) 土地公（公） God of the Soil

Tujia(zu) 土家族 Tujia ethnic group

Tushanwan 土山湾 ("T'ou-se-we" in Shanghai dialect) a small area in Xuhui District, seat of a Jesuit orphanage and arts and crafts school (1864–1960)

wai 外 external

Wang Mingzhen 王明真 (d. ca. 1880) Daoist master, founder of the White Clouds Monastery

wanyou zhenyuan 万有真原 the true source of all beings

wenmiao 文庙 lit., "temples of literature"; name given to the temple dedicated to Confucius in Shanghai and some other cities. The names given to state temples devoted to the cult of Confucius and the spreading of Confucian teachings during imperial times varied among cities and regions.

Wu Ruoshi 吴若石 (b. 1940) Father Josef Eugster (Swiss Catholic missionary living in Taiwan, founder of a method of reflexology)

wushi 巫师 medium, shaman

Wusong Jiang 吴淞江 Wusong River, also known as Suzhou Creek, a water tributary that passes through Shanghai's city center

Xiahaimiao 下海庙 Xiahai Temple

xian 县 district; county

Xiandai hanyu cidian 现代汉语词典 *Contemporary Chinese Dictionary*

xianghui 香会 pilgrimage to a sacred mountain or a temple; by extension, a network that organizes such excursions

xiangtou 香头 incense burner; leader of a *xianghui*

xiao miao 小庙 little temple; site where there are vestiges of a temple

Xiao Nian 小年 Little New Year (a time for cessation of all normal activities)

Xiao Taoyuan 小桃园 mosque in Huangpu District

xiaoqu 小区 residential community, micro-district

xibo 锡箔 tin-leaf ingots (burned as devotional, mostly funeral and ancestor-worship, offerings)

xie 邪 perverse

Xie Hua 谢华

xiejiao 邪教 heterodox cult

Xilin Chansi 西林禅寺 Xilin Temple

Ximalaya FM 喜马拉雅 FM Himalayas (FM radio station)

xin 心 heart; mind; heart-mind (considered as a whole)

xin zhai 心斋 fasting of the heart

Xinmei Ju 新梅居 halal restaurant in Shanghai

Xintian'an Tang 新天安堂 New Union Church

Xintiandi 新天地 a shopping and entertainment district in Shanghai, home to the site of the first congress of the Chinese Communist Party

xiuxing 修行 ascetic practice

xu 虚 vacuous (opposite of *shi* 实)

Xu Guangqi 徐光启 (1562–1633) statesman and scientist, Catholic convert

Xu Zhicheng 徐至成 (d. 1890) Daoist master

Xuhui 徐汇 district in Shanghai

Xujiahui 徐家汇 historic area in Shanghai, subdistrict of Xuhui. This area belonged to the descendants of Xu Guangqi and became the center of the Jesuit mission in Shanghai after 1843.

Xunhuo Shizijia 寻获十字架 True Cross

xuni 虚拟 virtual

Xunzi 荀子 *The Xunzi* (3rd century BCE)

Yan Kejia 晏可佳

Yan Weibing 严慰冰 contemporary teacher of muscle-bone strengthening techniques. *See also* yijinjing

Yang Huilin 杨慧林

Yang Laoye 杨老爷 Lord Yang. *See also* Yang Zhen

yang sheng 养生 nurturing life

Yang Zhen 杨震 Lord Yang (deity of the Jiangnan region)

Yaoshifo 药师佛 Medicine Buddha (Sanskrit, Bhaisajyaguru)

Yihao Chansi 颐浩禅寺 Yihao Zen Temple

yijinjing 易筋经 muscle-bone strengthening exercise. *See also* Yan Weibing

Yindu Miao 印度庙 Indian Temple (familiar name for the former Sikh *gurdwara* in Shanghai)

yingshen saihui 迎神赛会 procession and festive meeting for welcoming the gods

Yinyu Tingtang 音昱听堂 Octave (Well-Being Platform)

yinyuan 银元 silver dollar

Yi(zu) 彝（族） Yi ethnic group

Yong'en Tang 永恩堂 Yong'en Church

Yongfu An 永福庵 Yongfu Temple

youxi 游戏 game

Yu Cidu 余慈度 (1873–1931) Dora Yu (Pentecostal woman leader)

Yu Jin 俞晶

Yu Zhejun 郁喆隽

Yuanxiaojie 元宵节 Lantern Festival

Yuanying 园瑛 (1878–1953) Buddhist master, elected as the first chairman of the Buddhist Association of China in 1953

Yuhuang Dadi 玉皇大帝 Jade Emperor

Yulanpen 盂兰盆 Ghost Festival. *See also* Zhongyuanjie

yun 运 luck

Yuyuan 豫园 Yu Garden

zai guangzhong xinqi 在光中兴起 rising to the light

Zaojing Gongong 灶精公公 *See also* Zaoshen

Zaoshen 灶神 Kitchen God

zhai 斋 fasting; in ancient China, ritual purification

Zhang Jingqiao 张景桥 (17th century) Catholic convert

Zhang Liang 张靓 coauthor of *Shanghai Sacred* (Liang Zhang)

Zhangjialou 张家楼 Catholic parish in Pudong

zharou tixiang 扎肉提香 suspending gongs or incense burners attached to fishing hooks inserted into the forearms

Zhenchan 真禅 (1916–1995) Buddhist master, abbot of Jade Buddha Temple from 1979 until his death

zheng 正 right, orthodox (opposite of *xie*)

Zheng Mali 郑马利

Zhenguang 真光 *True Light*, magazine operated by the Baptist Publication Society (1902–40)

Zhengyan 证严 (b. 1937) Master Cheng Yen (Taiwanese Buddhist nun, teacher, and philanthropist)

Zhengyi 正一 Daoist School

Zhenyan 真言 Buddhist School (Japanese: Shingon)

zhili 直隶 (imperial) direct rule over a territory

Zhiye Chansi 知也禅寺 Zhiye Temple

Zhongguo hong 中国红 Chinese red

Zhongguo Jidujiao Xiehui 中国基督教协会 (Protestant) China Christian Council

Zhonghua Fojiao Zonghui 中华佛教总会 General Buddhist Association of China

Zhonghua Yishu Gong 中华艺术宫 China Art Museum (or China Art Palace). *See also* Dongfang Zhiguan

Zhongqiujie 中秋节 Mid-Autumn Festival

Zhongyuanjie 中元节 Ghost Festival. *See also* Yulanpen

zhou 咒 to curse

zhu 祝 to congratulate, to call for blessings upon

Zhu Xiaohong 朱晓红

Zhuangzi 庄子 *The Zhuangzi*

Zhujiajiao 朱家角 a water town in suburban Shanghai

zi 紫 purple

zifa donggong 自发动功 art of spontaneous movements (a form of tai chi)

Zongguan Miao 总管庙 General Manager Temple

zongjiao 宗教 religion

BIBLIOGRAPHY

Ammerman, Nancy Tatom. *Sacred Stories, Spiritual Tribes: Finding Religion in Every-day Life*. Oxford: Oxford University Press, 2013.

Arrault, Alain, and Tiziana Lippello. "In Memoriam: Monica Esposito (1962–2011): À Shanghai." *Cahiers d'Extrême Asie* 20 (2011): viii–x.

Aveline-Dubach, Natacha. "The Revival of the Funeral Industry in Shanghai: A Model for China." In *Invisible Population: The Place of the Dead in East Asian Megacities*, edited by Natacha Aveline-Dubach, 74–97. Lanham, MD: Lexington Books, 2012.

Bai Runsheng 白润生. "Yisilanjiao zai Shanghai" 伊斯兰教在上海 (Islam in Shanghai). *Journal of Shanghai Institute of Socialism* (Shanghai shi shehuizhuyi xueyuan xuebao 上海市社会主义学院学报), no. 2 (2008): 50–53.

Bell, Catherine. *Ritual: Perspectives and Dimensions*. New York: Oxford University Press, 2009.

Bellah, Robert N. "Civil Religion in America." *Daedalus, Journal of the American Academy of Arts and Sciences*, 1967, 1–21.

———. *Religion in Human Evolution: From the Paleolithic to the Axial Age*. Cambridge, MA: Belknap Press of Harvard University Press, 2011.

Berezkin, Rostislav. "The Connection between the Cults of Local Deities and Baojuan (Precious Scrolls) Texts in Changshu County of Jiangsu." *Monumenta Serica* 61, no. 1 (2013): 73–111.

Bergère, Marie-Claire. *Shanghai: China's Gateway to Modernity*. Stanford: Stanford University Press, 2009.

Betta, Chiara. "Myth and Memory: Chinese Portrayal of Silas Aaron Hardoon, Luo Jialing and the Aili Garden between 1924 and 1995." In *From Kaifeng . . . to Shanghai: Jews in China*, edited by Roman Malek, 375–400. Monumenta Serica Monograph Series, 46. Nettetal, Germany: Steyler Verlag, 2000.

Billioud, Sébastien, and Joël Thoraval. *The Sage and the People: The Confucian Revival in China*. Oxford: Oxford University Press, 2015.

Brindley, Erica Fox. *Music, Cosmology, and the Politics of Harmony in Early China*. Albany: State University of New York Press, 2012.

Brook, Timothy. "Xu Guangqi in His Context: The World of the Shanghai Gentry." In *Statecraft and Intellectual Renewal in Late Ming China: The Cross-Cultural Synthesis of Xu Guangqi (1562-1633)*, edited by Catherine Jami, Peter Engelfrief, and Gregory Blue, 72–98. Leiden: Brill, 2001.

Cao, Nanlai. *Constructing China's Jerusalem: Christians, Power, and Place in Contemporary Wenzhou*. Stanford: Stanford University Press, 2010.

Cao Zhongxing 曹中兴. "Shezhuang yu Shezhuang miao" 社庄与社庄庙 (The village and its temple). In *Pudong lao diming* 浦东老地名 (Old names of Pudong territories), 235–36. Shanghai: Shanghai Social Academy Publisher, 2007.

Certeau, Michel de. *The Practice of Everyday Life*. Translated by Steven F. Rendall. Berkeley: University of California Press, 1984.

Chan, Wing-Tsit. *A Source Book in Chinese Philosophy*. Princeton: Princeton University Press, 1963.

Chartier, Roger. *On the Edge of the Cliff: History, Language, and Practices*. Translated by Lydia G. Cochrane. Baltimore: John Hopkins University Press, 1997.

Cheng, Nien. *Life and Death in Shanghai*. London: Grafton Books, 1987.

Chopra, Radhika. "Robert Gardner's 'Forest of Bliss': A Review." *Visual Anthropology Review* 5, no. 1 (1989): 2–3.

Chu, Cindy Yik-yi. "China and the Vatican, 1979–Present." In *Catholicism in China, 1900–Present: The Development of the Chinese Church*, edited by Cindy Yik-yi Chu, 147–67. New York: Palgrave Macmillan, 2014.

Clarke, Jeremy. *The Virgin Mary and Catholic Identities in Chinese History*. Hong Kong: Hong Kong University Press, 2013.

Cochini, Christian. *Guide to Buddhist Temples of China*. Macao: Macao Ricci Institute, 2009.

Cristi, Marcela, and Lorne L. Dawson. "Civil Religion in America and in Global Context." In *The SAGE Handbook of the Sociology of Religion*, edited by James A. Beckford and N. J. Demerath, 267–92. London: Sage, 2007.

De Bary, William Theodore, ed. *Self and Society in Ming Thought*. New York: Columbia University Press, 1970.

Deng Zhenglai 邓正来. *Shimin shehui lilun de yanjiu* 市民社会理论的研究 (Studies on the theory of civil society). Beijing: China University of Political Science and Law Press, 2002.

Denison, Edward, and Guang Yu Ren. *Building Shanghai: The Story of China's Gateway*. Chichester, UK: Wiley-Academy, 2006.

Denton, Kirk A. "Museums, Memorial Sites and Exhibitionary Culture in the People's Republic of China." *China Quarterly* 183, no. 1 (2005): 565–85.

Des Forges, Alexander Townsend. *Mediasphere Shanghai: The Aesthetics of Cultural Production*. Honolulu: University of Hawai'i Press, 2007.

Douglas, Mary. *Natural Symbols: Exploration in Cosmology*. New York: Pantheon Books, 1982.

Durkheim, Émile. *The Elementary Forms of Religious Life*. Translated by Karen E. Fields. New York: Free Press, 1995 [1912].

———. *Professional Ethics and Civic Morals*. Translated by C. Brookfield. Westport, CT: Greenwood Press, 1957.

Eber, Irene. *Voices from Shanghai: Jewish Exiles in Wartime China*. Chicago: University of Chicago Press, 2008.

Elias, Norbert. *The Court Society*. Translated by Edmund Jephcott. Oxford: Basic Blackwell, 1983.

———. *The Society of Individuals*. Edited by Michel Schröter. Translated by Edmund Jephcott. Oxford: Basic Blackwell, 1991.

———. *What Is Sociology?* Translated by Stephen Mennell and Grace Morrissey. New York: Columbia University Press, 1978.

Elvin, Mark. "The Administration of Shanghai 1905–1914." In *The Chinese City between Two Worlds*, edited by Mark Elvin and G. William Skinner, 239–62. Stanford: Stanford University Press, 1974.

———. "Market Towns and Waterways: The County of Shang-hai from 1480 to 1910." In *The City in Late Imperial China*, edited by G. William Skinner, 441–73. Stanford: Stanford University Press, 1977.

Fan Ying 范荧. *Shanghai minjian xinyang yanjiu* 上海民间信仰研究 (Study on Shanghai folk beliefs). Shanghai: Shanghai People's Publishing House, 2006.

Fang Hao 方豪. *Zhongguo Tianzhu jiaoshi renwuzhuan* 中国天主教史人物传 (Biographies for the history of the Catholic Church in China). Shanghai: Guangxi Press of the Catholic Diocese of Shanghai, 2003.

Favraud, Georges. "Les 'Voies rapides surélevées,' *gaojia lu* 高架路: Structuration d'une aire de mobilité urbaine à Shanghai." In *Ethnographier l'Universel: L'exposition Shanghai 2010: Better city, better life*, edited by Brigitte Baptandier and Sophie Houdart, 33–69. Nanterre, France: Société d'ethnologie, 2015.

Feng Jingtao 冯锦涛. *Cong Guoji Libaitang kan Jidujiao yinyue zai Shanghai* 从国际礼拜堂看基督教音乐在上海 (Christian music in Shanghai seen from Shanghai Community Church). MA diss., Shanghai Conservatory of Music, 2005.

Feuchtwang, Stephan. "School-Temple and City God." In *The City in Late Imperial China*, edited by George William Skinner, 581–606. Stanford: Stanford University Press, 1977.

Fingarette, Herbert. *Confucius: The Secular as Sacred*. New York: Harper and Row, 1972.

Fogel, Joshua A. "The Recent Boom in Shanghai Studies." *Journal of the History of Ideas*, 71, no. 2 (2010): 313–33.

Franses, Henri. "Partial Transmission." In *Byzantine Things in the World*, edited by Glen Peers, 175–87. Houston: The Menil Collection, 2013.

Gao Hong 高虹. "Dangdai Shanghai 'laoban Fojiaotu' de gongyi cishan shijian yu gongmin yishi de jiangou" 当代上海'老板佛教徒'的公益慈善实践与公民意识的建构 (Charitable activities of Buddhist bosses and the structure of civil awareness in modern Shanghai). *World Religious Culture* (Shijie zongjiao wenhua 世界宗教文化), 4/2014 (2014): 102–7.

Gao Shining and He Guanghu. "The Central Problem of Christianity in Today's China and Some Proposed Solutions." Translated by Lawrence Braschi. *China Study Journal*, Spring/Summer 2011: 71–87.

Gao Zhengnong 高振农. "Lueshu Shanghai Yufochansi zai jiangou shehuizhuyi hexie shehui zhong suo qi de jiji zuoyong" 略述上海玉佛禅寺在构建社会主义和谐社会中所起的积极作用 (A brief presentation of the active role played by Shanghai Jade BuddhaTemple in building a socialist harmonious society). *Buddhism Culture* (Fojiao wenhua 佛教文化), 6/2005 (2005): 25–27.

Garbin, David, and Anna Strhan, eds. *Religion and the Global City*. Bloomsbury Studies in Religion, Space and Place. London: Bloomsbury, 2017.

Garrett, Shirley S. "The Chambers of Commerce and the YMCA." In *The Chinese City between Two Worlds*, edited by Mark Elvin and G. William Skinner, 213–38. Stanford: Stanford University Press, 1974.

Ge Zhuang 葛壮. "Hushang wailai liudong Musilin qunti de jingshen shenghuo" 沪上外来流动穆斯林的精神生活 (The spiritual life of migrant Muslim communities in Shanghai) *Journal of Social Sciences* (Shehui kexue 社会科学), 10/2011 (2011): 148–57.

———. "Jindai Shanghai shehui zongjiao de jiaorong jiaohui" 近代上海社会宗教的交融交汇 (Religious blending and interaction in the society of modern Shanghai). *Contemporary Religious Studies* (Dangdai zongjiao yanjiu 当代宗教研究), 4/2012 (2012): 27–36.

———. "Shanghai de chengshi fazhan yu zongjiao wenhua yingxiang" 上海的城市发展与宗教文化影响 (The impact of religious culture on Shanghai's urban development). *Contemporary Religious Studies* (Dangdai zongjiao yanjiu 当代宗教研究), 4/2009 (2009): 42–45.

———. "Shanghai de qingzhen yinshi wenhua" 上海的清真饮食文化 (Halal food culture in Shanghai). *Contemporary Religious Studies* (Dangdai zongjiao yanjiu 当代宗教研究), 4/2010 (2010): 21–27.

———. "A Survey of Modern Buddhist Culture in Shanghai." *Chinese Studies in History* 46, no. 3 (Spring 2013): 79–94.

Goodman, Bryna. *Native Place, City, and Nation: Regional Networks and Identities in Shanghai, 1853–1937*. Berkeley: University of California Press, 1995.

Goossaert, Vincent. *Dans les Temples de Chine: Histoire des cultes, vie des communautés*. Paris: Albin Michel, 2000.

———. "The Heavenly Master, Canonization, and the Daoist Construction of Local Religion in Late Imperial Jiangnan." *Cahiers d'Extrême Asie* 20 (2011): 229–45.

———. "Managing Chinese Religious Pluralism in Nineteenth-Century City God Temples." In *Globalization and the Making of Religious Modernity in China: Transnational Religions, Local Agents, and the Study of Religion, 1800–Present*, edited by Thomas Jansen, Thoralf Klein, and Christian Meyer, 29–51. Leiden: Brill, 2014.

Goossaert, Vincent, and Fang Ling. "Temples and Daoists in Urban China since 1980." *China Perspectives* 4/2009 (2009): 32–41.

Goossaert, Vincent, and David A. Palmer. *The Religious Question in Modern China*. Chicago: University of Chicago Press, 2011.

Grand Dictionnaire Ricci de la langue chinoise. Paris: Desclée de Brouwer, 2001.

Granet, Marcel. *La religion des Chinois*. 1922. Paris: Les presses universitaires de France, 1951.

Greenspan, Anna. *Shanghai Future: Modernity Remade*. Oxford: Oxford University Press, 2014.

Grimshaw, Anna. *The Ethnographer's Eye: Ways of Seeing in Anthropology*. Cambridge: Cambridge University Press, 2001.

Gui Guoqiang 桂国强. *Shanghai Chenghuang Miao daguan* 上海城隍庙大观 (An overview of the Shanghai City God Temple). Shanghai: Fudan University Press, 2002.

A Guide to Catholic Shanghai. Shanghai: T'ou-se-we Press, 1937.

Hamashima Atsutoshi. "Communal Religion in Jiangnan Delta Rural Villages in Late Imperial China." *International Journal of Asian Studies* 8, no. 2 (2011): 127–62.

Hamayon, Roberte. *Why We Play: An Anthropological Study*. Chicago: University of Chicago Press, 2015.

Harley, Lee. "An Existential Reading of Book 4 of the Analects." In *Confucius and the Analects: New Essays*, edited by Bryan W. Van Norden, 237–74. Oxford: Oxford University Press, 2002.

Harrison, Henrietta. *The Missionary's Curse, and Other Tales from a Chinese Catholic Village*. Berkeley: University of California Press, 2013.

Henriot, Christian. *Scythe and the City: A Social History of Death in Shanghai*. Stanford: Stanford University Press, 2016.

———. "Slums, Squats, or Hutments? Constructing and Deconstructing an In-Between Space in Modern Shanghai (1926–65)." *Frontiers of History in China* 7, no. 4 (2012): 499–528.

Herrou, Adeline. "La sagesse chinoise dans le développement urbain: Le temple taoïste des Nuages blancs de Shanghai et l'Exposition universelle 2010." In *Ethnographier l'universel, Shanghai 2010: Better city, better life*, edited by Brigitte Baptandier and Sophie Houdart, 283–331. Nanterre, France: Société d'ethnologie, 2015.

———. "Networks and the 'Cloudlike Wandering' of Daoist Monks in China Today." In *Religion in Contemporary China: Revitalization and Innovation*, edited by Adam Yuet Chau, 108–32. London: Routledge, 2011.

Hertzog, Alice, and Liz Hingley. "Belleville Bazaar." In *Rescripting Religion in the City: Migration and Religious Identity in the Modern Metropolis*, edited by Jane Garnett and Alana Harris, 77–84. Burlington, VT: Ashgate, 2013.

Herzfeld, Michael. *Cultural Intimacy: Social Poetics in the Nation-State*. New York: Routledge, 2005.

———. "The Performance of Secrecy: Domesticity and Privacy in Public Spaces." *Semiotica* 175 (2009): 135–62.

———. "Practical Piety: Intimate Devotions in Urban Space." *Journal of Religious and Political Practice* 1, no. 1 (2015): 22–38.

Hibbard, Peter. *The Bund Shanghai: China Faces West*. Hong Kong: Odyssey Publications, 2007.

Hingley, Liz. *Under Gods, Stories from the Soho Road*. Stockport, UK: Dewi Lewis Publishing, 2011.

Hingley, Liz, Benoît Vermander, and Liang Zhang. "(Re)locating Sacredness in Shanghai." *Social Compass* 63, no. 1 (2016): 38–56.

Hong, Zhaohui. *The Price of China's Economic Development: Power, Capital, and the Poverty of Rights*. Lexington: University Press of Kentucky, 2015.

Honig, Emily. "Burning Incense, Pledging Sisterhood: Communities of Women Workers in the Shanghai Cotton Mills, 1919–1949." *Signs* 10, no. 4 (1985): 700–714.

———. *Sisters and Strangers: Women in the Shanghai Cotton Mills, 1919–1949*. Stanford: Stanford University Press, 1986.

The Huainanzi: A Guide to the Theory and Practice of Government in Early Han China. Translated by John S. Major, Sarah Queen, Andrew Meyer, and Harold D. Roth. New York: Columbia University Press, 2010.

Huang, Weishan. "The Bodhisattva Comes Out of the Closet: City, Surveillance, and Doing Religion." *Politics and Religion Journal* 6, no. 2 (2012): 199–216.

Hunter, Alan, and Kim-Kwong Chan. *Protestantism in Contemporary China*. Cambridge: Cambridge University Press, 2007.

Ing, Michael David Kaulana. *The Dysfunction of Ritual in Early Confucianism*. Oxford: Oxford University Press, 2012.

Jackson, Isabella. "The Raj on Nanjing Road: Sikh Policemen in Treaty-Port Shanghai." *Modern Asian Studies* 46 (2012): 1672–1704.

Jami, Catherine, Peter Engelfriet, and Gregory Blue. *Statecraft and Intellectual Renewal in Late Ming China: The Cross-Cultural Synthesis of Xu Guangqi (1562–1633)*. Leiden: Brill, 2001.

Jansen, Thomas, Thoralf Klein, and Christian Meyer. *Globalization and the Making of Religious Modernity in China: Transnational Religions, Local Agents, and the Study of Religion, 1800–Present*. Leiden: Brill, 2014.

Jaschok, Maria, and Jingjun Shui. *The History of Women's Mosques in Chinese Islam: A Mosque of Their Own*. London: RoutledgeCurzon, 2000.

Jessup, James Brooks. *The Householder Elite: Buddhist Activism in Shanghai, 1920–1956*. PhD diss., University of California, Berkeley, 2010.

Jin Luxian. *Learning and Relearning, 1916–1982*. Vol. 1 of *The Memoirs of Jin Luxian*. Translated by William Hanbury-Tenison. Hong Kong: Hong Kong University Press, 2012.

Jin Ze 金泽. "Ruhe lijie zongjiao de 'shenshengxing'" 如何理解宗教的 "神圣性" (How to understand religious "sacredness"). *World Religious Culture* (Shijie zongjiao wenhua 世界宗教文化), 6/2015 (2015): 1–3.

Johnson, Linda Cooke. "Shanghai: An Emerging Jiangnan Port, 1683–1840." In *Cities of Jiangnan in Late Imperial China*, edited by Linda Cooke Johnson, 151–81. Albany: State University of New York Press, 1993.

Jue Xing 觉醒. "Dushi siyuan yu renjian Fojiao" 都市寺院与人间佛教 (Urban temples and humanistic Buddhism). *China Religion* (Zhongguo zongjiao 中国宗教), 1/2013 (2013): 48–51.

Kang Xiaofei. "Rural Women, Old Age, and Temple Work: A Case from Northwestern Sichuan." *China Perspectives* 4/2009 (2009): 43–50.

Keating, John Craig William. *A Protestant Church in Communist China: Moore Memorial Church Shanghai, 1949–1989*. Bethlehem, PA: Lehigh University Press, 2012.

Knyazeva, Katya, and Adam Sinykim. *The Old Docks*. Vol. 1 of *Shanghai Old Town, Topography of a Phantom City*. Shanghai: Suzhou Creek Press, 2015.

La Compagnie de Jésus en Chine: Le Kiang-Nan en 1869; Relation historique et descriptive; Par les missionnaires. Paris: E. de Soye, 1870[?].

La Servière, Joseph de. *Jusqu'à l'établissement d'un vicaire apostolique jésuite (1840–1856)*. Vol. 1 of *Histoire de la mission du Kiang-nan: Jésuites de la province de France (Paris) 1840–1899*. Shanghai: Imprimerie de Tou-sè-wè, 1914.

———. *Mgr Borgniet (1856–1862), Mgr Languillat (1862–1878)*. Vol. 2 of *Histoire de la mission du Kiang-nan: Jésuites de la province de France (Paris) 1840–1899*. Shanghai: Imprimerie de Tou-sè-wè, 1915.

Latourette, Kenneth Scott. *A History of Christian Missions in China*. New York: Macmillan, 1929.

Le Blanc, Charles. *Huai-nan Tzu: Philosophical Synthesis in Early Han Thought; The Idea of Resonance (Kan-Ying) with a Translation and Analysis of Chapter Six*. Hong Kong: Hong Kong University Press, 1985.

Lee, Joseph Tse-Hei, and Christie Chui-Shan Chow. "Christian Revival from Within: Seventh-Day Adventism in China." In *Christianity in Contemporary China: Socio-cultural Perspectives*, edited by Francis Khek Gee Lim, 45–58. London and New York: Routledge, 2013.

———. "Publishing Prophecy: A Century of Adventist Print Culture in China." In *Religious Publishing and Print Culture in Modern China 1800-2012*, edited by Philip Clart and Gregory Adam Scott, 51–90. Boston: Walter de Gruyter, 2015.

Lee, Leo Ou-fan. *Shanghai Modern: The Flowering of a New Urban Culture in China, 1930-1945*. Cambridge, MA: Harvard University Press, 1999.

Lefeuvre, Jean. *Shanghai: Les enfants dans la ville; vie chrétienne à Shanghai et perspectives sur l'Église de Chine, 1949-1961*. Tournai, Belgium: Casterman, 1962.

Leng, Xin, et al. "Contributing to the Construction of Social Morality and Harmonious Society: A Study of the Protestant Churches in Shanghai." *Ching Feng* 9, nos. 1–2 (2008–9): 175–206.

Lenoir, Yves, and Nicolas Standaert, eds. *Les danses rituelles chinoises d'après Joseph-Marie Amiot: Aux sources de l'ethnochorégraphie*. Brussels: Editions Lessius; Namur, Belgium: Presses universitaires de Namur, 2005.

Li, Huiping, et al. "Residential Clustering and Spatial Access to Public Services in Shanghai." *Habitat International* 46 (2015): 119–29.

Li, Jie. *Shanghai Homes: Palimpsests of Private Life*. New York: Columbia University Press, 2014.

Li, Shiqiao. *Understanding the Chinese City*. London: Sage, 2014.

Li Tiangang 李天纲. "Jiangnan zhenxiang jisi tixi zhong de difang yu guojia" 江南镇乡祭祀体系中的地方与国家 (The relationship between the local and the national in the sacrifice system of Jiangnan: A case study on Jinze Town, Suzhou Prefecture, and Songjiang Prefecture). *Journal of East China Normal University—Humanities and Social Science* (Huadong shifan daxue xuebao 华东师范大学学报), 4/2014 (2014): 69–78.

———. "Jiangnan zongjiao de xingshi—hunpo yu guichong" 江南宗教的形式—魂魄与鬼崇 (Religious form in regions south of the Yangzi River: Spirits and worship of demons). *Contemporary Religious Studies* (Dangdai zongjiao yanjiu 当代宗教研究), 3/2012 (2012): 1–11.

———. *Renwen Shanghai* 人文上海 (Humanistic Shanghai). Shanghai: Shanghai Education Publisher, 2004.

Liang, Samuel Y. *Mapping Modernity in Shanghai: Space, Gender, and Visual Culture in the Sojourners' City, 1853-98*. London: Routledge, 2010.

———. "Where the Courtyard Meets the Street: Spatial Culture of the Li Neighborhoods, Shanghai, 1870-1900." *Journal of the Society of Architectural Historians* 67, no. 4 (2008): 482–503.

Lin, Wei-cheng. *Building a Sacred Mountain: The Buddhist Architecture of China's Mount Wutai*. Seattle: University of Washington Press, 2014.

Lin Xiangping 李向平. "Renjian Fojiao de shenshengxing yu shehuixing—yi Xingyun Dashi de Fojiao sixiang wei zhongxin" 人间佛教的神圣性与社会性—以星云大师的佛教思想为中心 (The sacred and the social in humanistic Buddhism: Centering on the Buddhist thought of Master Xingyun). *Contemporary Religious Studies* (Dangdai zongjiao yanjiu 当代宗教研究), 1/2016 (2016): 4–13.

Liu, Cary Y. "Encountering the Dilemma of Change in the Architectural and Urban History of Shanghai." *Journal of the Society of Architectural Historians* 73, no. 1 (2014): 118–36.

Liu, Xun. *Daoist Modern: Innovation, Lay Practice, and the Community of Inner Alchemy in Republican Shanghai*. Harvard East Asian Monographs 313. Cambridge, MA: Harvard University Asia Center, 2009.

Liu Ping 刘平 and Jiang Linze 江林泽. "Panluan yu xiandaixing—Shanghai Xiaodaohui qiyi yu Shanghai xiandaihua de guanxi" 叛乱与现代性—上海小刀会起义与上海现代化的关系 (Rebellion and modernity: The relationship between the Shanghai Small-Sword Society uprising and Shanghai's modernization). *Historiography Research in Anhui* (Anhui shixue 安徽史学), 4/2014 (2014): 12–21.

Lu, Hanchao. *Beyond the Neon Lights: Everyday Shanghai in the Early Twentieth Century*. Berkeley: University of California Press, 1999.

Lu Zhongwei. "Huidaomen in the Republican Period." *Chinese Studies in History* 44, no. 1–2 (2010–11): 10–37.

Lukes, Steven. *Emile Durkheim: His Life and Work, a Historical and Critical Study*. London: Penguin, 1973.

Luo Wanshou 罗万寿. "Haifurun shijian" 海富润事件 (The Hai Furun case). In *Chinese Encyclopedias of Islam* (Zhongguo Yisilanjiao baikequanshu 中国伊斯兰百科全书), 206. Chengdu: Sichuan Lexicographical Press, 1994.

Ma Nuheng 马汝珩. "Cong Haifurun anjian kan Qianlong dui Huizu de tongzhi zhengce" 从海富润案件看乾隆对回族的统治政策 (Examining Qianlong's policy on ruling the Hui minority through the Hai Furun legal case). *Journal of Hui Muslim Minority Studies* (Huizu yanjiu 回族研究), no. 1 (1992): 8–12.

Macherel, Claude. "Le pain et la représentation sociale des processus vitaux: Identité alimentaire et altérité culturelle." *Université de Neuchâtel, Recherches et travaux de l'Institut d'ethonolgie*, no. 6 (1985): 213–30. http://hal.archives-ouvertes.fr/hal-00460407/fr, accessed 4 January 2014.

Madsen, Richard, and Fan Lizhu. "The Catholic Pilgrimage to Sheshan." In *Making Religion, Making the State: The Politics of Religion in Modern China*, edited by Yoshiko Ashiwa and David Wank, 74–95. Stanford: Stanford University Press, 2009.

Major, John S., Sarah Queen, Andrew Meyer, and Harold D. Roth, trans. *The Huainanzi: A Guide to the Theory and Practice of Government in Early Han China*. New York: Columbia University Press, 2010.

Makeham, John. *Lost Soul: "Confucianism" in Contemporary Chinese Academic Discourse*. Harvard-Yenching Institute Monograph Series, 64. Cambridge, MA: Harvard University Asia Center, 2008.

Mariani, Paul P. *Church Militant: Bishop Kung and Catholic Resistance in Communist Shanghai.* Cambridge, MA: Harvard University Press, 2011.

Meng, Yue. *Shanghai and the Edges of Empires.* Minneapolis: University of Minnesota Press, 2006.

Meyer, Maisie. "The Sephardi Jewish Community of Shanghai and the Question of Identity." In *Jews and China from Kaifeng . . . to Shanghai: Jews in China*, edited by Roman Malek. Monumenta Serica Monograph Series, 46. Nettetal, Germany: Steyler Verlag, 2000.

Mungello, David. E. "Reinterpreting the History of Christianity in China." *Historical Journal* 55 (2012): 533–52.

Névot, Aurélie. "Le Rouge de Chine (*Zhongguo hong* 中國紅): Une couleur subliminale." In *Ethnographier l'universel—l'exposition Shanghai 2010 "Better city, better life,"* edited by Brigitte Baptandier and Sophie Houdart, 103–36. Nanterre, France: Société d'ethnologie, 2015.

Okuyama, Michiaki. "'Civil Religion' in Japan? Rethinking the Arguments and Their Implications." *Religious Studies in Japan* 1 (2012): 61–77.

Palmer, David A. "From 'Congregations' to 'Small Group Community Building.'" *Chinese Sociological Review* 45, no. 2 (2012): 78–98.

———. *Qigong Fever: Body, Science, and Utopia in China.* New York: Columbia University Press, 2007.

Pan Mingquan 潘明权. "Shanghai zongjiao huodong changsuo de shehui dingwei he shehui guanli zouyi" 上海宗教活动场所的社会定位和社会管理刍议 (On the social positioning and social management of religious sites in Shanghai). *Contemporary Religious Studies* (Dangdai zongjiao yanjiu 当代宗教研究), 2/2014 (2014): 1–8.

Pan Tianshu and Liu Zhijun. "Place Matters: An Ethnographic Perspective on Historical Memory, Place Attachment, and Neighborhood Gentrification in Post-reform Shanghai." *Chinese Sociology and Anthropology* 43, no. 4 (2011): 52–73.

Pang, Laikwan. "The Dialectics of Mao's Images: Monumentalism, Circulation, and Power Effects." In *Visualizing China: Moving and Still Images in Historical Narratives*, edited by Christian Henriot and Wen-hsin Yeh, 407–35. Leiden: Brill, 2012.

Parsons, Gerald. *Perspectives on Civil Religion.* Milton Keynes, UK: Open University, 2002.

Perry, Elizabeth J., and Li Xun. *Proletarian Power: Shanghai in the Cultural Revolution.* Boulder, CO: Westview Press, 1997.

Pickering, W. S. F. *Durkheim's Sociology of Religion: Themes and Theories.* Boston: Routledge and Kegan Paul, 1984.

Pierard, Richard V., and Robert Dean Linder. *Civil Religion and the American Presidency.* Grand Rapids, MI: Zondervan Publishing House, 1988.

Prazniak, Roxann. "Weavers and Sorceresses of Chuansha: The Social Origins of Political Activism among Rural Chinese Women." *Modern China* 12, no. 2 (1986): 202–29.

Ristaino, Marcia R. *The Jacquinot Safe Zone: Wartime Refugees in Shanghai.* Stanford: Stanford University Press, 2008.

Robertson, Roland. "Globalization, Theocratization, and Politicized Civil Religion." In *The Oxford Handbook of the Sociology of Religion*, 451–77. Oxford: Oxford University Press, 2009.

Roy, Ananya, and Aihawa Ong, eds. *Worlding Cities: Asian Experiments and the Art of Being Global*. Hoboken, NJ: Wiley-Blackwell, 2011.

Ruan Renze 阮仁泽 and Gao Zhennong 高振农. *Shanghai zongjiao shi* 上海宗教史 (The religious history of Shanghai). Shanghai: Shanghai People's Publishing House, 1992.

Scheid, John. *Les dieux, l'État et l'individu: Réflexions sur la religion civique à Rome*. Paris: Seuil, 2013.

Schilling, Robert. "Sacrum et profanum: Essai d'interprétation." *Latomus* 30, no. 4 (1971): 953–69.

Schneider, Arnd, and Christopher Wright, eds. *Between Art and Anthropology: Contemporary Ethnographic Practice*. London: Bloomsbury, 2010.

Shen, Vincent. "Dao in the City." In *The Natural City — Re-envisioning the Built Environment*, edited by Ingrid Stefanovic and Stephen Scharper, 117–35. Toronto: University of Toronto Press, 2012.

Shi, Xijuan. "Christian Scholar Xu Guangqi and the Spread of Catholicism in Shanghai." *Asian Culture and History* 7, no. 1 (2015): 199–209.

Shiu, Herry, and Leah Stokes. "Buddhist Animal Release Practices: Historic, Environmental, Public Health and Economic Concerns." *Contemporary Buddhism* 9, no. 2 (2008): 181–96.

Shun, Kwong-loi. "Ren 仁 and Li 禮 in the Analects." In *Confucius and the Analects: New Essays*, edited by Bryan W. Van Norden, 53–72. Oxford: Oxford University Press, 2002.

Smith, S. A. "Talking Toads and Chinless Ghosts: The Politics of 'Superstitious' Rumors in the People's Republic of China, 1961–1965." *American Historical Review* 111, no. 2 (2006): 405–27.

Suhr, Christian, and Rane Willerslev. "Can Film Show the Invisible? The Work of Montage in Ethnographic Filmmaking." *Current Anthropology* 53, no. 3 (2012): 282–301.

Sun Weiqiao 孙尉乔. "Wu guishu de Fojiao yigong? Cong Fojiao yigong kan Fojiao xintu guishu zhuangtai" 无归属的佛教义工? 从佛教义工看佛教信徒归属状态 (Buddhist volunteers who do not belong? Looking at the sense of belonging of Buddhist believers from the viewpoint of volunteers). *Contemporary Religious Studies* (Dangdai zongjiao yanjiu 当代宗教研究), 2/2016 (2016): 7–13.

Tang Zhongmao 唐忠毛. "Minguo Shanghai jushi Fojiao cishan de yunzuo moshi, tedian yu yiyi" 民国上海居士佛教慈善的运作模式、特点与意义 (The operational mode, characteristics, and significance of Shanghai lay Buddhist charity in the Republican period). *Journal of Social Sciences* (Shehui kexue 社会科学), 10/2013 (2013): 150–59.

Tarroco, Francesca. "The City and the Pagoda: Buddhist Spatial Tactics in Shanghai." In *Handbook of Religion and the Asian City: Aspiration and Urbanization in the Twenty-First Century*, edited by Peter van der Veer, 37–51. Berkeley: University of California Press, 2015.

Tong, Joy Kooi-Chin. "Christian Ethics and Business Life: An Ethnographic Account of Overseas Chinese Christian Entrepreneurs in China's Economic Transition." In

Christianity in Contemporary China: Socio-cultural Perspectives, edited by Francis Khek Gee Lim, 169–82. London: Routledge, 2013.

Tsu, François-Xavier. "La vie des pêcheurs du Bas-Yangtse." In *Mémoires et Documents*, 60–158. Paris: Centre de documentation géographique et cartographique, 1952.

Tweed, Thomas A. "Crabs, Crustaceans, Crabiness, and Outrage: A Response." *Journal of the American Academy of Religion* 77, no. 2 (2009): 445–59.

———. *Crossing and Dwelling: A Theory of Religion*. Cambridge, MA: Harvard University Press, 2006.

Veer, Peter van der, ed. *Handbook of Religion and the Asian City: Aspiration and Urbanization in the Twenty-First Century*. Berkeley: University of California Press, 2015.

———. *The Modern Spirit of Asia: The Spiritual and the Secular in China and India*. Princeton: Princeton University Press, 2014.

Vendassi, Pierre. *Chrétiens de Chine: Affiliations et conversions au XXIème siècle*. Renne, Frances: Presses universitaires de Rennes, 2016.

———. "Mormonism and the Chinese State." *China Perspectives* 1/2014 (2014): 43–50.

Vermander, Benoît. "From Ethnography to Theology: Religious Communities in Contemporary Shanghai and the Tasks of East Asian Theology." *Korean Journal of Systematic Theology* 39 (2014): 7–35.

———. "Jesuits and China." *Oxford Handbooks Online*, 2015. doi:10.1093/oxfordhb/9780199935420.013.53.

———. "The Law and the Wheel: The Narrative of Falun Gong." In *Creeds, Rites and Videotapes, Narrating Religious Experience in East Asia*, edited by Elise Anne DeVido and Benoît Vermander, 151–83. Taipei: Taipei Ricci Institute, 2004.

———. "Religious Revival and Exit from Religion in Contemporary China." *China Perspectives*, 2010/1 (2010): 4–15.

———. "Une société civile aux caractéristiques chinoises: Citoyenneté et gouvernance en débat." AFRI, *Annuaire français de relations internationales*, 217–30. Paris: La documentation française, 2012.

Vermander, Benoît, and Xie Hua. "Avec leurs voix propres: Portrait par eux-mêmes de jeunes catholiques des villes chinoises." *Nunc* 31 (2013): 25–28.

Wakeman, Frederic. *Policing Shanghai, 1927–1937*. Berkeley: University of California Press, 1995.

Wakeman, Frederic, and Wen-hsin Yeh, eds. *Shanghai Sojourners*. China Research Monograph 40. Berkeley: University of California Press, 1992.

Wasserstrom, Jeffrey N. *Global Shanghai, 1850–2010: A History in Fragments*. Abingdon, UK: Routledge, 2009.

Welch, Holmes H. *Buddhism under Mao*. Cambridge, MA: Harvard University Press, 1972.

Wendling, Thierry. *Ethnologie des joueurs d'échecs*. Paris: Presses universitaires de France, coll. Ethnologies, 2002.

Wickeri, Philip. *Seeking the Common Ground: Protestant Christianity, the Three-Self Movement, and China's United Front*. Maryknoll, NY: Orbis Books, 1988.

Wiest, Jean-Paul. "Les jésuites français et l'image de la Chine au XIXème siècle." In *La*

Chine entre amour et haine, edited by Michel Cartier, 283–308. Paris: Desclée de Brouwer, 1998.

Xi, Lian. *Redeemed by Fire: The Rise of Popular Christianity in Modern China*. New Haven: Yale University Press, 2010.

Xiong Yuezhi 熊月之. "20 shiji Shanghai shi yanjiu" 20 世纪上海史研究 (Historical research on twentieth-century Shanghai). *Journal of Shanghai Administration Institute* (Shanghai xingzheng xueyuan xuebao上海行政学院学报), 1/2000 (2000): 92–105.

Yang, Der-Ruey. "From Ritual Skills to Discursive Knowledge: Changing Styles of Daoist Transmission in Shanghai." In *Religion in Contemporary China: Revitalization and Innovation*, edited by Adam Yuet Chau, 81–107. London: Routledge, 2011.

Yang, Fenggang. "Lost in the Market, Saved at McDonald's: Conversion to Christianity in Urban China." *Journal for the Scientific Study of Religion* 44, no. 4 (2005): 423–41.

———. "Religion in China under Communism: A Shortage Economy Explanation." *Journal of Church and State* 52, no. 1 (2010): 3–34.

Yang Rongbin 杨荣斌. *Minguo shiqi Shanghai Huizu shangren qunti yanjiu* 民国时期上海回族商人群体研究 (A study of the Hui merchant community of Shanghai at the time of the Republic of China). Beijing: Social Sciences Academic Press of China, 2014.

Yang Wenyi 杨文怡. "Xinxing ling'en chengshi jiaohui tezheng yanjiu—ji yu dui Shanghai diqu xinxing gongshang tuanqi yu jiating jiaohui de kaocha" 新兴灵恩城市教会特征研究—基于对上海地区新兴工商团契与家庭教会的考察 (Research on the characteristics of emerging charismatic city churches—based on an investigation of emerging business fellowships and home churches in Shanghai). BA thesis, Fudan University, Shanghai, 2016.

Yu Jianrong. "Desensitising the Christian House Churches." Translated by Lawrence Braschi. *China Study Journal* (Autumn/Winter 2008): 34–50.

Yu Jianxing 郁建兴, Jiang Hua 江华, and Zhou Jun 周俊. *Zai canyu zhong chengzhang de Zhongguo gongmin shehui* 在参与中成长的中国公民社会 (Chinese civil society growth out of participation). Hanghzou: Zhejiang University Press, 2008.

Yu Zhejun 郁喆隽. *Shenming yu shimin—Minguo shiqi Shanghai diqu yingshen saihui yanjiu* 神明与市民—民国时期上海地区迎神赛会研究 (Deities and city dwellers—research on popular processions in Shanghai during the Republican era). Shanghai: Shanghai Joint Publishing Company, 2014.

Zhang Hua 张化. "Shanghai Fojiao xuexi Jidujiao chengyin yanjiu" 上海佛教学习基督教成因研究 (Research on the causes of the study of Christianity by Buddhism in Shanghai). *Contemporary Religious Studies* (Dangdai zongjiao yanjiu 当代宗教研究), 1/2017 (2017): 31–38.

Zheng Tuyou 郑土有 and Liu Qiaolin 刘巧林. *Hucheng xingshi: Chenghuang xinyang de renleixue kaocha* 护城兴市: 城隍信仰的人类学考察 (Anthropological inquiry on the cult of the city god). Shanghai: Shanghai Lexicographical Publishing House, 2005.

Zhou Jin 周进. *Shanghai jiaotang jianzhu ditu / Shanghai Church* 上海教堂建筑地图. Bilingual. Shanghai: Tongji University Press, 2014.

Zhu Hongbo 朱鸿伯, ed. *Chuansha xian zhi (Chuansha County Chronicles)* 川沙县志 (上海市川沙县志编修委员会). Shanghai: Shanghai People's Press, 1990.

Zuo, Jiping. "Political Religion: The Case of the Cultural Revolution in China." *Sociology of Religion* 52, no. 1 (1991): 99–110.

Zuo Yuhe 左玉河. "Zhongguo jindaishi yanjiu de fanshi zhizheng yu chaoyue zhi lu" 中国近代史研究的范式之争与超越之路 (The paradigm controversy in research on Chinese modern history and a way of overcoming it). *Historical Monthly* (Shixue yuekan 史学月刊), 6/2014 (2014): 55–71.

INDEX

city planners. *See* urban planning

civic sacredness, 34–39, 133

civil religion, 33–34

"common-trade associations" (*gongsuo*), 19

compounds (*daochang*): Buddhist, 97–104, 98*map*; Catholic, 79–80, 87–92, 88*map*; in Chuansha New Town, 81–83; home worship and, 110; Islamic, 83–87, 84*map*; Jewish, 105–7; meaning of, 79–81; Protestant three-church network, 92–97, 94*map*; Sikh *gurdwara*, 107–9, *plate 23*

Confucianism, 150–51, 156–57

Confucius, 9, 181

Confucius Temple of Jiading, 37*map*, 39, 157

conversion, 121–24, 173–75

Cultural Revolution: bridge shrines and, *plate 36*; Daoism and, 61; mosques and, 20, 129; *qigong* ban, 154; St. Nicholas Church and, 58

Dai Lizhen, 113, *plate 26*

Daodejing, 185

Daoism: Communist regime and, 27; Cultural Revolution and, 61; festivals, 45–46; married masters, 64; music in, *plate 46*; Quanzhen and Zhengyi schools, 26, 64, 209n43; renewal in, 26; schooling and discursive legitimacy of, 151–54, *plates 39*; temples, defined, 209n43

Daoist masters (*daoshi*), 64

Daoist National Association, 61, 151

deaf congregation, 117–18

deity worship (*jishen*) vs. ancestor worship, 47

Deng, Cora, 25

Denton, Kirk, 74–75

Disney Resort, Shanghai, 35, 36*map*, 123

Diwali, 124, *plate 29*

Dizang (bodhisattva), 51

dong ("movement"), 183–85

Dong Qichang, 18

Dongfang Yue, 182–83

Dongling Temple, 57*map*

Dongxiang ethnic minority, 130

Dongyue (Supreme God of Mount Tai), 148, 150

Dongyue Temple, 57*map*, 148, 152*map*, 153

door gods (*menshen*), 112

Double Yang Festival (Chongyangjie), 51–52, 148

Douglas, Mary, 203n12

Dragon-Boat Festival (Duanwujie), 50

Durkheim, Émile, 5–10, 51, 188, 216n32

Duzhu Taitai (Mistress of the soil), 115, 212n6

dwellers and nomadism, 183–85, 189

Eaglewood Pavilion (Chenxiang Ge), 57*map*, 61–62, 98*map*

East China Theology College (Huadong Shenxueyuan), 95–96

East Shanghai Church, 57*map*, 94*map*

Easter: Easter Vigil, 139; at migrant church, 122–23; Orthodox, 58, *plate 9*; Tomb Sweeping Festival overlapping with, 49–50, 122

eating. *See* food and communal eating

Eid al-Adha (Festival of Sacrifice), 54–55, 83–85, *plates 8, 17*

Eid al-Fitr (Breaking-the-Fast Feast), 54, 83

Elders' Day, 51–52

Eliade, Mircea, 5

Eternal China, 38

Eugster, Josef (Wu Ruoshi), 141–42

Expo Shanghai 2010, 38, 58

Fagushan Monastery (Taiwan), 101

Fahua Pagoda and Confucius Temple, 40

Falun Gong movement, 154, 155

Fan Zhongliang, 138

feast days. *See* calendar and feast days; *specific holidays*

Feast of the Nativity, Orthodox, 58

figuration, 13

fire ceremonies, 160, 169–70, *plate 42*

xuni ("virtual"), 180–83

Xunzi, 185

Yan Weibing, 156

Yang, Der-Ruey, 151

Yang Fenggang, 31

Yang Zhen (Lord Yang), 148, 149, 150

Yang Zhen Temple, 148–50

Yangpu Mosque, 129

Yangzhen Temple, 152*map*

Yi minority, 55

Yihao Temple, 98*map*, 147, 149

Yindu Miao ("Indian Temple"), 107–8

yingshen saihui processions, 60

yoga, 165–71, 214n45

Yongfu An, 98*map*, 101–2

Young John Allen Memorial Church, 94*map*, 95–96, *plate 27*

Yu Cidu, 25

Yu Garden, 47, 59, 61

YWCA and YMCA, 24, 25

Zaoshen or Zaojing Gongong (Kitchen God), 45, 46

Zen One Clubhouse, 126–27, 156

Zen/Chan Buddhism, 74, 76, 126–27

Zhang Jingqiao, 89

Zhangjialou Church (Sacred Heart of Jesus Church), 79–80, 88*map*, 89–91, 131–32, 141, 172, *plate 11*

Zhenchan, Venerable, 76

zheng ("right"), 177–78

Zhengyi School of Daoism, 26, 64, 209n43

Zhenru Temple, 98*map*

Zhenyan tradition of Buddhism, 76

Zhiye Temple, 72–73, 98*map*

Zhongshan Church, 71

zhu (to congratulate; call for blessings upon), 8–9

zifa donggong ("art of spontaneous movements"), 154

Zongguan Temple, 152*map*